SRFLIS series in library science / ed. by Dr K P Singh ; no.7

LIBRARY CLASSIFICATION AND S R RANGANATHAN :
A Guide

Library Classification and S R Ranganathan : A Guide

M. P. Satija
Formerly Guru Nanak Dev University

Compiled and Edited by
Daniel Martínez-Ávila
São Paulo State University (UNESP), Marília, Brazil
and
Rosa San Segundo Manuel
Universidad Carlos III de Madrid, Spain

Ess Ess Publications
New Delhi

LIBRARY CLASSIFICATION AND S R RANGANATHAN:
A Guide

ISBN: 978-81-936074-7-3

First Published 2018

Published by:
Ess Ess Publications
4831/24, Ansari Road,
Darya Ganj,
New Delhi-110 002.
INDIA
Phones: 23260807, 41563444
Fax: 41563334
E-mail: info@essessreference.com
www.essessreference.com

Cover Design by *Patch Creative Unit*

Printed and bound in India

Dedicated to
DOCUMENTATION RESEARCH AND TRAINING CENTRE,
Bengaluru
Its
Founder
Faculty, Past and Present
Students, Past and Present
In Commemoration of the 125th Birth Anniversary of
S R RANGANTHAN

Contents

Preface

Sharpness in thinking, clarity in expression, expedition in response, and exactness in communication depend ultimately on the deliberate expression of the innate power of deliberate classification. — **Ranganathan, *Prolegomena*, 1967, p. 547.**

S R Ranganathan stays put in our thoughts and work even nearly half a century after his death. Some of his theories and methods were for his times, but most of them are relatively perennial, and quite a few are finding new applications and relevance in the digital age. Some of his work is classic with lofty ideas which always engender new thoughts for the present age. His Colon Classification, last published disastrously in 1987, may not survive as a specific system, or is perhaps already dead, but its methods have already pervaded the body and soul of all knowledge organization systems (KOS). Ranganathan brought a paradigm shift in library classification theory and practice and extended its reach much beyond the library precincts. Facet analysis is the order of the day, not only in library classification but also in organizing and searching e-databases and the web—the untamed sea of knowledge. It not only guides the designing of databases but also in structuring the expressed ideas[1,2]. It has truly been said by

---

1. Neelameghan, A. (1992). "Applications of Ranganathan's general theory of knowledge classification in designing specialised databases." *Libri* 42(3): 202-226.

2. Neelameghan, A.(1975). *Presentation of Ideas in Technical Writing*. New Delhi: Vikas Publishing House, 189 p.

Ingetraut Dahlberg that there has been no real advances in knowledge organization since Ranganathan, though some improvements and simplifications have been made over his methods. In India classification, mostly through its formal teaching in library schools did keep its foot down when elsewhere in the world faith in its relevance and need was dwindling. And we Indians working under his long shadow have proved right. Now the world is experiencing a second Golden Age of Classification and Indexing in the world wide web environment. In fact faceted classification prophesized as the basis of all knowledge organization systems and tools in mid 1950s is proving visibly true today. Classification has bounced back with a vengeance. Eugene Garfield (1925-2017) aptly said Ranganathan is to library science what Einstein is to physics.[3]

These articles written over the last two decades try to present a brief summary and importance of Ranganathan's work in classification, though by no means his best. It is difficult to come out with the best of a treasure in an ocean. He left a huge body of classification literature, full of thought provoking with multidimensional applications. Apart from the Classification Research Group (CRG) disciples his work has inspired many a genius in our profession. A glimpse of the cornucopia of his work is given in a bibliography on the Colon Classification by M P Satija and Amrik Singh (1994), and true tributes to his importance have been offered from time to time by the greats of our profession[4]. Apart from a summary and chronology of his classification work these

3. Garfield Eugene. (1984). "Current Comments. A Tribute to S. R. Ranganathan, the Father of Indian Library Science. Part 2. Contribution to Indian and International Library Science." *Current Contents* 7, February 13: 3-7; and *Essays of an Information Scientist* 7: 45-49. Available at: http://www.garfield.library.upenn.edu/essays/v7p045y1984.pdf

4. Dudley, Edward. (1974). *S R Ranganathan, 1892-1972.* London: Library Association.

essays portray the current scene on classification studies practices and literature in India and in KO in general. Lastly it makes a hearty plea to know, value, preserve and perpetuate his legacy bequeathed on us—a legacy which has brought glory to the Indian LIS profession. Terminology in simple language may help the novices to learn and understand the basis of Ranganathan's work. There may be repetition of ideas in some chapter which has been deliberately maintained to make every chapter an independent read. In nutshell the book is a reminder of his greatness, relevance and our enduring debt to him.

Thanks are to Dr. Daniel Martínez-Ávila and Prof. Rosa Segundo for collating this work; and to Prof. Devika Madalli and Dr. B. Dutta (Both of DRTC) for being the author of the earlier version of chapter 4 published in KO/ISKO 2014. Thanks to Mr. Harish Chander (DU Scholar) for his help in proof reading.

— M P Satija

The International Relevance of Ranganathan

The classics are the books that come down to us bearing upon them the traces of readings previous to ours, and bringing in their wake the traces they themselves have left on the culture or cultures they have passed through.

— **Ítalo Calvino,** *Why Read the Classics?*, **1991**

The work of S.R. Ranganathan has made a huge impact around the world that is still pretty much alive today. International Knowledge organization and the classification field would not be the same without Ranganathan and his philosophy. Not only his Colon Classification and his writings were revolutionary during his time (as acknowledged by international peers such as Jesse Shera, the British Classification Research Group, and others), but the relevance of his legacy also includes a school of brilliant Indian scholars such as Dr. M.P. Satija that have carried the torch over the years and have continuously put the intellectual capital of the country in the spotlight. Even today, Library and Information students from distant countries such as Spain, Portugal, or Brazil look at India in amazement and admiration because of the work of Ranganathan. Anyone who wants to specialize in classification anywhere in the world must study Ranganathan and the Indian school, regardless the system that is used in their country and the specificity of their culture. The international relevance of the Colon Classification and Ranganathan's work is universal.

In Spain, Library and Information Science was not

formally taught in universities until the 1970s. With a very few exceptions, there was virtually no research and knowledge on the advances in classification until those years. New trends, author, and theories were not known as the country was immersed in situation of political and intellectual darkness. There was an almost total ignorance of topics and ideas related to new classification systems during Ranganathan's life. Only the Universal Decimal Classification (UDC) was used and known in practice. When Spanish Universities and scholars caught up and began implementing Library and Information Science programs, researchers found a vast amount of information to explore, including the whole *ouvre* of Ranganathan to prepare the curricula. The Indian legacy was not easy for the newbies, but its value made the effort worthy. Indeed, although most of the new generation of Spanish researchers in classification at the time, such as Rosa San Segundo, began their career studying the UDC, they quickly realized that Ranganathan's work was the only way to acquire real expertise in classification. While Rosa San Segundo's Ph.D. at Universidad Complutense de Madrid initially focused on the UDC, Universidad Carlos III de Madrid Professor Virginia Cano advised her that a doctoral dissertation on classification without tackling Ranganathan would never be complete. Two years after, Prof. Virginia Cano would join the Department of Communication and Information Studies at Queen Margaret College in Edinburgh, Scotland. As a result, Rosa San Segundo's Ph.D. dissertation[5] was the

5. San Segundo, Rosa (1993). *Teoría e historia de la clasificación bibliotecaria en España, siglos XIX y XX*. Madrid: Universidad Complutense de Madrid. Available http://eprints.ucm.es/1784/1/S3019501.pdf. Also published as a book: San Segundo, Rosa. (1996). *Sistemas de Organización del conocimiento: La organización del conocimiento en las bibliotecas españolas*. Madrid: Universidad Carlos III; Boletín Oficial del Estado. Available http://e-archivo.uc3m.es/bitstream/10016/4256/2/sansegundo_sistemas_1996.pdf.

first publication in Spanish dealing with Ranganathan's Colon Classification.

Another important event in relation to the dissemination of Ranganathan and his Colon Classification in Spain was the visit of Prof. Kaula in 1992. He gave a talk at Universidad Carlos III de Madrid entitled "Introduction to Colon Classification," and also at other Spanish institutions such as Fundación Germán Sánchez Ruipérez and Universidad Complutense de Madrid. These talks were the first conferences in Spain that were specialized in Ranganathan and the Colon Classification. For the first time, Spanish students had the opportunity of learning about the system from an Indian authority (and indeed, given the isolation of the country during the previous decades, it is very likely that this was the first time that many of those students had contact of any kind with a person from India). Professor Kaula began his talks introducing the life of Ranganathan, which was quite unique and different from what people in Spain were used to. This provoked a great interest in Ranganathan's life and the Indian culture among the students. Then, he proceeded to summarize the Colon Classification including its terminology, structure, notation, main classes, categories, rounds and levels, and all the theoretical aspects that underlie system. For a better understanding of these concepts, Kaula gave many examples that were familiar to Spanish students, including fields of knowledge and everyday situations they could relate. These talks made a huge impact in Spain and after Kaula's visit several authors published papers on Ranganathan and the Colon Classification[6]. The work of

---

6. As examples: San Segundo, Rosa. (1998). "Conferences given by professor Kaula and their impact on teaching of classification." In, P.P. Rawat, O.P. Gupta and V. Venkatappaiah, eds., *Current Developments in Library and Information Science: Papers presented in honour of Prof. P.N. Kaula on his 71st Birthday*; San Segundo, Rosa. (1996). "The impact of Ranganathan's Work in

Ranganathan became a main influence in the writings and teaching of some of the most relevant LIS senior scholars in Spain, including Emilia Currás and Antonio García Gutiérrez (who in 2016 received the SRFLIS World Library Leaders Life Time Achievement Award). Rosa San Segundo's students, including Daniel Martínez-Ávila, also had contact with the work of Ranganathan and his followers from day one. In this sense, another of the biggest influences and main ambassadors of the legacy of Ranganathan has been Prof. Satija and his Satija Research Foundation for Library and Information Science. Between 2012 and 2013, before the economic crisis and bad management hit the school, Rosa San Segundo tried to get funding to bring Prof. Satija to Universidad Carlos III de Madrid. Although the visit could not happen due to unrelated issues, Daniel Martínez-Ávila was lucky to meet him and attend to one of his talks in 2013 at the University of Wisconsin-Milwaukee, in the United States. That was the beginning of a good and fruitful relationship that brought several collaborations including the present book.

This book is a compendium of some of the essential writings by M.P. Satija on Ranganathan and the Colon Classification. Each paper has been selected by Satija himself and sequenced in a logical order to make the study of Ranganathan and his philosophy more comprehensible for everybody, including experienced scholars and students of every level. However, although there is a logical sequence of papers, it is not necessary to read the book from beginning to end as each chapter speaks on a different matter and has

---

Spain." In P.N. Kaula, Krishan Kumar et. al., eds., *International and Comparative Librarianship and Information Systems: Ranganathan Memorial Volumes*: and Currás Puente, Emilia. (1995). "Teorías de clasificación del Dr. Ranganathan bajo postulados de ciencia sistemática." *Boletín de la ANABAD*, 45(4): 145-168.

some repetition of key and basic concepts. In some way, this book can also be used as a reference book, including a glossary of terms and papers on the different aspects of Ranganathan's philosophy. Each paper has been updated and improved to make each chapter a stand alone master class on one of the facets of one the most influential authors in the history of Library and Information Science and classification by another one of the most important authors in the field. It is an honor for us to be able to participate in this prestigious project that we hope that will keep on influencing scholars around the world.

Thanks to Prof. M P Satija and the Satija Research Foundation for Library and Information Science for making this project possible.

Daniel Martínez-Ávila
Rosa San Segundo

1

S. R. Ranganathan (1892-1972): A Global Indian Library Thinker

Not so long ago India was considered among the world leaders in library science education and research. Librarians across the world expectedly looked towards India for some conceptual and practical innovations in the area of information organization and retrieval. Dr. Shiyali Ramamrita Ranganathan Iyer, deservedly known as the father of Indian Library Movement, literally revived the proud tradition of ancient India to attract scholars from far and wide to learn from our savants. Such an inspiring genius was born to Mrs. Sitalakshmi and father N. Ramamrita on August 12, 1892 in aVedama Iyer Brahmin family of village Shiyali in the Thanjavur district then in Madras presidency. Vedama Iyers are said to have migrated long ago from the North. He was eldest of the three brothers and one sister. One brother died very young. His actual name can be construed to be Ranganath. In Tamil culture "an", "am" or "ar" are honorific suffixes to the personal names. Family was poor, but cultured and deeply religious. Early death of his father, a small farmer, made his life strewn with difficulties. He was brought up by his maternal grandfather who was an elementary school teacher. Wading his way through hardships, he completed his schooling in 1909 creditably, and later passed M.A. in mathematics in 1916 from Madras Christian College. In childhood Ranganathan was poor health-wise and financially, but made good his inborn shortcomings with undaunted efforts, determination, and the gift of good memory. While in college he came under the tutelage of his mathematics professor Edward B. Ross who was a Scottish missionary. Ross helped him financially, gave moral support, and above all trained his mind in the art of thinking *ab initio*. Ranganathan always treated Ross as his intellectual father and his portrait remained with the family wherever they moved. On earning a teaching degree in 1917 he became a teacher of mathematics in government colleges of the Madras Presidency. He loved mathematics and teaching, both. Life was going on, and he was already past thirty without any inkling of the great task ahead that the Providence had assigned him.

Suddenly in 1924, he crossed over to librarianship which in those days was not a career for active scholars and ambitious persons. Profession of Librarianship did not exist then. He received training in librarianship from the University College, London, there he is said have read all the books in the college library available on the subject of librarianship. He was impressed and influenced by his teachers like W.C.B. Sayers (1881-1960), though syllabus and the teaching methods did not satisfy him. He also undertook a tour of British libraries to gain a firsthand knowledge of their working and services. He returned home in 1925 with his mind swarming with new ideas. After that, neither he nor library science remained the same. His new found profession provided him intellectual, social and spiritual fulfillment, and huge fame later. Librarianship became his vocation and avocation to the exclusion of all other worldly engagements. Then library science curricula and teaching methods did not satisfy his inquiring mind trained in science and mathematics. Nevertheless, he was very much impressed by the variety, extent and intensity of library services provided to each British citizen by the legislation based British libraries network. He set before himself the twin tasks of providing wide library facilities at *par* with the British services to every Indian on statutory basis. This was a utopian goal which is still incomplete and unattainable. The second aim was to make library science true to the name of science by writing it anew on rigidly scientific lines. From the very day, he totally occupied himself with work for the noble goals he had set before himself. Librarianship also provided him spiritual sustenance. He modernized the Madras University library to provide unheard and unimagined library and information services to the students and faculty. Later such services were extended to the Madras elite at their door steps by home delivery of books service—a very novel idea then. It was a master stroke in library marketing. The foremost indigenous need was to create a social awakening for the value of libraries. He started, what we call now, library advocacy. He talked to people whatever be their social rank, to spread the gospel of the social value of library services, work and library sciences. He availed every opportunity, platform, personal contacts and available media to convince the statesmen, scholars, bureaucrats and laymen alike that libraries are depositories of our culture, and an apparatus of social memory. Libraries are indispensable to uplift a nation socially, democratically, economically and educationally—whatever be its social, economic and literacy conditions.

In the beginning, his was the one-man library movement. In his many books he proposed many plans and worked tirelessly for an integrated countrywide system of public and academic libraries. He was opposed to desultory establishment of libraries. In 1928 he founded, with prominent Madras citizenry, the Madras Library Association (MALA) with the twin aims of promoting library movement and to generate trained work force for the libraries to run on scientific lines. He succeeded in both so much so that the MALA school was taken over by the Madras University and upgraded it to university diploma—the first university library science course in India. Between 1940s and 1950s he adeptly drafted many library plans and library bills to suit Indian conditions, and wrote many books on the organization of libraries and role of libraries in adult education and national development. He was of the strong conviction that libraries are a force in education including adult education. His dream was to provide free book service to all Indians, and to make India a republic of books and libraries. Political leadership respected him, but looked upon libraries as luxury of the educated class in a mostly illiterate nation struggling with many economic and political problems after the Independence from the British rule in1947. There was no money for his massive plans. He, an incorrigible optimist, never gave in despite successive failures, and even personal discomfitures. At last in 1948, the library legislation was enacted by the then Madras state. Now library legislations exist in nineteen Indian states, namely, (1) Tamil Nadu –1948 (2) Andhra Pradesh -1960 (3) Karnataka -1965 (4) Maharashtra -1967 (5) West Bengal - 1979 (6) Manipur - 1988 (7) Kerala - 1989 (8) Haryana - 1989 (9) Mizoram -1993 (10) Goa -1993 (11) Gujarat - 2000 (12) Odessa– 2002 (13) Uttarakhand - 2005 (14) Rajasthan - 2006 (15) Uttar Pradesh - 2006 (16) Chhattisgarh- 2007 (17) Puducherry-2007 (18) Bihar-2008 (19) Arunachal Pradesh-2009. Many states are on their way to legislation. But the state of libraries and their services is far from his dreams. The all-India library system that he wanted to build has not come up. Libraries here and there are not linked in any nationwide system. The information, library and book policy has not yet been finalized. We have a Central National Library, national libraries for different subjects such as arts, science, agriculture, medicine; there are legal depositories of books, state and city libraries, but there is no library structure. There is no scheme of cooperation, there is unnecessary duplication of our meager library resources. UGC's multimillion 'Libraries and Information Network' (INFLIBNET) has not yet brought the academic libraries under a truly inter-connected network. The bibliographical activities of the nation are far from adequate. Yet the model he proposed is still seminally valid, and his dream will continue to inspire and guide the Indian library leaders. He would have been happy to see the recognition the National Knowledge Commission (2005-2008) has given to the value of libraries to make India a knowledge society. Establishment of the National Mission on Libraries in 2012 to frame library and information policy, and prepare long term plans and strategies for development of the library sector is a right step to implement the recommendations of the Knowledge Commission. But it was only he who with his selfless efforts, vision, high stature, right connections and convincing power that he got academic status for university and college librarians for which we are eternally under his debt. He also got the subject and substance of library science recognized among the academia, intelligentsia, and the government.

Crusader in him never stifled the scientist he was. He possessed a radical and fertile mind. His deliberations on the theory of library science metamorphosed its very face. In his first book *The Five Laws of Library Science* (1931, 2nd ed., 1957), now a classic (reprinted many times), he gave library science its normative principles:

- Books are for use
- Books are for all
- Every book its reader
- Save the time of the reader
- A library is a growing organism.

These simple looking laws have profound implications for library services and planning, and are as true as laws of any social science.

This book is a sum and summary of his entire library philosophy and became the fountain head of all his later writings. By induction, deduction and other methods of intellectual elaboration he carved out, as simple corollaries of the Laws, canons, principles, postulates and implications for all branches of library science from book selection to library administration and documentation to knowledge organization. Five laws are equally applicable to information networks and digital libraries. Authors after authors in the world have attested to their applications in the electronic and digital environment. His range was amazingly ecumenical and vision universal.

By the mid-1940s he had done his seminal work by writing on all aspects of the discipline such as library administration, book selection, reference service, cataloging code and cataloging theory, and the most famous *Prolegomena to Library Classification* (1937, 1957, 1967). His later work was simply further elucidation and improvement. He was a prolific as well as an innovative writer with uncanny insights and synthetic capacity of the mind. The full volume of his writings measures up to 60 books and 2000 papers, apart from many reports. His Colon Classification (1933), based on the concept of facet analysis, has been acknowledged as a greatest breakthrough in library classification. Its principles are still taught in all the library schools the world over. In 1957 an international conference held in England accepted facet analysis as the basis of information retrieval both in manual and automated systems. His work has gained so much acceptance that it forms the very bedrock of new researches in library science, and finds applications in new fields such as artificial intelligence, expert systems and knowledge representation. Facet analysis has found many concrete applications in organizing databases and networked resources on the world wide web. He is to library science what Einstein is to physics, says Eugene Garfield (1925-2017), a great information scientist. His work has been considerably furthered by some of his British and Indian disciples. International library experts and organizations such as UNESCO and International Standards Organization (ISO, The Hague) always sought and valued his advice. His influence in international librarianship was all pervasive. Perceptible library historians have acknowledged and elucidated his concrete influence first on British and through it on American librarianship. He had been quite a familiar figure in international library organizations such as, UNESCO, FID and IFLA. He was made honorary emeritus vice president of International Federation for Documentation (FID, the Hague) as well as the (British) Library Association (now, CILIP) London. It is believed that without his advice the UN library at NewYork would have been another US library. He proselytized to his theories many a fine brain such as Bernard Palmer (1910-1979) Education Officer of the (UK) Library Association, through him to whole of the British librarianship led by luminaries like J. Mills, B.C. Vickery, D.W. Langridge, and D.J. Foskett. His own teacher called him as the foremost grammarian of library classification. In the US he cast visible influence on the greats like, Jesse Shera, Eugene Garfield, Pauline Atherton, John Comaromi, Nasser Sharify, and Michael Gorman, to name a few. Above all, the American Library Association(ALA) while sending greetings on his birth centenary celebrations in 1992 acknowledged that he was "instrumental in establishing closer relations between the East and West, and encouraging cooperation at all levels of librarianship and library education..." The ALA described him as the librarian to the world.

In March 1945 Ranganathan left the Madras University. The same year, he joined the Banaras Hindu University on the invitation of S. Radhakrishnan (1888-1975) then its Vice-Chancellor later the President of the Republic of India. On the request of Sir Maurice Gwyer (1878-1952), an eminent jurist, Chief Judge of Federal Courts (now Supreme Court) and Vice-Chancellor of Delhi University, he joined therein 1947 as an honorary professor. At Delhi, he promoted higher education and research in library science. With his sole vision and efforts Delhi University became the first in the entire British Commonwealth to institute Master and Doctoral degrees in library science. That was in 1947. From 1944 to 1953, he unanimously remained President of the Indian Library Association to which he gave professional outlook, functions and agenda for future work. That is still considered the golden period of this 85 years old all India organization of professional librarians.

He donned many a hat at a time — a revolutionary thinker, philosopher, educationist, preacher, doer, missionary, teacher, a librarian, and above all a crusader. He worked single-mindedly and tirelessly for the development of libraries and library science in India. More than purveyor of information and knowledge he valued libraries as instruments for all-round development of the country. At heart he was an internationalist, a humanist who saw libraries as a force in world peace and international cooperation. Though he remained engaged in academics and research all his life, yet his role in public libraries movement, library legislation for a national network of libraries accessible to one and all remains critically important. He won for librarians a professional identity. Revered gratefully as Father of Indian Library Movement, he got us social and academic recognition with his selfless efforts and political links. In his life time he raised the library profession to great heights of academic respect and social responsibility. He knew it will not be possible to attract talented and meretorious persons to the professions unless it gets social status, academic recognition and better pay scales.

The crusader in Ranganathan organized people around him. He guided and inspired his library colleagues in intellectual work and to work for the library movement. He formed associations, organized conferences, established small and inner research circles to meet regularly when he was at Madras, Delhi, and Bangalore. Of these the Library Research Circle at Delhi (1950-53) is the most famous. He ardently believed in the value of team work, conferences and associations to develop and strengthen the emergent Indian library profession. From 1955 to 1957 he lived in Zurich and obtained first-hand knowledge of the use of library services to industry and R&D units. It was another active period internationally and intellectually. All eminent librarians of Europe visited him for discussions and advise. In 1962, the Government of India founded for him the Documentation Research and Training Centre (DRTC) at his convenient place, Bangalore to carry on his research and to train librarians in the advance work of information science and services. Now a world famous center, the DRTC is considered his "crowning accomplishment" (Garfield). He died on 27th September 1972 at Bangalore after a brief illness due bronchitis.

In his lifetime he had become a household name, and a legendary figure in library circles in India and abroad. Library experts in advanced countries were keen to confer with and listen to him. Invitations were pouring in from various countries. Sponsored by the British Council and the Rockefeller Foundation in 1948, he visited Europe and North America, and many times thereafter to participate in international meetings, conferences, and to deliver lectures or to advise library organizations. He always remained the focus in any gathering he participated. He was a confident and voluble speaker, and Westerners saw in him an embodiment of Eastern wisdom and intellect. They fondly addressed him *Guru*. His work got acceptance so much so that in 1957 an international conference of librarians held at Dorking, England deliberated and scrutinized his work. His theory of classification became the general theory of classification for information retrieval. He received universal recognition for his work cutting across political borders and mental prejudices that discount the intellectual work emanating from developing countries. So penetrating was his influence, and personality so peerless that American librarians reverently addressed him as "Librarian to the World". British librarians named his lifetime as "Ranganathan Age" He is the architect of the Indian library profession who bequeathed us a rich legacy. Describing his Colon Classification and its underlying theory as "monumental accomplishment" the eminent librarian D.W. Langridge (1925-2001) said that Ranganathan's "systematization in bibliographic classification surpassed the achievement of any European or American". We continue to live in his shadow.

He won laurels and acclaims at home and abroad for his single-minded devotion, creativity, and revolutionary work. Inventory of his awards and honors is long beginning with the title of *Rao Sahib* in 1935 by the British Government. Important among them include *Padmashri* in 1957 in the very first year of institution of this award, honorary D.Litt. from the University of Delhi (1948) and University of Pittsburgh (1964), National Research Professorship in

Library Science (1965), and a two-volume festschrift by an international committee (1962), Honorary Vice-Presidentship of the British Library Association (1957); and Membership of honor of the International Federation for Documentation, the Hague (1957), and inclusion of his portrait in the ISI "Cathedral of Man". Personal tributes vary from being known as founder of a distinguished school of thought to bringing cultural cooperation between the East and the West; and to enrichment of English language with his new terminology. In 1985, a successful and widely participated conference on Ranganathan's philosophy and relevance was held in New Delhi. Experts from Asia, Europe, South Africa and North America endorsed his continued relevance in present times. It was the first international library conference devoted to the work of an individual. In 1992 the International Society for Knowledge Organization (ISKO) and the International Federation of Library Associations (IFLA, the Hague) held their general conferences in India to celebrate his birth centenary. Government of India issued a commemorative postal stamp in his honor on the occasion. Many festschrifts and books explaining his contributions were released and many international journals such as *Libri, Knowledge Organization* brought out special issues on his work to commemorate the occasion.

As a man, he was deeply religious, strikingly simple and modest, living a spartan life. Parsimony and austerity were his hallmarks. He never even owned a house, nor a car. He always and vehemently abhorred intoxicants and flesh food — a true yogi. But in 1957, he donated his savings of one lakh (hundred thousand) rupees (then a tremendously huge sum!) to Madras University for the promotion of library education. Thereafter, he frequently gave away his accumulated wealth to the library profession in India. In 1963 he established the Sarada Ranganathan Endowment in Library Science for promotion of library movement. It is a very active Bangalore based organization. Temperamentally, he was a mystic and a philosopher. Most of his writings are inspired and intuitive. He wrote that his classic *Prolegomena to Library Classification* (1937) came out whole as an egg—that is he wrote it in one sitting. As a teacher he was par excellence. His method was Socratic to train the minds of his students in the art of thinking. He used to say a teacher is like a midwife who should bring out ideas already within the students. He always taught with anecdotes. He taught life in the guise of library science. More than facts and figures, he taught us attitude, spirits and the scientific temperament. He believed in the oneness of knowledge and interconnectedness of everything under the sun. He too often quoted the poet Francis Thompson (1859-1907):

All things by immortal power
Near or far,
Hiddenly
To each other linked are,
That thou canst not stir a flower,
Without troubling of a star.

Steeped in Indian philosophy, he saw the entire universe from flowers to stars linked in a Great Chain of Being. In his intellectual work he practiced the Vedic principle of *Ekavayata* - a sort of strong systems approach which emphasizes continuity and interconnected of entities in this universe. Intuition and flair are its main instruments. It provides a holistic approach to the problems of life and to the universe of knowledge. This accounts for the seminal unity of his work. Accordingly, on the spiritual side he saw the entire humanity as one Big Family. For him libraries and free flow of information were the instruments to promote peace and enlightenment. The scientist was a spiritualist at heart. His contribution to information science is enduring; and his niche is secure amongst the immortals of the library science world. He is a national hero in the august company of Dr. CV Raman and Guru Rabindra Nath Tagore. But his achievements in the then budding discipline of library science were much more momentous, as he built the profession from scratch. Raman and Tagore had something to build on, but Ranganathan had nothing, except opportunities before a visionary. With his vision and intellect Ranganathan created something new and multidimensional. He built a mountain with many peaks where even a mole did not exist. As a pioneer he took the library profession to its glorious heights.

Standing on the threshold of information society, we love the man for his dedication and humility; marvel the thinker for the profundity and enigmatic energy of his mind, remember the statesman for his vision and crusades; and awfully admire the librarian for his immense faith in power of libraries and free flow of information to enrich life in every human endeavor and to perpetuate world peace, civilization and culture.

An Appeal

The Government of India has launched a "Make in India" programme, but we have also to preserve, perpetuate, innovate and market what we already have.

The Library and Information Science profession in India must rise to the occasion to bring home the value of Ranganathan's work to the people who matter – the Government, politicians, and the Society at large.

Our hallowed legacy bequeathed to us by Dr S Ranganathan is squandering. It should not happen in a civilized country proud of its ancient civilization.

In days when the research agencies are liberal in funding research and academic activities, thanks to RUSA, we must make hay while this sun of grants shines.

There should be a National Mission for Revival of Ranganathan Legacy (NMRRL).

Appropriate agencies must be approached by the Indian library organizations and centers, especially by the National Mission on Libraries.

Let us all join to create another movement to make known, perpetuate and innovate what one man, Ranganathan bequeathed to us.

REFERENCES

Dudley Edward. (1973). *Ranganathan, S.R. 1892-1972*. London: Library Association, 1973 (1992 reprint).

Garfield Eugene. (1984). "Current Comments. A Tribute to S. R. Ranganathan, the Father of Indian Library Science. Part 2. Contribution to Indian and International Library Science." *Current Contents* 7, February 13: 3-7; and *Essays of an Information Scientist* 7: 45-49. Available at: http://www.garfield.library.upenn.edu/essays/v7p045y1984.pdf

Girja Kumar. (1992). *S.R. Ranganathan: An Intellectual Biography*. New Delhi: Har-Anand.

Langridge, D.W. (1991). "Classifying knowledge." In Meadows, A.J. (ed.), *Knowledge and communication: Essays on the Communication Chain*. London: Library Association Publishing, pp.1-18.

Satija, M.P. (1992). *S.R. Ranganathan and the Method of Science*. New Delhi.: Aditya, 1992.

Satija, M.P. (2011). "Remembering the Work of Ranganathan for Academic Libraries and Library Education." *SRELS Journal of Information Management* 48(3): 245-250.

Satija, M.P. (2016). "National Mission for the Revival of Ranganathan Legacy (NMRRL): An Appeal." *Library Herald* 54(3): 257-260.

Satija, M.P. (2017). "Colon Classification" *ISKO Encyclopedia of Knowledge Organization*. Accessible at http://www.isko.org/cyclo/colon_classification; and *Knowledge Organization* 44(4): 291-307.

Sri Ram, Chandra (2017). "Dr S R Ranganathan: An Intimate Biographical Essay" *Library Herald* 55(1): 2-13

Yogeshwar, R. (2001). *S.R. Ranganathan: Pragmatic Philosopher of Information Science: A Personal Biography*. Mumbai: Bhartiya Vidya Bhavan.

2

Colon Classification (CC)

STRUCTURE

ABSTRACT

Shiyali Ramamrita Ranganathan (1892-1972) has been called the father of the Indian library movement. He developed the revolutionary Colon Classification (CC) from 1924 to 1928, which was published in seven editions from 1933 to 1987. In this article the evolution of CC through its seven editions is discussed. The unique features of CC are described, including the work in idea, verbal, and notational planes. Tools for designing and evaluating a system are enshrined in his 55 canons, 22 principles, 13 postulates, and 10 devices (Indian Statistical Institute 2012, 34-38). Semantic and syntactic relations are enshrined in his order of main classes, Principles of Helpful Sequence in arrays, PMEST facet formula fitted with rounds and levels of facets, and other principles, such as the famous wall-picture principle for citation order of facets, and numerous devices for improvising class numbers for nonexistent isolates and potential subjects. Briefly explained are facet and phase analyses and number building with its notational base of 74 characters and symbols. It concludes with a discussion of the extent of application of CC in libraries, its contribution to the science of classification, and a view of its future.

2.1. INTRODUCTION

Mathematician turned librarian Dr. S. R. Ranganathan (1892–1972) is deservedly called the father of the Indian library movement. Internationally recognized as the most prolific library thinker and innovative librarian of his time, his exemplary dedication and uncanny insights won him the acclaim of his peers the world over. His work forms the bedrock of an influential theory of the wide discipline of knowledge organization. His extensive work on all aspects of library science was epoch-making, and created a paradigm next in importance only to the pioneering work of Melvil Dewey (1851–1931), who is often considered the father of modern librarianship. Ranganathan's views, appeals, and the research findings he communicated through books, journals, reports, international seminars, and lectures, have pervaded, and still constitute, the core of our current knowledge of the subject. His books, on almost all branches of library and information science, are librarians' lore. This chapter focuses on his Colon Classification (CC) and does not cover faceted classification in general, or the biography of Ranganathan.

2.2. A BRIEF HISTORY OF THE EDITIONS OF COLON CLASSIFICATION

The Colon Classification (CC), conceived and originally developed from 1924 to 1928, and initially applied in the Madras University Library, was first published in 1933 (Ranganathan 1933) by the Madras Library Association (founded by Ranganathan in 1928). The latest edition, and the first published after the death of Ranganathan, was the seventh (Ranganathan 1987). Being a mathematician and a close student of an inspiring teacher W. C. B. Sayers (1881–1960) in the School of Librarianship, University College London, Ranganathan was most attracted to classification studies. In his later work, he perceived many similarities between classification and mathematics (Ranganathan, 1939b). At the same time, practical classification by the Dewey Decimal Classification (DDC) did not satisfy his orderly mind. That being a "mark and park" system without any professed theory, he could assign more than one class number to a document, especially those dealing with compound and complex subjects. For example, "Anatomy of flowering plants" could either be given the class number of "Plant anatomy" or "Botany of flowering plants." It was a problematic option by default for all such compound subjects. In his view, this defeated the purpose of classification itself. Besides this, Ranganathan also found only a nominal representation of Indian subjects in the scheme. WASPish (White, Anglo-Saxon, Protestant) bias in Dewey's system, as it is in other western systems, is well-known, even today (Comaromi and Satija, 1985). Indeed all KO systems are cultural and temporal in their making (Judge 1983; Sahadath, 2013).

First, Ranganathan realized that the aftermath of World War I, 1914–1919, had brought in the emergence of specialized, micro, and interdisciplinary subjects, which the existing classifications failed to cope with. He diagnosed that DDC, because of its enumerative nature and 17th century roots, was a classification suited to the nineteenth century linear, mono-dimensional kind of literature (cf., Ranganathan 1961, pp. 81-83). An enumerative classification by default is not able to assign coextensive class numbers to most compound and complex subjects except to some by coincidence (Parrochia and Neuville 2013, p.14). Knowing the malady, the remedy could not have been far away. The problem occupied his mind relentlessly. In 1924, Ranganathan happened to visit Selfridge's department store in London, and accidentally stumbled on a demonstration of a Meccano toy kit. The salesman was making different toys from the same kit by permutation and combination of the blocks, strips, nuts, and bolts. That triggered his mind to adopt a similar technique to design different class numbers from the same subject concepts to suit individual documents (Indian Statistical Institute 2012). This idea later brought a paradigm shift in classification theory, practice, and research. He visualized that all knowledge is comprised of some basic and discrete concepts (call these building blocks of the universe of knowledge), which could be combined to construct class numbers to specifically suit a document, instead of assigning it a predetermined ready-made sort of pigeonhole class number. Connecting symbols in the form of punctuation marks served as his nuts and bolts to string together discrete concepts. Sayers at once commended the idea of the new technique, but warned him of the labour and patience required for the huge task ahead (Maltby 1975, p.191). Back home in 1925, as the first trained librarian of Madras University, he developed and applied his scheme to that library, and gained long and first-hand experience of its applications and problems, including comments from the library's users. As already stated, CC was first published in 1933. The second edition (Ranganathan 1939a), was important as it clearly laid down the theory and methods of CC as already published in his magnum opus, the *Prolegomena to Library Classification* (Ranganathan 1937). The third edition of CC (Ranganathan 1950) came out when Ranganathan had moved to Delhi University and was in the second phase of his writing career. In Delhi, he attracted a band of young and faithful follower librarians and organized them into a formal group named Library Research Circle; they considerably advanced research in classification, and applied his KO systems and methods in their libraries (Parthasarthy 1952). Colon Classification was widely adopted in Delhi libraries. This led him to delve deep into his classification theory at a somewhat more abstract level with his colleagues, disciples and students. New advances were published in conference volumes and serials of the Indian Library Association of which he was the president (1944-1953). He had the power to descend from the phenomenal level down to the seminal level (Ranganathan 1967a, p.395). After long experience and a constant quest to generalize the various facets, in 1952 he came out with his famous, although debatable, theory of "five and only five fundamental categories in the universe of knowledge." In the earlier editions, the facets were named variously in different main classes, e.g., problem facet, institution facet, substance facet, etc. (Ranganathan 1939, 1.85-1.151). In the fourth edition (Ranganathan 1952) these were highly generalized by an intuitive process of abstraction, and named as personality, matter, energy, space, and time, famously known as PMEST. It was a masterstroke in generalizing myriads of facets to a few seminal categories. It is considered as the least number of categories for any bibliographic classification postulated so far. The fifth edition (Ranganathan 1957a) was proposed as two volumes of basic and depth versions, but only the basic version was published. Later Ranganathan realized the non-viability of publishing depth schedules in book form (Indian Statistical Institute 2012). By the time the sixth edition was published (Ranganathan 1960), CC had reached its pinnacle of glory, exemplified by the International Study Conference on Classification Study and Information Retrieval, held at Dorking, England in 1957, which exclusively discussed his theories with wide approval. The Classification Research Group (CRG, London formed in 1952) declared its manifesto of faceted classification as the basis of all future information retrieval systems. Ranganathan's philosophy and method of facet analysis achieved wide acceptance, though only a few believed the doctrine of five fundamental categories. The term facet was used differently by different scholars and classification schemes, and it still continues so. The sixth edition, later issued with amendments (Ranganathan 1963), remains the most popular, used and stable edition. It is the one taught in all Indian library schools. The seventh edition (Ranganathan 1987), which was published posthumously and edited by his long time research assistant, Professor M.A. Gopinath (1940-2013), was considered by many to be confused and inconsistent in structure and notation. On the whole, this edition has been discarded by the Indian library profession (Satija 1990). Nevertheless, it brought many metamorphic changes to aspects such as basic subjects, categories, common isolates, and notation, though to no avail.

2.3. THREE VERSIONS OF COLON CLASSIFICATION

Gopinath (1972) conveniently grouped the seven editions into three versions in the line of evolution of facetisation of the system:

2.3.1. Version 1 (1933–1950): Rigidly Faceted Era

During this period, the facet formula was rigid and predetermined. The colon was the only connecting symbol for all the facets. That is, until the fourth edition (Ranganathan 1952) the only connecting symbol was the colon; even the absent facets had to be indicated by dummy colons, e.g., 2::::N for "Libraries in twentieth century". Here the first three colons indicate the absence of matter, energy and space facets, the last colon is the connecting symbol for the time facet, i.e., twentieth century. It made the class numbers unwieldy and even slippery. An inadvertent extra colon could land the book in an alien place, thus misplacing it. Some adversaries made fun of the cluttering of colons.

2.3.2. Version 2 (1950–1963): Analytico-Synthetic Era

As stated earlier, the fourth edition became a milestone with the postulation of the five fundamental categories and generalizing them concretely as PMEST. Each category was indicated by a distinct connecting symbol. Hence, the absence or presence of any category was self, or automatically indicated. For example, the above class number is now denoted as 2'N —the apostrophe being the indicator symbol for the category of Time. It means that all other categories, namely P, M, E, and S are visibly absent. It brought simplicity and brevity to the notation by doing away with the rigidity of the facet formula.

2.3.3. Version 3 (1963–1987): Freely Faceted Era

This period was devoted to the close study of the properties and structure of the universe of subjects. The matter category was split into three sub-categories: Matter-Property, Matter-Method and Matter-Material. Discovery of new common isolates, the concept of speciators to further differentiate a facet into species, and the development of highly hospitable sector notation and devices for improvising class numbers made CC more flexible. This led Ranganathan to declare it as a freely-faceted analytico-synthetic scheme, which is a sort of a self-perpetuating system. A self-perpetuating system is one that needs least revision, and which allows forging of new isolates as needed with the help of inbuilt devices. The new version has a virtually infinite capacity to incorporate new subjects at their proper places with the help of hospitality devices for the creation of new isolate numbers. However, even though CC is a truly postulate-based analytico-synthetic classification, and a highly faceted classification, history has proved that no classification can be self-perpetuating. The theory or concept of a self–perpetuating KO system is inherently flawed.

2.4. FEATURES OF CC

The CC is a general scheme, which aims to classify by discipline (a method adopted and perpetuated by DDC) all subjects and all forms of library documents - books, periodicals, reports, pamphlets, microforms, and electronic media - in all kinds of libraries. For bibliographic records and micro-subjects, requiring depth classification, its potential becomes even greater. The scheme is described as an analytico-synthetic as opposed to an enumerative classification system. Enumerative systems provide an exhaustive top down list of all subjects recorded at a given time. In contrast, the CC system lists, in bottom-up way, concepts which are to be combined in a pre-set order, to construct a class number co-extensive with the subject of the document. This objectively formulated and dynamic theory for designing and evaluating classification systems is enshrined comprehensively in his magnum opus *Prolegomena to Library Classification* (1937/1957a/1967a), and later summarized in a paper (Ranganathan 1964). For designing a classification system, Ranganathan divided the whole work into three successive planes, named Idea, Verbal and Notational planes. The idea plane is the message, the verbal its expression, and the notational plane is its visible representation in shorthand symbols.

2.4.1. Three Planes of Work

Prior to Ranganathan, classification design was considered as an intuitive field, the domain of a few inspired geniuses. This is quite obvious from the work of Melvil Dewey (1851–1931), C.A. Cutter (1837–1903), and J.D. Brown (1862–1914). H. E. Bliss (1870–1955), who was singularly dedicated to classification studies, did base his Bibliographic Classification (1944–1953) on some concretely formulated principles which Ranganathan viewed as static theory. The first edition of CC was mostly based on intuition and unstated principles. Later he justified this approach by his belief that in the real world a practice precedes its theory: poetry emerged much earlier than poetics (Satija 1992, 87-88). To elaborate in his own words:

> Design work of any kind has to draw largely from intuition unmediated as far as possible by the intellect or by rules framed by intellect. In its general makeup, a scheme of library classification will have to come out whole as an egg from the intuition of a classificationist of the creative variety. The intellectual classificationist can only polish it with the aid of a theory germane to it (Ranganathan 1961, pp 79-80).

Nevertheless, Ranganathan soon crystallized the unconscious theory that had gone into the making of his CC from 1928 to 1933. This theory was precipitated in his magnum opus, *Prolegomena to Library Classification* (1937). Through comparative approach and by identifying the best practices in existing systems, he formulated a panoply of canons and postulates for designing and evaluating classification systems. Structuring his theory into canons was obviously borrowed from Sayers whom he always regarded as the first grammarian of library classification (Ranganathan 1961, p.76). In 1950, a great breakthrough was achieved in the design of classification by dividing it in three succeeding phases, called planes: idea plane, verbal plane, and notational plane. Guided by basic laws of thinking and the overarching *Five Laws of Library Science* (1931) the work in each plane is executed by a total of 55 canons, 22 principles, and 13 postulates. Ranganathan (1967a, pp.53-71) makes clear distinctions between these terms. In addition, there are 10 devices to improvise notations for non-existing concepts or terms in the schedules.

2.4.1.1. Idea Plane

It is a thinking, policy, and decision-making phase; a paramount plane which is both a map and foundation of the system's design. The quality of work done here genetically determines the quality of the ultimate product.

Here intellectual analysis of the subject is done; characteristics are selected to break down the subject of the document into facets, and ultimately into isolates, arranged discretely and systematically into arrays and chains. An isolate is the smallest unit of knowledge in CC; whereas a facet is a group of isolates, denoted by an umbrella term, obtained by the application of a single characteristic to a set of entities. The types and quality of characteristics, and the order in which these are to be applied, are determined by the seven Canons of Characteristics. These canons mandate that characteristics chosen as the basis of division should be able to divide, and be relevant to the ultimate purpose of classification, concrete, objective, ascertainable and permanent; successively characteristics should be applied in order of general to specific in order of their relevance and importance.

Once facets and their isolates are formed by the application of characteristics, the function of the next set of canons is to arrange terms in arrays and chains in filiatory sequence. An array is a set of cognate entities of equal rank arranged in some systematic and predictable order. For this, Ranganathan formulated rules for formation of arrays of entities. These are: Canon of Exhaustiveness that an array should be inclusive of all the classes. Canon of Exclusiveness lays down that an entity should belong to one and only one array - it will avoid cross classification. This is only required for shelf classification as for classifying databases and designing Online Public Access Catalogs (OPACs), cross classification is a boon. Cross classification allows a virtual document to be kept at more than one place. Principles of Helpful Sequence mandate that facets and isolates of an array should be arranged in a predetermined logical or utilitarian sequence, or the one which is expected by the majority of the users. Historical events should be arranged chronologically, while UN member states can be put in an alphabetical order; living species may be arrayed in the order of their evolution (Principle of increasing complexity); chemical elements can be arranged by their atomic numbers. Coins can be arranged by their face value. Geographical entities can be arranged by the principle of spatial contiguity, as in a map. Ranganathan discovered eight options to arrange entities in a helpful order. A chain is a sequence of entities in a constantly decreasing order of their extension. For example, World—Asia—South Asia—India—North India—Delhi is a chain of classes. The Canon of Decreasing Extension means a chain should move from broader to narrower or from general to specific classes; and the Canon of Modulation means no link in the chain should be missed. Division of a universe should be gradual, proximate and finely calibrated. In the above chain, we should not jump from India to Delhi omitting North India. At the end of the work here we have a finely woven and exhaustive systematic network of all concepts with nodes and links. But still all is nebulous, and in an intangible and un-named amorphous form.

2.4.1.2. Verbal Plane

Then the theater moves to the verbal plane - to articulate the findings of the idea plane in unambiguous language. Language is the dress of thought, aptly said Dr. Samuel Johnson (1709–1784). Ranganathan (1962, Sec.A1) believed this and always exhorted librarians to learn and use technical terminology for effective communication. Terms used to express a science, or a phenomenon, should be current and free of homonyms and synonyms. Ranganathan vehemently laid down that terms used for a classification system should be made free of homonyms and synonyms; that is a term must be unique to the concept, and should be expressed and read in its context. He also said that the terms should mostly be neutral, not opinionated or critical, meaning that a classification term should not be value-ridden. As an example, classification systems should not use the terms major/minor authors to categorize them, as DDC did in its 14th edition (1942). Ironically, the terminology in the CC is now quite dated, which poses problems in chain indexing—a famous system invented by Ranganathan to derive subject headings from class numbers.

2.4.1.3. Notational Plane

Of the three planes, the notational plane is the most visible, so much so that many people mistake it for the classification *per se*. Ranganathan expected much from a notational system in terms of its capacity and sophisticated multitasking to represent and denote complex ideas. He vainly aspired that the notation should faithfully and comprehensively translate the subject of a document into a language of ordinal symbols. For him, classification was also a sort of translation. He overloaded his notation with onerous work and expected it to be very powerful, but relegated it to be the servant of the idea plane. In fact it is the faithful executor of the idea plane. However, he laid down that notation in a class number should be brief, simple and easy to write, remember (for a short time), and pronounce. These are optional qualities, not present in his system. More essentially, it should be expressive of subject structure (both hierarchical and faceted), and above all it should be hospitable to new subjects. This latter quality in Ranganathan's notation is in abundance—achieved at the high price of being unwieldy and too complex. Considered a high-water mark in the development of library classification notations, his notation is highly mixed and uses decimal, sector, and group notation. It is rigorously hierarchical, extremely hospitable and depicts the facets and categories in a transparent manner. Notation is highly hospitable both in always and chains by the use of many hospitality devices. His notation is highly mnemonic even down to the seminal level—e.g., unity, God, world are always denoted by 1; diseases and mechanical breakdown will get the same number, as will medical cures and mechanical repairs in their different main classes. As another example, G; 3, I; 3; , K; 3, and L; 3 represent general, plant, animal, and human physiology, respectively. Similarly, fuel/energy (machines), feed (animals), and food (humans) may get the same number wherever they occur in different schedules. Ultimately the notational plane is frighteningly complex and was much ahead of its time for shelf classification. Nevertheless, it is quite suited to computerized databases where the notational complexity does not matter.

2.4.2. Notation

The mixed notation in CC-7, comprising 74 symbols and characters (60 semantic and 14 indicator) has been divided into the following six species (Ranganathan 1987, p.33)

1	A/Z (Roman capitals)	26
2	Δ (Greek Delta)	01
3	0/9 Indo-Arabic numerals used decimally	10
4	a/z Roman lower case (i,l,o excluded)	23
5	* " ← Indicator symbols with anteriorising value	03
6	& ' . : ; , - = → + ( ) Ordinary indicator symbols	11 = 74

Asterisk, double inverted comma, backward arrow, ampersand, inverted comma, dot, colon, semicolon, comma, hyphen, equal to, forward arrow, plus, and parentheses (composed of two digits), respectively.

The notational base of CC is the widest ever in any library classification system. On this count, the CC-7 notation is wide based, thus very spacious and accommodating, though it has made the notation, and consequently the system, quite complicated - which has become detrimental to its popularity.

2.4.3. Division of Knowledge in CC

The CC presumes the entire body of knowledge woven into a system, and considers there to be an evolutionary unity in it. All knowledge is one, Ranganathan learnt from the Vedas (1700-500 BCE). The structure that ultimately emerges from CC is both traditional and revolutionary at once. But in the end it is not Vedic or Eastern in its appearance or working. The fact that Ranganathan recognizes and uses the existence of time-honored main and canonical classes, makes his scheme look steeped in the Western disciplinary tradition going back to Francis Bacon (1561-1626). Ranganathan identified three types of subjects in the universe of knowledge: basic, compound and complex, analogous to chemical substances. Basic subjects are unitary subjects, such as physics, thermodynamics, economics, Marxian economics, Homeopathy medicine, music, law, and library science. Compound subjects are basic subjects with subdivisions or additional facets, e.g., velocity of light, transport economics, guitar music, or law of marriage, and libraries in India. Compound subjects of varying degree are virtually infinite in number. Complex subjects are mostly interdisciplinary in nature, e.g., mathematics for engineers, geophysics, medical geography, or comparative physiology. Ranganathan postulated that every subject, be it of any type or level, has a basic subject that forms the first, or the base, facet in constructing a class number. CC further divides basic subjects into:

Main basic subjects

Non-main basic subjects

and further divided them into 10 species. On the basis of their modes of formation the following 10 types of basic subjects have been identified (Satija, et al 2014)

1	*Main basic subjects*	2	*Non-main basic subjects*
1.1	Traditional (Law, Physics)	2.1	Canonical classes (Algebra, Geometry)
1.2	Newly emerging (Library & Information Science)	2.2	System constituents (Marxian economy)
1.3	Fused (Biotechnology)	2.3	Environment constituents (Desert farming)
1.4	Distilled (Research methodology)	2.4	Special constituents (Gerontology)
1.5	Subject bundles (Ocean sciences)		
1.6	Agglomerates (Social sciences)		

2.4.3.1. Complex Subjects

A complex subject is a two-phased subject depicting mostly interdisciplinary relations. Six types of phase relations have been identified:

Type	*Indicator digits*	*Example*	*Class number*
General	a	Relation of political science with history	V &aW
Bias	b	Psychology for doctors	S & b L
Comparison	c	Physics compared with chemistry	C & c E
Difference	d	Difference between Christianity and Islam	Q, 6 & d7
Tool	e	Mathematical physics	C & e B
Influencing	g	Influence of Mahatma Gandhi on John Lennon	NR,56,N"w N40 & g zG

These relations can occur at three levels, namely: between two main classes for interdisciplinary subjects (e.g., Phase relation: chemistry and physics); between two foci of the same facet (e.g., Intra-facet relation: Islam and Judaism); and between two isolates of the same array within a facet (Intra-array relation: Catholics and Protestants). Therefore, there are 6 × 3 = 18 such relations in all. The number of relations does not seem comprehensive, but it should be noted that phase relations supplement other relationships depicted through PMEST, citation order, hierarchy, and helpful-sequence principles (Satija 2001). The general phase relation comprehends any relationship not expressed through the other five, while other relations are obvious. Definitive rules for primary and secondary phases and constructing their class numbers ensure the expression of the relationships in a mathematically precise and consistent way (Ranganathan 1987, 33). Ampersand "&" is the indicator symbol for phase relation, while each of 18 relations has its own indicator symbol a/y.

2.4.3.2. Main Classes and Their Order

Knowledge is the librarian's merchandise; our stock-in-trade. Understanding its nature and manner of growth is as vital to a classificationist as is the study of anatomy to a surgeon. Ranganathan's research in social epistemology has been lauded as an everlasting "intellectual contribution to the underlying philosophy of librarianship" by the late Jesse H. Shera (1903–1982) (Shera 1970, p.106). Ranganathan made pioneering studies of the mode of growth of subjects, mostly to attune his system to the growing universe of knowledge. He laid great emphasis on the order of knowledge and consequently on the arrangement of basic subjects in his CC. For him, the essence of library classification lay first in systematic arrangement, then in a helpful sequence of subjects and documents. A classification must depict the structure of knowledge. The first division of knowledge in CC is into traditional disciplines, which he arranges in the order of their evolution as academic studies, namely:

Science and technology

Humanities

Social sciences

The social sciences are the most recent academic disciplines to emerge; science and technology, however, were studies (of curiosity) of even primitive and cave dwelling humans.

The disciplines are further divided into sub-disciplines, namely:

B*Z	Maths and physical sciences
G*Z	Biosciences
K*Z	Animal sciences
L*Z	Medical sciences
MZ*Z	Humanities and social sciences
MZ*ZZ	Humanities
S*Z	Behavioral sciences
T*Z	Social sciences

Within each discipline CC has an order of main classes meticulously based on objectively stated principles. An overview of main classes in the CC is as follows:

A/B Science/Mathematics	Δ Spiritual experience & Mysticism
C/D Physics/Engineering	N/O/P Fine arts/Literature/Language
E/F Chemistry/Chemical technology	Q/R Religion/Philosophy
G/H Biology/Geology	S/T Psychology/Education
I/J/K/L Botany/Agriculture/Zoology/ Medicine	U/V Geography/History W/X Political Science/Economics
M Useful arts	Y/Z Sociology/Law

These main classes are in fact preceded by Generalia and Form classes a/z, and newly emerging classes 1/9, e.g.,

a	Bibliography	1	Universe of knowledge
k	General encyclopedias	2	Library science
m	General periodicals	3	Book science
p	Conference proceedings	4	Mass communication
w	Biographies	8	Management science
z	Generalia classes		

Sciences (including technologies) in classes A–M have been arranged in order of their increasing concreteness: B, Mathematics, is the most abstract of the sciences, while M, Useful arts, which includes crafts and applied technologies, is the most concrete in the group. Within A/M, theory and practice alternate: theory always precedes practice or its applications. For example, B, Mathematics, precedes C, Physics, which in turn precedes D, Engineering. E, Chemistry precedes F, Chemical technology. Similarly, I, Botany is followed by J, Agriculture. This internal arrangement is based on the principle of dependency, first promulgated by Auguste Comte (1798–1857). Unlike Dewey, Ranganathan preferred to collocate the theory with the practice of a subject. Indeed the Library of Congress Classification (1899/1940+) followed this principle prior to Ranganathan. In the humanities, which are spread over main classes N–S, the arrangement is in order of increasing richness of subject content. The order of social sciences, in main classes T–Z, is of increasing artificiality of their laws: Z Laws, being legislative and subject to frequent modifications, is considered the most artificial of the social sciences. One may fault this arrangement. For example, economic and social laws are not artificial but are based on long observed human nature and thus should not come so far down in the order of classes.

In an article published prior to the release of CC, R.S. Parkhi (1933, 87) commended and explained its arrangement of main classes as logical and evolutionary. Elucidating his viewpoint, he described the Generalia class as the complete miniaturized view of knowledge that precedes the entire universe of knowledge. B Mathematics pervades every science, indeed the queen of sciences. Physical sciences C–F study the matter and forces that constitute this universe. G, Biology is vital science. Classes H–K are in evolutionary order of life on our planet. Classes L–P are application subjects for the well-being and prosperity of humankind. Classes from Q, Religion to T, Education are for the moral and social development of individuals, which in fact depend upon the correct application of classes L–P, which in turn depend on classes A–K. Classes U–Z study the geographical and social sciences, the latest areas of knowledge to engage academicians. Here W Politics (and Government) precedes the creation and distribution of wealth in X, Economics, while Y, Sociology, and Z, Law keep society internally safe, intact and sustainable.

2.4.3.3. Triangular Representation of Main Classes

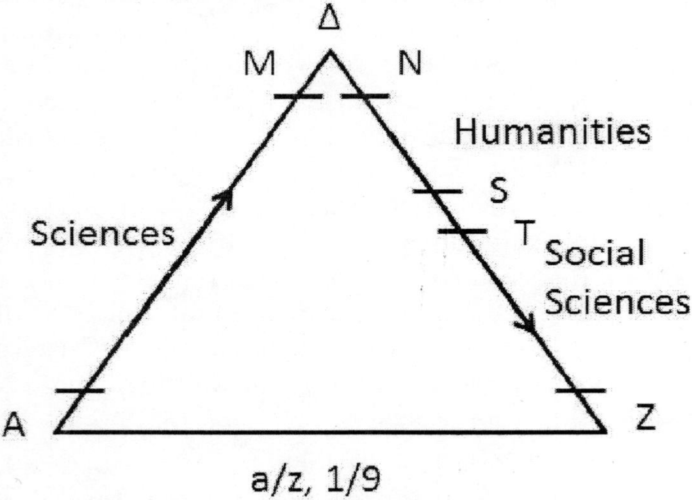

CC subsequently added the main class Δ (Greek letter Delta), Spiritual experience and mysticism, positioned between the sciences on the one hand and the humanities and social sciences on the other side of the triangle. The Δ is at the confluence of two different streams of knowledge, the sciences, and the humanities, the two different cultures of C.P. Snow (1905–1980). Ranganathan, (who personally believed in many supernatural phenomena and extra-sensory existents (Yogesawar 2001, pp.219-224)) treats spiritual experience as the fountainhead and summation of all knowledge, thus refuting Snow's theory of two cultures of sciences and humanities.

The library philosopher and classificationist H.E. Bliss (1870–1955) endeavored to discover a permanent order of main classes based upon what he called scientific and educational consensus. In fact no consensus can ever be permanent, since knowledge is a socially created and driven entity. Therefore, there cannot be any pre-existing order of main classes in Nature. The spatial order of subjects and their social value varies from society to society and from time to time. It has very aptly been observed that we "have to replace continually a classification by another one, according to the perception of more basic links between objects, and to the discovery of new indices of classification in the course of time" (Parrochia and Neuville 2013, p.18). The Renaissance placed a premium on humanities, while the Industrial Revolution gave the prime place to science and technology. In the 19th century theology was the queen of academic subjects only to be dethroned by research trends post the two World Wars. In the classification system (BBK) of the Soviet Union, Marxism was given the first place in any division of knowledge. Ranganathan based his Order instead on concrete and objectively stated principles. These principles are helpful in placing ever-emerging new main classes at their logically apt places in the array of main classes. The number of basic subjects has increased to about 800 in CC-7 without any problem of getting them to their rightful place in the lengthy array of basic subjects (Ranganathan 1987, pp.57–66)

2.4.3.4. Division of a Main Class

A main class is further split into [P], [M], and [E] categories, whereas categories of [S] and [T] are common to all the subjects in the universe of knowledge. Categories are further instantiated into facets, and facets into the ultimate isolates specific to that class. Very traditional main classes are divided into canonical classes, not directly into categories. Obviously canonical classes are traditional or classic divisions of an old main class. For example, mathematics has been divided into the canonical classes of arithmetic, algebra, geometry, etc., whereas physics is divided into heat, light, sound, electricity, etc. Canonical classes of a main class have their own facets and isolates. Some of the main classes have systems, specials, and environmental main classes. These amplified basic classes precede the categories as the basic facet in the facet formula.

2.4.3.5. Division of the Universe of Knowledge (UK)

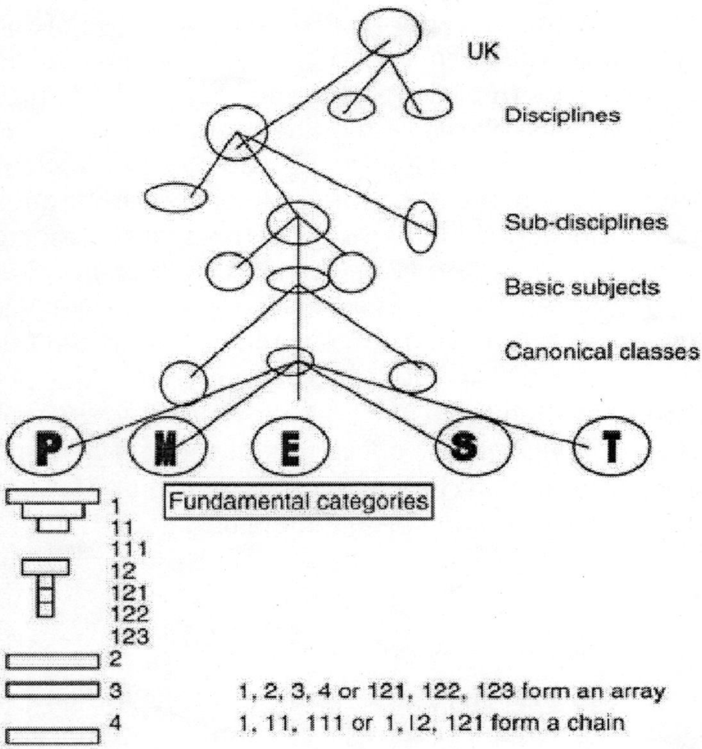

It may be noted that Ranganathan is very traditional in the division of knowledge up to the canonical classes

2.4.3.6. Facet analysis

Facet analysis as developed by Ranganathan is at the

core of CC philosophy and methods. Class numbers for compound or complex subjects are not listed ready-made. These have to be synthesized, or tailor-made, on the basis of the specific subject of the document. Ranganathan has given eight standard and interlocking steps to turn a raw title (as it appears on the document) into a coextensive class number based on the subject content and form of the document (Ranganathan 1987, pp.14-18). First of all, the specific subject of a document has to be determined. Ranganathan (1967a, p.174) defines the specific subject of a document as the one whose extension and intension are square with its subject content, but does not outline practical procedure for its determination. Ranganathan calls it an intuitive or trial-and-error act for which there can be no specific rules. Indeed, it requires flair, and is learned continuously from experience. Nevertheless, a specific subject is to be determined from the title, subtitle, preface, table of contents, or even by reading the text, as when applying other knowledge organization systems (Koford 2017, p.10). Subject analysis process is the same for all KOSs. The raw title may be augmented by key words or phrases, if necessary, to fully indicate the specific subject of the document.

Next, the subject proper must be separated from the common isolates, which represent the tangible bibliographic elements of the document, or viewpoint of the author. Then the main class in which the specific subject falls is determined. Main classes and other basic classes are postulated by the system —these are the givens, not to be challenged by a classifier. Ranganathan postulates that every subject belongs to one and only one basic subject, which forms the first facet (Ranganathan 1960, Sec.12, p.1.42). Then starts the facet analysis *per se* into PMEST categories. The system suggests identification and separation of the categories in a subject in the order from [T] to [P], moving from the easily recognisable category to the most elusive one. Broader categories are further resolved into specific facets.

Categories tend to evade definition. Their nature is somewhat elusive, though not metaphysical. These are still postulated and require much experience and flair to recognize them. For example, the personality category occurs in all the main classes, yet it is difficult to say what in general it is. The nature or constituents of categories vary from main class to main class. Their deceptive nature is clear from the fact that what had been the energy category in the fourth to sixth editions became, all of a sudden, the matter category in the seventh edition. At times it is utterly confusing to categorize an entity clearly. For example, in the class music, musical instruments such as guitar, drum, flute, etc., are designated as matter category, so are books and other documents in library science. Therefore, if something puzzles us, the only solace seems to acquiesce in the way desired by Ranganathan. The Postulate of Impersonation of categories adds to the confusion—that is, a category may masquerade as some other category, e.g., a country is [P] in N Fine arts, V History and Z Law, but [S] in other social sciences. Also the context changes the category: Gold is [M] in numismatics but [P] in E Chemistry and HZ Mineralogy. In practical classification we start with identifying [T] and come down to [P] via [S], [E] and [M]. Time indicated by the apostrophe, is chronological, diurnal, or seasonal. Its examples are twentieth century, medieval period, summer season, or morning time, etc. Space indicated by a dot is the manifestation of geographical and political areas or population clusters, for example, Asia, London, French speaking countries, NATO, G-8, hilly or desert areas, Iberian Peninsula, or Colorado valley. Energy, indicated by a colon, manifests actions, activities, processes, and problems. For example, treatment, storage, diseases, teaching, management, or grammar etc. are instances of energy. Earlier [M] was confined to the material of the entity, such as wooden chairs, marble sculpture, or gold coins. In the latest edition Ranganathan has widened the scope of matter by recognizing three variants of this category:

Matter-Property [M-P].

Matter-Method [M-M].

Matter-Material [M-Mt].

For all the three the indicator symbol is ";" semicolon. Of all the fundamental categories, personality [P] is the most concrete, but, paradoxically, the most difficult to recognize. Like human personality it is a complex entity and thus elusive. It is wholeness of the subject of the document. Ranganathan recommended the Residual Method to spot it in the facet analysis of a subject. It means that after identifying [T], [S], [E], and [M], categories, if anything still remains in the residue, then it might be personality - as a corollary of the "five and only five fundamental categories" But this method does not work all the time, especially when there are more facets than categories. M.A. Gopinath (1985) later maintained that the residual method was no longer necessary for this purpose. Personality is incarnate in persons (individuals or groups), communities, nations, institutions, animal and plant families, body organs, chemical substances, agricultural produce, languages, literary works, religions, art styles, political systems or ideologies, laws and the like. It is indicated by a comma.

2.4.3.7. Facet Formula: Citation Order

Rounds and levels of facets : It is not necessary for the subject of a document to be composed of all five categories. It may encompass any number of categories from one to five depending upon how far it is compounded or micro. On the other hand, a category may also occur more than once in the same subject. A category may manifest itself in more than one concept in micro subjects. Recurrence of a category is accounted for and accommodated by the ingenious postulate of Rounds and Levels. The PMEST formula is, in fact, comprised of many so called rounds and levels of facets. For example, in class O, Literature, the category [P] personality occurs four times (Language, Form, Author, and Work), each at the same hierarchic level. In the subject, 'Treatment of human diseases', both diseases and treatment are manifestations of the first and second rounds of energy, respectively, in the sixth edition. A subject aspect 'Summer of 2018' manifests two levels of Time facet. Thus, in a facet formula, facets of the same category may occur more than once to be accommodated in a logical citation order. Ranganathan (1960, 1.27-1.28) postulated that:

- Space and time occur only in the last round of the facet formula; they can have levels ;
- Categories [P], [M], and [E] can occur in various rounds;
- Levels occur only within a round;
- Within a round [P] and [M] can also occur at many levels;
- Energy always completes a round and has no level, but only rounds.

To mechanize the arrangement of categories and their recurring but scattered facets, Ranganathan after a long trial, finally settled on the general, all encompassing, and very handy facet formula famous as PMEST. Rounds of categories and, within a round, levels, are arranged by the Principle of Dependency, which Ranganathan formulated as the Wall-Picture principle: Since there cannot be any mural without a wall, so the wall is made the first facet. The master Wall–Picture principle has various corollaries formulated in such axiomatically worded principles as the

Whole–Organ principle (whole–part relationship) and the Cow–Calf principle (principle of appurtenance) to arrange rounds and levels of facets; the more complex Actand-Action-Actor-Tool principle is obtained by a mix of the above principles. Actand or Actee is someone on which action is performed. For example, Actand is a patient on which Action (surgery) is performed by the Actor (doctor) with laser (Tool).

In the sequence, the basic facet, invariably represented by the main class or its amplification by system (Sm), environment (Env), or specialization (Sp), precedes other facets. The grand general facet formula may be represented as follows:

> (BF), [1P1], [1P2], [1P3], [1P4]; [1M1]; [1M2]; [1M3]: [E], [2P1], [2P2]; [2M1]: [2E], [3P1]... : [3E]. [S1].[S2]'[T1]'[T2]

Numbers prefixed to a category indicate its round, while numbers suffixed to a category indicate its level, e.g., [2M1] is 2nd round 1st level Matter.

In the current edition of CC, the total number of facets and their general sequence is as follows (Ranganathan 1987, 49-51):

> Field of study → System → Environment → Specials → Object of study → Kinds/Parts of object → Properties of object → Action on the object → Kind of action → Method of action → Agent of action → Instrument of action → Space → Space qualifier → Time → Time qualifier.

2.4.3.8. Absolute Syntax: Quest for a Holy Grail

In his spirited quest for discovering a natural order of facets, Ranganathan proposed the idea of an "absolute syntax of facets," by which he meant a sequence in which component facets of a subject "arrange themselves in the minds of the majority of persons" (Ranganathan 1987, pp.579-582). Indeed, he conjectured that absolute syntax may be the "same for a large majority of persons irrespective of their mother tongues," so that absolute syntax and linguistic syntax do not necessarily coincide. He further believed that absolute syntax was close to his own PMEST citation order, arrived at by rigorous postulates and principles. The basic question is whether there exists such an absolute syntax of ideas in the minds of the majority of adults, free from the constant influence of the mother tongue and its grammar as impressed on human minds since infancy. Yet there is no empirical evidence that it exists at all. Nevertheless, as Iyer (1995, p.184) asserts, "If a particular way of structuring a subject can be easily understood in translation to another language, regardless of the linguistic variations of individual tongues, then an absolute syntax may exist at some level." Arthur Maltby (1975, p.199) points out that Ranganathan believed in knowledge synthesis rather than in its mere division for mapping and information retrieval; this makes the search for the absolute syntax of ideas worth pursuing by a highly varied interdisciplinary group of researchers.

2.4.3.9. Synthesis

Analysis is followed by synthesis of facets in an analytico-synthetic classification. For any document, first of all subject *per se* is to be separated from common isolates denoted by Roman lower case, and added after the subject facets with their own indicator symbols. These are the two types: anteriorising and posteriorising.

Anteriorising Common Isolates (ACIs) denote forms of documents, e.g.,

a	bibliography	r	administration report
k	encyclopedia	s	statistics
m	periodical	t	commission report
		x	collected works

These are added with a connecting symbol (indicator) double inverted comma ["], and documents fitted with ACI file anterior to core documents. Posteriorising Common Isolates (PCIs) which denote associations, centers, critical studies, are further instances of three types: Personality, Matter-Property, and Energy.

b14	calculation
aTc	critical study
t	educational/research institutions or learned societies

These are added with their respective indicator symbols of cornma, semicolon, and colon respectively, and take the document to a backward position:

2;5 'P"a	Bibliography of twenty-first century library classification
2;5"k1,P1	ISKO Encyclopedia of knowledge organization (IEKO)
2;5.1,g,N9	International Society for Knowledge Organization (ISKO)
2.73,g,M7	American Library Association (ALA)
2.73,g,M7,1;3	Functions of the President of the ALA
2,J1*Z. 73:a T	Assessment of U.S. academic libraries
E*Z: aR	Research in chemical sciences
Y;aa	Theories of sociology

Class numbers look like lengthy algebraic equations, or even unwieldy and surrealistic. Savor a few:

20th century bibliography on Merchant of Venice by Shakespeare

O,111, 2J64, M+V" aN

Homeopathy for treatment of heart diseases of old people living in high altitudes

L-L-9Un4-9E, 32; 4:6

A history of the Association of Commonwealth Universities

T,18.1=CN48,g, 9N" v

The US armament policy towards Pakistan from 1975 to 2017

V, 73; 1844X=M1'P17←N75

India's foreign policy towards Muslim countries

V, 44; 181= (Q, 7)

Sociological abstracts

Y" a" m73, N

(Mind the punctuation marks!). Ranganathan sacrificed the brevity and simplicity of notation to make the notation extremely hospitable, and to produce finely coextensive class numbers. His motto was "be minute, be minute, and be too minute". Most classifiers are afraid of the notation, and find the varying synthesis rules quite baffling. All that make the system unpopular, even dreaded. But to the initiated classifying by the CC is mind stimulating.

2.4.3.10. Shelf Arrangement

Principle of Inversion : CC follows the Principle of Inversion first used by the Universal Decimal Classification (UDC). It means that the citation order of facets in the facet formula is the reverse of their arrangement on the shelves. To elaborate, though the [T] is the last facet in the PMEST citation order, the subjects fitted with only [T] will file before [S] category, which in turn will file before [E], and so on. In the PMEST facet formula, categories are arranged in order of decreasing concreteness: [P] Personality is the most concrete and [T] Time the most abstract, or least concrete; [E] Energy lies midway, being as much concrete as it is abstract. On the shelves or in a classified bibliographic database, however, the order of subjects is from general to specific, that is, from abstract to concrete, i.e., from [T] to [P]. Overall order on the shelves within a class comes out to be:

General treated generally

General treated specially

Special treated generally

Special treated specially

This order is achieved ingeniously by fixing the ordinal value of semantic and indicator symbols, e.g., the ordinal value of the indicator for [T] is less than that of [S], and so on. The other class numbers are arranged in the ascending order of a/z, 0/9 and A/Z.

2.4.3.11. APUPA Pattern

Within a given specific class CC arranges documents on the shelves in a regular pattern, what is termed the APUPA pattern (Satija 2001, 208-209). The letters of this acronym stand for different pockets of documents in a given and related class: The A on both ends of the acronym represents Alien (or related) subject zones; Ps denote Penumbral regions. The first Penumbral area comprises associated documents such as bibliographies or dictionaries which are preliminaries to the U region proper —which houses pithy core subject documents. U is the Umbral region, having core documents on the subject. The second P region accommodates advanced documents such as advances in the subject, critical studies, research organizations or centres for the advancement of the discipline. Obviously such documents are studied after comprehending the core documents in the U region. The general APUPA pattern is achieved by postulating two kinds of common isolates: Anteriorizing Common Isolates (ACIs) and Posteriorizing Common Isolates (PCIs). Common isolates are like the standard subdivisions of DDC or form and viewpoint common auxiliaries of the UDC, which are attachable to any class, irrespective of its specificity. Documents having Anteriorizing Common Isolates are not the subject proper, but form approaches to a subject. They include, for example, bibliographies, synopsis, histories, and glossaries of a subject. Documents fitted with ACIs are filed anterior to the subject proper. This forms the first penumbral region, having less of the subject proper. Then follows the proper, pure, one hundred percent subject with all its subdivisions. For example, basic, compound and complex subjects constitute the umbral region in the pattern. This is followed by another penumbral region formed by fitting documents lying in the umbral region with PCIs. These are documents about the subject that are best read by advanced students or researchers after the mastery of the core subject (U). These include educational and research institutes in the subject, critical reviews, and recent advances in the subject. Thus the umbral region is surrounded on both sides by penumbral regions of differing natures, which in turn are flanked by two different alien regions on both the ends. The APUPA pattern, unique to CC, is one of the most logical, pedagogically useful, and beautiful arrangements of documents on the shelves. It uniformly and constantly weaves a perceptible pattern of documents on the shelves, or of their surrogates in a bibliography. The arrangement is so impeccable that it is appropriate to say that to browse a CC classified library is 'itself an education' (Palmer 1961, pp.206-207). Ranganathan (1967b, pp.61-62) claims that it reduces noise while locating documents on the shelves, or retrieval of their surrogates in a classified database. This has been achieved by investigating deeply the varied forms of documents and arranging them within a given class in a progressively pedagogic way.

A	P	U	P	A	P	U	P	A	P	U	P	A	P	U	P	A	P	U	P	A	P	U	P	A

APUPA on the shelves is a continuum from A/Z classes.

2.4.3.12. Index

The sixth edition had many subject indexes, but the seventh has none attached to it. CINDEX, a machine readable index to CC-7 on a CD in UNESCO's WINISIS, was issued in 2002. It is waiting to be incorporated into the print edition (Ranganathan 1987).

2.4.3.13. Book Numbers

The CC espouses a comprehensive and sound chronological book number system for the sub-arrangement of documents by the year of publication. It was based on a chronological system devised by W.S. Biscoe (1853-1933) and endorsed by his mentor Melvil Dewey. But Ranganathan's system is much more systematic, sophisticated and comprehensive in its approach. He made it an integral part of Colon Classification, and also provided a Canon of Book Number (Ranganathan 1967a, p.503) to make it mandatory for every classification system, and every library to make it an integral part of the call number. The broader formula for book numbers is [L][F][Y].[V]-[S];[C]:[g] —standing for language, form, year of publication, volume, supplement, copy and commentary respectively, of the book. Each of the first three facets has its own schedule of isolates, while rest of the facets are represented by their inherent numeral in order to construct the book number for the document. It helps to keep together a book and all its associated volumes, copies, supplements and commentaries. For example, a 2017 book of quotations in the French language (irrespective of its subject) will get the book number x122Q7. In practice this elaborate looking but mechanical and mnemonic system, most of the time turns out very brief book numbers, even of just two digits. By all accounts it is the most systematic book numbering system ever devised (Satija, 2015a).

2.5. REVISION, USE, STATUS AND FUTURE

2.5.1. Revision and use

Despite being promoted as India's national scheme of classification by some patriotic enthusiasts (Parkhi 1965),

CC is not a widely used system in India. The DDC outranks any other system in popularity in the country. Though no register of its users has been maintained, according to a very favorable estimate some 24% of libraries were using the CC system in India in the 1960s. No new library is adopting it as it is dated and there is no support from any institution for troubleshooting. The quick succession of six editions from 1933 to 1960 also led people to view it as an experimental system, rather than a stable one, and still in the making. Nevertheless, Colon Classification class numbers are given as a bibliographic element in entries in the Indian National Bibliography (Satija 1986). It badly needs revision (Raghavan 2015), but there is no national committee or substantive institutional backing to advise or to take responsibility for its revision or publication. Efforts to revive and revise it have been to no avail, because of the enormity of the task, and the lack of collective efforts and enthusiasm of its adherents (Satija 2015b). It is now repeatedly reprinted by a commercial publisher for legions of students. Its theory and practice is still taught in all the Indian library schools, partially out of deference to the legacy of Ranganathan, but mostly due to its sound theory applicable in the practice of other systems such as the DDC and UDC. In India it has been the most popular system for writing and research as evidenced by the largest bibliography on it (Satija and Singh 1994). More than a dozen textbooks on CC in English and in some Indian languages have been published for students.

2.5.2. Status and Future

The system is based on postulates and principles integrated into a coherent, fully and finely developed theory of classification. Francis Miksa (1998, p. 67) aptly says that Ranganathan "treated library classification as a single unified structure of ideas which followed from a cohesive set of basic principles." For this, Ranganathan evolved appropriate principles and forged precise tools. The theory of CC is, in fact, considered as the theory of classification in general, and is taught in many library schools the world over. The contribution of CC lies in its facet analysis technique, the concept of fundamental categories, three plans of work, and a raft of practical postulates and hospitality devices. Above all, it provides scientific and concrete guidelines for the construction of any new classification system (Vickery 1960; Ranganathan 1964). Many depth and special classification systems have been designed using CC methods, as listed by Kaula and Prasad (1981) and the Indian Statistical Institute (2012). It can be used to design other indexing vocabularies such as thesauri, subject headings (through chain indexing), or depth classifications for micro subjects. Its facet analysis is immensely helpful in query formulation for better recall and precision of output in any retrieval system (Neelameghan 1993; Suman 2014). Some search engines and Web directories are using Ranganathan's approach with good results for retrieval on the Web (La Barre 2007; Tunkelang 2009). Glassels (1998) for one wonders if Ranganathan anticipated the WWW and search engines. Ellis, David, and Ana Vasconcelos (1999) have lucidly explained the use of Ranganathan's theories for organising and searching the web. Advances in classification theory and practice in the online environment very much depend on facet analysis (Slavic 2008). Apart from two very comprehensive bibliographies on Ranganthan one by Das Gupta (1967) and other by Satija and Amrik Singh (1994), there are numerous bibliometric studies on Indian library literature. In all such studies Ranganthan dominates the scene with his enduring contribution. However four important studies, two before the Google era (Finks and Haug, 1992; Lancaster et al, 1992) and two very recent ones studying Ranganthan's presence in databases Smiraglia (2014), Das and Mishra (2015) attest his continuing relevance and international popularity. Finks and Haug who measured quantitative impact of Ranganathan on North American librarianship found that 72 of all the 122 publications which cited Ranganathan were on classification. They further endorsed Eugene Garfield's findings of 1984 that *Prolegomena* received most of attention of all his works in the US and Canada. Lancaster's team made citation analysis of Ranganthan's writing from 1956 to 1990 to report that his influence continues intact: "Citations to the *Prolegomena...* (95), *Colon Classification* (69) and *Five Laws...* (28) account for more than a third of the total citations (690)". They further observed, "Facet analysis and subject structuring get substantial references, including computer generation of thesaurus, deep structure indexing systems and expert systems design". Impressed by depth and breadth of his contribution they concluded that hardly anyone can match his diversity of contributions to LIS field. Smiraglia (2014) employing domain analysis technique to the references of the last three decades in the database of the *Web of Science* (WoS) shows Ranganathan's legacy in the 21st century is leading the knowledge organization (KO) domain to a new territory. He empirically reviews and maps Ranganathan's influence on research in KO to demonstrate with evidence that facet analysis is "fuelling its popularity in K O systems and web engineering". His research shows Ranganathan's ideas form starting discussion to the current era of progress in K O. His legacy is an integral part of the 21st century research in this widening domain. Das and Mishra almost came out with similar results finding Prolegomena, CC and Five laws as the most popular and highly cited works in the Google Scholar (GS), Web of Science, and Scopus databases. Quantitatively they reported citations: Prolegomena 748 (GS), 127 (WoS), Five Laws 671 (GS), 87 (WoS), and the CC 559 (GS), 177 (WoS). His other books such as *Elements of Library Classification* (1940s), *Philosophy of library*

Classification (1950s), and *Classification and communication* (1950) also continue to be considerably cited all over the world. Relevant journal articles in these databases discuss the theories of facet analysis and faceted classification systems. They found out "Many authors also discuss Ranganathan's theoretical framework in today's context, analysing his influence in designing modern ICT-enabled information systems and retrieval techniques". Citations also indicate that his theories are contextual in semantic web applications, designing search interfaces, organizing and accessing web resources and other specialized databases. This study also documented that his seminal work continues to guide us to formulate multidimensional and multimodal information architecture to design semantic web and ontologies. "Ranganathan's principles can be applied for multilingual knowledge representation, and designing efficient search and retrieval interfaces for the common netizens", they find out further (Das and Mishra 2015, p.298). In view of such studies nothing could be more appropriate than ALA's 1992 tribute describing Ranganathan as the "librarian to the world".

There is, on the other hand, also important criticism of the theoretical status of CC. Parrochia and Neuville (2013, pp.15-16) wrote:

> The advantages of CC are numerous. The first one is a greater flexibility in determining new subjects and subject numbers. But CC improves on the enumerative systems in several other ways. One of them is the concept of phases which allows classifiers to readily combine [...] However, many problems have confronted Colon Classification. In particular, we must understand that the secret model of Ranganathan is, in fact, crystallography. Facets,

> i.e. small components of larger entities or units, are similar to flat faces of a diamond which reflect the underlying symmetry of the crystal structure, so that the general structure of Ranganathan Classification, as that of faceted classification in general, is a kind of permutohedron. [...] This means that the determinations of the Colon Classification are not unequivocal ones, and that the same subject may be classified in many different ways.

Parrochia and Neuville (2013, p.17) also found that

> Since the 1950s, several decades of research in Information Science did not solve anymore the problem of a general theory of classifications in library science, a dense and active research field in the last century (see [Dhyani 1999]). For instance, between 1951 and 1961, when S.R. Ranganathan was the "Rapporteur général" of the Committee on General Theory of Classification of the International Federation for Documentation, which was formed in 1950 on his initiative, he (see, for instance, [FID. 1954]) and some other scientists such as de Grolier (see [Maniez 1991]) wrote some interesting reports, while the members of the Classification Research Group (Farradane, Fairthorne, Vickery, Foskett and others), were working on their own. But the search for a new universal standard classification, such as the original type of alphanumeric and pronounceable symbolization advocated by de Grolier in those years, remained a utopia. Twenty or thirty years later, it was still out of reach (see [de Grolier 1970 and 1988]) and more recently, some author was

even wondering whether such a classification is possible (see [Mai 2002]).

2.5.3. Conclusion

The CC seems to confirm the sad experience that success of KOS is related less to their theoretical and research based qualities than to the strength of support for maintaining systems. The survival of the system in its present state seems uncertain because of long and callous neglect. The DDC is considered less advanced, but is the most successful classification. The BISAC system (Martínez-Ávila 2016) is also becoming influential because of its support from the publishing industry. Although CC introduced a methodology of classification that has many advantages, and that remains a strong and distinct approach in knowledge organization, some of its assumptions are regarded by many today as utopian, or even undesirable. The idea of providing a universal standardized classification of knowledge seems to be in conflict with the realization that all KO systems are cultural and temporal in their making.

Having already subtly pervaded the making of new systems and getting sublimated into a theory, CC has achieved *nirvana* from bodily avatar. Transcending the cycle of life and death, it has become a subliminal tool of information retrieval and knowledge mapping.

ACKNOWLEDGMENT

I offer my sincere thanks to Dr. Daniel Martínez-Ávila for editing the references and to Prof. Birger Hjørland for his practical help in drawing my attention to many references and providing full texts of some of them. Finally thanks to Prof. Vanda Broughton for careful proofreading of the manuscript and to Prof. Claudio Gnoli for further suggestions. Thanks are again to the Editors of IEKO for first publishing it.

REFERENCES

Bliss, Henry E. (1938). "Review of Prolegomena to Library Classification by S. R. Ranganathan." *Library Quarterly* 8(4): 299-303.

Broughton, Vanda(2018): Facet Analysis. London: Facet Publishing, 224p

Comaromi, John P. and Mohinder P Satija. (1985). "History of the Indianisation of the Dewey Decimal Classification." *Libri* 35(1): 1-20.

Das, Anup Kumar and Sanjaya Mishra. (2015). "S. R. Ranganathan in Google Scholar and Other International Databases." *Annals of Library & Information Studies* 62(4): 290-298

Dhyani, Pushpa. (1999). "Library Classification in Computer Age." *DESIDOC Bulletin of information Technology* 19(3): 5-13

Ellis, David and Ana Vasconcelos. (1999). "Ranganathan and the Net: Using Facet Analysis to Search and Organise the WorldWide Web." *Aslib Proceedings* 51(1): 3-10.

FID. (1954). International Federation for Documentation—Committee on 'General Theory of Classification' Rapporteur generale: S.R. Ranganathan. Minutes of the First Meeting. Report 4 to the 21st Conference of the FID, 1954. *Revue de la documentation* 21: 3-5.

Finks, Lee W. and James D. Haug. (1992). "Ranganathan's contribution to American librarianship" In Sharma, R.N., ed., *S. R. Ranganathan and the West*. New Delhi: Sterling Publishers, pp.71-97.

Glassel, Aimee. (1998). *Was Ranganathan a Yahoo* https://scout.wisc.edu/scout/toolkit/enduser/archive/1998/euc-9803

Gopinath, M. A. (1972). "The Colon Classification." In Arthur Maltby, ed., *Classification in the 1970's*. London: Clive Bingley, pp. 53-85.

Gopinath, M. A. (1985). "Relevance of Ranganathan's Postulational Approach in the Identification of Key concepts in the Newly Formed Subjects and its Implications to Intellectual Organisation of Information." In Tanjavur Srinivasarengan Rajagopalan, ed., *Ranganathan's Philosophy: Assessment, Impact and Relevance*. New Delhi: Vikas, 153-181.

de Grolier, Éric. (1970). "Quelques Travaux Récents en Matière de Classification Encyclopédique." *Bulletin des Bibliothèques de France* 15(3): 99–126.

de Grolier, Éric. (1988). "Taxilogie et Classification: un Essai de Mise au Point et Quelques Notes de Prospective." *Bulletin des Bibliothèques de France* 6(6): 468–489.

Hjørland, Birger. (2013). "Facet Analysis: The Logical Approach to

Knowledge Organization." *Information Processing and Management* 49(2): 545-557.

Indian Standards Institution. (1964). *Glossary of Classification Terms. New Delhi: Indian Standards Institution. (IS: 2550-1963).* (Indian Standards Institution is now renamed Bureau of Indian Standards. Ranganathan was the chairman of the ISI Committee and de facto the author of this glossary). https://law.resource.org/pub/in/bis/S07/is.2550.1963.pdf

Permanent webcite: http://www.webcitation.org/6ovd7NkGg

Indian Statistical Institute. (2012). *Dr. S. R. Ranganathan's Fifty Years of Experience in the Development of Colon Classification.* Bangalore: Indian Statistical Institute, Bangalore Centre. http://WWW.isibang.ac.in/~library/portal/Pages/chp1.pdf (Accessed on 5 march 2017). Permanent webcite: http://www.webcitation.org/6ovdax2pD

Iyer, Hemalata. (1995). *Classification Structures.* Frankfurt: IndeksVerlag.

Judge, Anthony J.N. (1984). "Functional Classification." *International Classification* 11(3): 145

Kaula, Prithvi N. and Prasad, H.N. (1981). "Classification Literature in India: An Analysis Trend." *International Classification* 8(3): 145-149.

Koford, Amelia Bowen. (2017). "Engaging an Author in a Critical Reading of Subject Headings." *Journal of Critical Library & Information Studies* 1(1): 10

La Barre, Kathryn. (2000). "Bliss and Ranganathan: Synthesis, Synchronicity or Sour Grapes?" In Nancy J. Williamson, Clare Beghtol and Lynne Howart, eds., *Dynamism and Stability in Knowledge Organization: Proceedings of the Sixth International Conference of the International Society for Knowledge Organization Toronto, July 13-15, 2000.* Wurtzburg: Ergon, 157-163.

La Barre, Kathryn. (2007). "Faceted Navigation and Browsing Features in New OPACs: Robust Support for Scholarly Information Seeking?" *Knowledge Organization* 34(2): 78-90.

Lancaster, F.W., et al. (1992). "Ranganathan's influence examined bibliometrically", *Libri* 42(3): 268-281

Mai, Jens-Erik. (2002). "Is Classification Theory Possible? Rethinking Classification Research." *Advances in Knowledge Organization* 8, 472–478.

Maltby, Arthur. (1975). *Sayers Manual of Classification for Libraries*, 5th ed. London: Andre Deutsch.

Maniez, Jacques. (1991). "A Decade of Research in Classification." *International Classification* 18(2): 73–77.

Martínez-Ávila, Daniel. (2016). "BISAC Subject Headings List." *Knowledge Organization* 43(8): 655-662.

Miksa, Francis L. (1998). *The DDC, the Universe of Knowledge and the Post-Modern Library*. Albany, NY: Forest Press.

Morville, Peter and Louis Rosenfeld. (2007). *Information Architecture - for the World Wide Web*. 3rd ed. Sebastopol, CA: O´Reilly Media, Inc.

Moss, Wilfred Raymond. (1964). "Categories and Relations: Origins of Two Classification Theories." *American Documentation* 15(4): 296–301

Neelameghan, A. (1993). "Application of S. R. Ranganathan's Postulates and Principles of the General Theory of Knowledge Classification to Database Design and Information Retrieval." *International Cataloguing and Bibliographic Control* 22(3): 46-50.

Palmer, Bernard Ira. (1961). "Classification as a Foundation Study of Librarians" In Douglas J Foskett and Bernard Ira Palmer, eds., *The Sayers Memorial Volume*. London: The Library Association, 202-212.

Parkhi, R. S. 1933. "Colon Scheme of Library Classification." *Modern Librarian* 3(2): 85-88.

Parkhi, R. S. (1965). "Colon Classification: the National Scheme of Classification for India." In Prithvi N. Kaula, ed., *Library Science Today: Ranganathan Festschrift*. Bombay: Asia, 94-98.

Parkhi, R. S. (1972). *Library Classification: Evolution of a Dynamic Theory*. Delhi: Vikas Publishing House. (Completed by Ranganthan after Parkhi's death).

Parrochia, Daniel and Pierre Neuville. (2013). *Towards General Theory of Classification*. Basel: Birkhauser.

Parthasarathy, S. (1952). "Memoirs of Library Research Circle (Delhi)." *Annals of Indian Library Association* 2: 153-159.

Raghavan, Koti. S. (2015). "The Colon Classification: A Few Considerations on its Future." *Annals of Library & Information Studies* 62(4): 231-238.

Ranganathan, S. R. (1933). *Colon Classification*. [First edition]. Madras: Madras Library Association.

Ranganathan, S. R. (1937). *Prolegomena to Library Classification*. Madras: Madras Library Association. (A second edition was Ranganathan 1957b; a third edition was Ranganathan 1967a).

Ranganathan, S. R. (1939a). *Colon Classification, second edition.* Madras: Madras Library Association and London: E. Goldston, Ltd.

Ranganathan, S. R. (1939b). "Impact between Mathematics and Library Science." *Modern Librarian* 10: 22-33.

Ranganathan, S. R. (1944). *Library Classification: Fundamentals and Procedures, with 1008 graded examples and exercises.* Madras: Madras Library Association.

Ranganathan, S. R. (1945). *Elements of Library Classification.* Poona: N.K. Publishing House. (A second edition edited by B. I Palmer was published in 1959 by the Association of Assistant Librarians, London; A third edition was published in 1967 by Asia Publishing House, Bombay).

Ranganathan, S. R. (1950). *Colon Classification.* Third Edition. Madras: Madras Library Association.

Ranganathan, S. R. (1951a). *Classification and Communication.* Delhi: University of Delhi.

Ranganathan, S. R. (1951b). *Philosophy of Library Classification.* Copenhagen: Ejnar Munksgaard.

Ranganathan, S. R. (1952). *Colon Classification.* Fourth Edition. Madras: Madras Library Association and London: Blunt.

Ranganathan, S. R. (1957a). *Colon Classification.* Vol. 1, Basic Classification. Fifth Edition. Madras: Madras Library Association.

Ranganathan, S. R. (1957b). *Prolegomena to Library Classification.* Second Edition. London: Library Association.

Ranganathan, S. R. (1960). *Colon Classification: Basic Classification.* Sixth Revised Edition. Bombay: Asia Publishing House, 3 parts in one volume. (Reissued 1963 with a10-page annexture of amendments).

Ranganathan, S. R. (1961). "Library Classification on the March." In Douglas J Foskett and Bernard Ira Palmer, eds., *The Sayers Memorial Volume,* ed. London: The Library Association, 72-95.

Ranganathan, S. R. (1962). *Elements of Library Classification,* 3rd ed. Mumbai: Asia.

Ranganathan, S. R. (1963). *Colon Classification: Basic Classification.* Sixth Revised Edition. Bombay: Asia Publishing House. (Reissued version of Ranganathan (1960) with a10-page annexture of amendments).

Ranganathan, S. R. (1964). "Design of Depth Classification: Methodology." *Library Science with a Slant to Documentation* 1(1): 1-42.

Ranganathan, S. R. (1965). *A Descriptive Account of the Colon Classification*. New Brunswick, N.J.: Graduate School of Library Science, Rutgers State University. (Published again in 1967 in India by Asia Publishing House, Bombay).

Ranganathan, S. R. (1967a). *Prolegomena to Library Classification*, 3rd ed. Mumbai: Asia Publishing House.

Ranganathan, S. R. (1967b). *A Descriptive Account of the Colon Classification*. Mumbai: Asia Publishing House.

Ranganathan, S. R. (1971). *Colon Classification*. Seventh Edition.: A preview. Bangalore: Sarada Ranganathan Endowment.

Ranganathan, S. R. (1987). *Colon Classification*. Seventh Edition. Basic and Depth Version ed. by Malur Aji Gopinath. Bangalore: Sarada Ranganathan Endowment.

Sahadath, Catelynne. (2013). "Classifying the Margins: Using Alternative Classification Schemes to Empower Diverse and Marginalized Users." *Feliciter* 59(3): 14-17.

Satija, M. P. (1986). "Use of Colon Classification." *International Classification* 13(2): 88-92.

Satija, M. P. (1990). "A Critical Introduction to the Seventh Edition (1987) of the Colon Classification." *Cataloguing & Classification Quarterly* 12(2): 135-138.

Satija, M. P. (1992). "Classification and Ranganathan: A Chronology 1924–1992." *International Classification* 19(1): 3-6.

Satija, M. P. (2001). "Relationships in Ranganathan's Colon Classification." In Carol A. Bean and Rebecca Green, eds., *Relationships in the Organization of Knowledge*. Dordrecht: Kluwer, pp. 199-210.

Satija, M. P. (2015a). *Book Numbers: Indian and Cutter*. New Delhi: Viva Books.

Satija, M. P. (2015b). "Save the National Heritage: Revise the Colon Classification." *Annals of Library & Information Studies* 62(4): 239-248

Satija, M. P. and Amrik Singh. (1994). *Bibliography of Colon Classification, 1930-1993*. New Delhi: M.D. Publications.

Satija, M. P., Devika P. Madalli and Biswanath Dutta. (2014). "Modes of Growth of Subjects." *Knowledge Organization* 41: 195-204

Shera, Jesse. H. (1970). *Sociological Foundation of Librarianship*. Mumbai: Asia.

Slavic, Aida. (2008). "Faceted Classifications: Management and Use." *Axiomathes* 18(2): 1-15.

Smiraglia, Richard P. (2014). "Prolegomena to a new order: A domain-analytical view of the influence of S R Ranganathan on knowledge organisation" In K S Raghavan and A Neelameghan, eds., *Knowledge Organisation: from libraries to Web.* New Delhi: Ess Ess., pp.7-18

Spang-Hanssen, Henning. (1974). "Kunnskapsorganisasjon, Informasjonsgjenfinning, Automatisering og Språk." In *Kunnskapsorganisasjon og Informasjonsgjenfinning.* Oslo: Riksbibliotektjenesten, pp.11–61.

Suman, Aparajita (2014). *From Knowledge Abstraction to Management Using Ranganathan's Faceted Schema to Develop Conceptual Frameworks for Digital Libraries. Oxford , U K:Chandos,272p*

Tunkelang, Daniel. (2009). *Faceted Search.* San Rafael, CA: Morgan & Claypool Publishers.

Vickery, Brian C. (1960). *Faceted Classification: A Guide to the Construction and Use of Special Schemes.* London: Aslib.

Yogeshwar, Ranganathan. (2001). *S R Ranganathan: Pragmatic Philosopher of Information Science: A Personal Biography.* Mumbai: Bhartiya Vidya Bhavan.

APPENDIX-I

Chapters refer to the *Prolegomena,* 3rd ed. (1967).

1	GENERAL LAWS
11	Laws of Interpretation (Chap DC)
12	Laws of Impartiality (Chap DD)
13	Law of Symmetry (Chap DE)
14	Law of Parsimony (Chap DF)
15	Law of Local Variation (Chap DG)
16	Law of Osmosis (Chap DH)
2	LAWS OF LIBRARY SCIENCE
21	Books are for Use (Sec DB1)
22	Every Reader His book (Sec DB2)
23	Every Book Its Reader (Sec DB3)
24	Save the Time of the Reader (Sec DB4)
25	Library is a Growing Organism (Sec DB5)

3	CANONS OF CLASSIFICATION
31	Canons for Work in the Idea Plane (Part E)
311	Canons for characteristics (Chap EB, EF)
3111	Canon of Differentiation (Chap EC)
3112	Canon of Relevance (Chap ED)
3113	Canon of Ascertainability (Chap EE)
3114	Canon of Permanence (Chap EF)
34312	Canons for Succession of Characteristics (Chap EG/EK)
3121	Canon of Concomitance (Chap EH)
3122	Canon of Relevant Succession (Chap EJ)
3123	Canon of Consistent succession (Chap EK)
313	Canons for Array (Chap EL/EQ)
3131	Canon of Exhaustiveness (Chap EM)
3132	Canon of Exclusiveness (Chap EN)
3133	Canon for Helpful Sequence (Chap EP)
3134	Canon of Consistent Sequence (Chap EQ)
314	Canons for Chain (Chap ER/ET)
3141	Canon of Decreasing Extension (Chap ES)
3142	Canon of Modulation (Chap ET)
315	Canons for Filiatory Sequence (Chap EU)
3151	Canon of Subordinate Classes (Sec EU1)
3152	Canon of Co-ordinate Classes (Sec EU2)
32	Canons for Work in the Verbal Plane (Part G)
321	Canon of Context (Chap GB)
322	Canon of Enumeration (Chap GC)
323	Canon of Currency (Chap GD)
324	Canon Reticence (Chap GE)
33	Canons for Work in the Notational Plane (Parts J/L)

331 Basic Canons for Notation (Part J)
3311 Canon of synonym(Chap JB)
3312 Canon of Homonym (Chap JC)
3313 Canon of Relativity (Sec JD1)
3314 Canon of Uniformity (Sec JD2)
3315 Canon of Hierarchy (Sec JE1)
3316 Canon of Non-Hierarchy (Sec JE2)
3317 Canon of Mixed Base (Sec JF1)
3318 Canon of Pure Base (Sec JF2)
33191 Canon of Faceted Notation (Sec JG2)
33193 Canon of Co-extensiveness (Sec JH1)
33194 Canon of Non Co-extensiveness (Sec JH2)
332 Canons for Mnemonics (Part K)
3321 Canon of General Mnemonics (Chap KA)
3322 Canon of Alphabetical Mnemonics (Chap KB)
3323 Canon of Scheduled Mnemonics (Chap KC)
3324 Canon of Systematic Mnemonics (Chap KD)
3325 Canon of Seminal Mnemonics (Chap KE)
333 Canons for Growing Universe (Part L)
3331 Canon of Extrapolation in Array (Chap LC)
3332 Canon of Interpolation in Array (Chap LD)
3333 Canon of Extrapolation in Chain (Chap LF)
3334 Canon of Interpolation in Chain (Chap LG)
34 Canons for Book Classification (Parts U/V)
341 Canon of Book Number (Sec UB2)
342 Canon of Collection Number (Sec VB6)
343 Canon of Distinctiveness (Sec VC3)
4 POSTULATES OF CLASSIFICATION (Part R)
41 Postulated for Facets (Chap RB/RJ)

411 Postulate of Fundamental Categories (Sec RB1)

412 Postulate of Basic Facet (Sec RC1)

413 Postulate of Isolate Facet (Sec RD1)

414 Postulate of Rounds for Energy (See RH1)

415 Postulate of Rounds for Personality and Matter (See RH2)

416 Postulate of Rounds for Space and Time (Sec RH3)

417 Postulate of Level (Sec RJ1)

42 Postulates for facet Sequence

421 Postulate of First Facet (Sec RK1)

422 Postulate of Concreteness (Sec RK2)

423 Postulate of Facet Sequence within a Round (Sec RK3)

424 Postulate of Facet Sequence within Last Round (Sec RK 4)

425 Postulate of Level Cluster (Sec RK5)

5 POSTULATES FOR SUB-FACETS

51 Postulates for Sub-Facets in a Basic Facet

511 Postulate of Main Sub-facet in a Basic Facet

512 Postulate of Primary, Non-Main Sub facet in a Basic Facet

513 Postulate of Sub-facets , other than the Main and Primary ones, in a Basic Facet.

52 Postulates for Sub-Facets in an Isolate Facet

521 Postulate of Primary Sub-Facet in an Isolate Facet

522 Postulate of Qualifier Sub-Facets in an Isolate Facet

6 PRINCIPLES FOR FACET SEQUENCE AND SUB-FACET SEQUENCE (CHAP RM/RN)

61 Wall-Picture Principle (Sec RM1)

62 Whole-Organ Principle (Sec RN1)

63	Cow–Calf Principle
64	Actand-Action-Actor-Tool Principle (Sec RNS)
7	PRINCIPLES FOR HELPFUL SEQUENCE
71	Principle of Chronology and Evolution
711	Principles of Later-In-Time (Chap FB1)
712	Principle of Later-In-Evolution (Chap FC1)
72	Principle of Spatial Contiguity (Chap FD)
721	Principle of Bottom-Upwards (Sec FD21)
722	Principle of Top-Downwards (Sec FD22)
723	Principle of Left and Right (Sec FD31)
724	Principle of Right and Left (Sec FD32)
725	Principle of Clockwise Direction (Sec FD41)
726	Principle of Counter-Clockwise Direction (Sec FD42)
727	Principle of Periphery to Centre (Sec FD51)
728	Principle of Centre to Periphery (Sec FD 52)
7291	Principle of Away-from-Position (Sec FD6)
73	Principle of Quantity (Chap FE)
731	Principle of Increasing Quantity (Sec FE1)
732	Principle of Deceasing Quantity (Sec FE2)
74	Principle of Increasing Complexity (Chap FE1)
75	Principle of Canonical Sequence (Chap FC)
76	Principle of Literary Warrant (Chap FH1)
78	Principle of Alphabetical Sequence (Chap FJ1)

Source : http://www.isibang.ac.in/~library/portal/Pages/chp1.pdf

APPENDIX-II

List of important books on Classification by S R Ranganathan,1933-1972

Colon Classification. Madras: Madras Library Association, 1933. The last edition done by Ranganathan was the 6th (1959), again issued with amendments in 1963, and published by Asia Publishing House, Bombay (Now in its 7th ed., 1987 published posthumously).

Prolegomena to Library Classification. Madras: Madras Library Association, 1937 (Now in its 3rd ed.) (1967) published by Asia Publishing House, Bombay. Its 2nd ed. (1957) was brought out by the Library Association, London.

Library Classification: Fundamentals and Procedures, with 1008 graded examples and exercises. Madras: Madras Library Association, 1944.

Elements of Library Classification. Poona: N.K. Publishing House, 1945 (Now in its 3rd ed., 1967), published by Asia Publishing House, Bombay. Its second edition edited by B.I Palmer was published in 1959 by the Association of Assistant Librarians, London

Classification and Communication. Delhi: University of Delhi, 1951.

Philosophy of Library Classification. Copenhagen: Ejnar Munksgaard, 1951.

Indian Standards Institution. 1964. Glossary of Classification Terms. New Delhi: Indian Standards Institution. (IS:2550-1963). (Indian Standards Institution is now renamed Bureau of Indian Standards. Ranganathan was the chairman of the ISI Committee and de facto the author of this glossary). https://law.resource.org/pub/ in/ bis/S07/is.2550.1963.pdf

Indian Standards Institution (1964). *A Descriptive Account of the Colon Classification.* New Brunswick, N.J.:

Graduate School of Library Science, Rutgers State University, 1965 (Published again in 1967 in India by Asia Publishing House, Bombay).

Colon Classification, 7th ed.: A preview. Bangalore: Sarada Ranganathan Endowment,1971,52p.

Library Classification: Evolution of a Dynamic Theory. Delhi: Vikas Publishing House, 1972 (Started by R S Parkhi, but completed by Ranganthan after Parkhi's death).

APPENDIX-III

Some important articles in chronological order

Ranganathan, S.R. (1947). "Classification and international documentation." *Revue de la documentation* 14:154-177

Ranganathan, S.R. (1949). "Self-perpetuating scheme of classification." *Journal of Documentation* 4:223-244

Ranganathan, S.R. (1951). "Colon Classification and its approach to documentation." In: Shera, J.H. and Egan, M.E., eds, *Bibliographic organization*. Chicago, IL: University of Chicago, pp. 94-108.

Ranganathan, S.R. (1952). "Library classification: its added uses." *Libri* 2: 31-36

Ranganathan, S.R. (1951). "General theory of classification." *Abgila* 2:1-8

Ranganathan, S.R. (1953). "General theory of classification." *FID Review of documentation* 20:13-18

Ranganathan, S.R. (1958). "Library classification glossary." *Annals of Library Science* 5:65-112

Ranganathan, S.R. (1959). "Classifying, indexing, coding." *Annals of Library Science* 6: 99-104

Ranganathan, S.R. (1960). "Colon notation and Indian scripts." *Library Herald* 3: 55-60; 265-269; 387

Ranganathan, S.R (1960). "Standards for classification." *Annals of Library Science* 7: 90-96

Ranganathan, S.R. (1961). "Sayers and Donker Duyvis: theory and maintenance of library classification." *Annals of Library Science* 7: 85-99

Ranganathan, S.R. (1961). "Library Classification on the March." In Douglas J Foskett and Bernard Ira Palmer, eds., *The Sayers Memorial Volume.* London: The Library Association, pp. 72-95

Ranganathan, S.R (1963). "Classification research no longer a toddler." *Annals of Library Science* 10: 85-96

Ranganathan, S.R. (1964). "Design of Depth Classification: Methodology." *Library Science with a Slant to Documentation* 1(1): 1-42.

Ranganathan, S.R. (1964). "Subject headings and facet analysis." *Journal of Documentation* 20: 109-119.

Ranganathan, S.R. (1965). "General and special classification." *International Study Conference on Classification Research (2nd: 1964:Elsinore) Proceedings,* pp.81-93.

Ranganathan, S.R. (1965). "Barbara Kyle and the classification of sociology." *Journal of Documentation* 21: 271-274.

Ranganathan, S.R. (1965). "Library classification on the march." *Herald of Library Science* 4: 84-91.

Ranganathan, S.R. (1965). "Library classification through a century." *Library Science with a Slant to Documentation* 2: 1-30.

Ranganathan, S.R. (1965). "Colon Classification." In Thomas Landau, ed., *Encyclopedia of librarianship*,3rd ed. London: Bowes, pp.112-117.

Ranganathan, S.R. (1967). "Hidden roots of classification." *Library Science with a Slant to Documentation* 4: 1-26.

Ranganathan, S.R. (1968). "Basic subjects and their kinds." *Library Science with a Slant to Documentation* 5: 97-133.

Ranganathan, S.R. (1968). "Choice of a scheme for classification." *Library Science with a Slant to Documentation* 5: 1-69.

Ranganathan, S.R. (1969). "Colon Classification, 7th edition (1971): a preview." *Library Science with a Slant to Documentation* 6: 193-242.

Ranganathan, S.R. (1969). "Developments in the use of digits in Colon Classification." *Library Science with a Slant to Documentation* 6: 1-38 (with Dr M A Gopinath).

Ranganathan, S.R. (1972). "Colon Classification notational system: towards a plan for its productive use." *Library Science with a Slant to Documentation* 9: 1-37.

Ranganathan, S.R. (1972). "Comparative study of schemes for library classification." *Lib.sc with a slant to documentation* 9: 289-315.

Ranganathan, S.R. (1972). "Impact of growth in the universe of subjects on classification." *FID/CR Report* No.12. Copenhagen: Denmark centre for Documentation, 1-12.

3

Call, Book and Collection Numbers: Ranganathan's Chronological System

STRUCTURE

1. Elements of documents
    1.1 Definition
2. Chronological Book numbers
    2.1 Advantages of chronological systems
3. Ranganathan's system
    3.1 [L] Language Facet; 3.1.1 Omission of the language facets
    3.2 [F] Form Facet
        3.2.1 Omission of Form Facets
    3.3 [Y] Year Facet
        3.3.1 [A] Accession part of the year number
    3.4 [V] Volume Number of the Document
    3.5 [S] Supplement Number of the Document
    3.6 [C] Copy Number of the Document

3.1. ELEMENTS OF DOCUMENTS

S.R. Ranganathan is of the view that a document comprises of Gross body (Physical carrier) Subtle body (language, style, viewpoint, presentation, etc.) and the Soul (knowledge and subject). These days classification of documents though is based on their subject contents, viz., knowledge, yet the oddities and realities of the physical and subtle bodies of the documents cannot and should not be ignored. In a library, one cannot arrange books distinctively without accounting for these physical peculiarities. Therefore, it is generally seen that a class number alone fails to individualize a book in a library or a reference in a bibliography, howsoever deep a classification may be. Many books in a library may get the same class number by virtue of having the same specific subject. In such cases to assign a unique individual place to a given document - as it is the requirement of every library - these documents are given a further notation, also called External Notation.

3.1.1. Definition

This external notation based on some non-subject considerations, used to arrange documents within a given specific class number, is known as a Book Number. Function of a book number starts from where that of a class number ends. A book number for a document has a meaning in the context of its class numbers. Therefore a book number is a satellite of the class number. Book number may be based on either some or all of the considerations such as author, title, edition, language, format, physical form or the year of publication. Supplement, concordance, volume, or copy numbers too may have to be considered. In many schemes of classification and consequently in libraries book numbers get only insignificant treatment - even step motherly behavior. Not only this, many schemes are silent on the issue. The DDC in its earlier editions included a scheme of book numbers. Since the 12th edition, it has been abandoned leaving the libraries to use any standard or locally devised methods of book numbers. Therefore, it has prompted classifiers to use any locally devised arbitrary method of giving book numbers.

3.1.2. Functions of Book Numbers

Book numbers individualize a book so that it "may be quickly and accurately placed, called for, found and charged" wrote Melvil Dewey in 1898. Miss Bertha R. Barden (1937) in her enduring study of book numbers has described the following six uses of book numbers which are wonderfully valid to this day:

1. To sub arrange books in order on the shelves.
2. To provide a brief and accurate call number for each book.
3. To locate a particular book on the shelf.
4. Provide a symbol for charging books to borrowers.
5. To facilitate the return of books on the shelves.
6. To assist in quick identification of a book when inventories are taken. It helps in stock-taking.

In addition to these, an author number also brings together all the books by one author in one specific subject. A chronological book number will clearly portray the development of a subject over a given period. Book numbers are indispensable for a shelflist.

3.2. CHRONOLOGICAL BOOK NUMBERS

There are two major systems of book numbers namely alphabetical and chronological. Chronological book numbers have their origin in accession arrangement first proposed by Melvil Dewey. His assistant W.S. Biscoe in 1885 put forward a method to sub arrange books by the year of publication. It has since become an accepted alternative to Cuttering. Though the antecedents of Biscoe's method can easily be seen in Dewey's accession method but Biscoe credited Cutter and others of its times for the basic ideas of his time tables. The year of publication which is essential basis of Biscoe's method is converted for brevity and simplicity into alphanumeric notations from the following table:

A	B.C.E.	J	1830-1839	S	1920-1929
B	C.E.1-999	K	1840-1849	T	1930-1939
C	1000-1499	L	1850-1859	U	1940-1949
D	1500-1599	M	1860-1869	V	1950-1959
E	1600-1699	N	1870-1879	W	1960-1969
F	1700-1799	O	1880-1889	X	1970-1979
G	1800-1809	P	1890-1899	Y	1980-1989
H	1810-1819	Q	1900-1909	Z	1900-1999
I	1820-1829	R	1910-1919		

Year of copyright is taken for this purpose. Some of the years are translated into notations as follows:

1900	Q0	1925	S5	1961	W1
1993	Z3	1999	Z9		

Another great librarian James Duff Brown (1862-1914) proposed another chronological system in the first edition of his Subject Classification (1906). His 'Extended Date Table' subarranged books by year of publication denoted by two small alphabets as follows:

aa-az	1450-1475	na-nz	1788-1813
ba-bz	1476-1501	oa-oz	1814-1839

ka-kz	1710-1735	xa-xz	2048-2073
la-lz	1736-1761	ya-yz	2074-2099
ma-mz	1762-1787	za-zz	2100-2125

For example, 1762 is denoted by ma, 1787 by mz, 1995 by uz, 2000 by ve. This table is not known to be used anywhere else.

3.2.1. Advantages of chronological systems

1. Users usually wish to get the latest material or the oldest, or pertaining to a certain span of time, accordingly they may get their material gathered at one place. It, therefore, satisfies the Fourth Law of Library Science by saving the time of the users in locating books.
2. Knowledge is growing, documents are increasing in number, thus library is a growing organism. When books on a given specific subject are arranged in their sequence of their publication year, this sort of arrangement helps to trace the development of a subject over a given period. Therefore, such a sub arrangement is helpful in writing trend reports, state-of-the-art reports and history of a given subject. This sort of arrangement satisfies the Fifth Law of Library Science.
3. When as per the Fifth Law, a Library grows, some old books may not be of use to the common users. Therefore, chronological book numbers may help in weeding out obsolete books, belonging prior to a certain date. Therefore, it again helps to satisfy the Fifth Law of Library Science.
4. Similarly, on many more counts the supremacy of a

chronological book numbers can be listed. Melvil Dewey recommending system by Biscoe in 2nd edition of the DDC wrote "It's advantage is in presenting the historical development of the subject... in science it has a special value..."

3.3. RANGANATHAN'S SYSTEM

It was Ranganathan who brought the chronological system to its perfection. Like his classification system his book number system is minute and systematic. In the facet formula of book number, Ranganathan has provided even obscure and rarely occurring oddities in books. Besides the year of publication, his book number takes notice of language, form, volume number, supplement, copy number and critical commentary, if any. The colon book number facet formula along with the indicator digits is:

[L] [F] [Y] [A] . [V]-[S] ; [C] : g[EVN]

Wherein

L - Language of the document.

F - Form of the document.

Y - Year of publication of the document.

A - Accession part of the year number.

V - Volume number of the document.

S - Supplement number of the document.

C - Copy number of the document.

g - Evaluation Number

EVN - Accession part of the evaluation number.

Apparently the formula is quite complex and it looks that the resulting book number would be quite lengthy. Far from this, in practice the CC book number is very simple and brief; and it is estimated that about 90 per cent of the book numbers consist only of two digits for the year number. Other facets are only occasionally geared into service.

Position and role of various facets in the book number formula are as follows.

3.3.1 [L] Language Facet

It is worth noting that the first characteristic to subdivide a given specific class is the language. So, in this way all the documents in one language having the same class number come together. Since most of the library users are monolingual, they find together at one place all the books in their language. This saves their time.

The language isolates are the same as meant for the general CC schedule [as given on pages 2.26-2.27 (Chapter 5) (CC-6)]. For example,

111	English	153	Punjabi
113	German	156	Gujarati
122	French	157	Bengali
123	Spanish	3	Dravidian languages
142	Russian	31	Tamil
15	Sanskrit	35	Telugu
152	Hindi		

3.3.1.1. Omission of the language facet

In many cases, as enumerated below, the language number is omitted:

(a) There is no need of language facet for books in the favored language of the library. Favored language of the library is either the mother-tongue or the official language. In other words, it is the language in which most of the holdings of the library are written. For example, in India, English is the favored language in majority of the libraries. Since the majority of the books in the library are in the favored language, so most of the books will not need this facet. This makes for brevity and simplicity of the book number.

(b) Book Numbers for books in the main classes Literature and Linguistics do not require the language facet as the language number is already present in the class number, and as such it will be superfluous to repeat it. In cases of language inequality the language facet in book number may be needed.

Language inequality is a situation when a critical book on literature or linguistics is written in other than its original language. For example, Shakespeare in Hindi or French, for that reason in any language other than English is a case of language inequality. Similarly, a book on French grammar or history of Spanish language written, say, in English are another cases of language inequality. Prem Chand's Godan in any language other than Hindi is a case of language inequality.

(c) Lastly the language facet may be omitted from the booknumber of serial/periodical publications.

3.3.2 [F] Form Facet

The form facet represents the mode of presentation of the subject in the document. It is what Ranganathan calls the subtle body of the document. For example, a book may be all pictures; another may be a practical manual; yet another may be merely a tabulated data. In ancient India, books on medicine and astronomy were written in verse form. List of forms can be multiplied and in this age of information revolution and multimedia many new forms of documents are being invented and introduced. Isolate numbers, consisting of Roman smalls usually followed by an Indo-Arabic numeral have been enlisted on page 2.3 (Chapter 02) of CC-6 (1963). For example,

a5	Alphabetical	h2	Histogram
a6	Chronological	p1	Lecture
b	Index	p7	Symposium
c	List	q	Code
d	Databook	v	Practical

f	Picture	w1	Verse
f953	Cinema film	w2	Drama
g	Plan	w4	Letter
h	Graph	x	Quotation

Ranganathan's list is not exhaustive as many more form of documents are available these days.

3.3.2.1. Omission of Form Facet

However, the Form number is omitted in the books which are in the favored form of the library. In a general library, printed cuboid books in prose make the popular Form category. Hence majority of the book numbers are without this facet, too. For example, a book on economic progress through "graphs" will get the form facet 'h' in book number and a lecture will get the facet number p1 in book number, but any ordinary book will get no form facet.

3.3.3 [Y] Year Facet

This is the indispensable facet, as no Colon Book Number is without it. This facet denotes the year of publication of the book. For this purpose, Ranganathan has designed a special chronological table from 1880 to 2119 to provide brief isolate numbers for this facet. This table, given at page 1.13 of CC-6, 1963, is as follows:

A	Before 1880	P	2000-2009
B	1880-1889	Q	2010-2019
C	1890-1899	R	2020-2029
D	1900-1909	S	2030-2039
E	1910-1919	T	2040-2049
F	1920-1929	U	2050-2059
G	1930-1939	V	2060-2069
H	1940-1949	W	2070-2079
J	1950-1959	X	2080-2089
K	1960-1969	Y	2090-2099
L	1970-1979	ZA	2100-2109
M	1980-1989	ZB	2110-2119
N	1990-1999		

Letters I and O are not used to avoid confusion with 1 and 0 respectively.

In the Table every digit from B onwards spans a decade; and a particular year is denoted by adding the year number of that decade to the decade digit. For example, 1987 is M7, 1969 is K9, 2000 is P0 and 2005 is P5 and 2010 is Q0. Therefore, a book on Lectures on Economics published in 2014 will be plQ4; and a book on Lectures on Economics in Hindi published in 2011 will be 153 p1Q1.

Similarly the book number for a document published in 1973 in film form in Russian language will be

142 f953L3

where 142 is Russian language, f953 is film, L3 is 1973

3.3.3.1 [A] Accession part of the year number

This is a device to distinguish more than one book published in the same year, same language and same form having the same class number. This consists in adding 1, 2, 3, etc., for the 2nd, 3rd, 4th, etc., book to the year number of the book number. For example, the first book on Physics published in 1987 will have the class number M7; and the second will have M71; and the 3rd, M72 and so on. Again, let us say, in 2013 several books on the history of Hindi literature were published. All will have the class number O152v. Their book numbers in order will be:

Q3 for the 1st book

Q31 for the 2nd book

Q32 for the 3rd book

Q33 for the 4th book

Q3n-1 for the nth book

This device is not much used except for a very current and popular topic say, computers, environment, biotechnology, etc.

3.3.4 [V] Volume Number of the Document

Many books especially the reference books and other source documents are completed in many volumes. Quite obviously all the volumes of a 'book' need to be placed together. To do this, Ranganathan suggests to put 1, 2, 3, etc., for the first, second and third volume, etc., after the accession part of the year number facet. Volume Number is preceded by a dot (.). Suppose we have a book Palgrave's Dictionary of Economics in 3 Volumes published in 2004. Each volume will have the book number:

P4.1 1st Volume

P4.2 2nd Volume

P4.3 3rd Volume

3.3.5 [S] Supplement Number of the Document

Sometimes it happens that to update a book, or to correct the earlier one, or to add some latest development in the field, a supplement to original book is issued. Sometimes more than one supplement may be issued successively. Need to keep together the original and the supplements is pretty obvious. A supplement separated from its original book is like a child lost in a fair. So, to keep the host and the associated books together Ranganathan prescribed a symbol hyphen (-) followed by the supplement Number. In the formula it comes after the Volume [V] facet. The supplement will bear the year number [Y] of the original book, and not the actual year of its publication. Let us say, a book published in 2009 has two supplements issued in 2010 and 2011. Their book numbers will respectively be:

P9 Original Book

P9-1 1st supplement

P9-2 2nd supplement

If the book is multivolumed then the supplement is placed after the last volume unless specified otherwise. The supplement number will be:

P9.1	1st volume
P9.2	2nd volume
P9.2-1	1st supplement (2009)
P9.2-2	2nd supplement (2011)

It is a simple but very effective device to keep the parent and associated books together.

3.3.6 [C] Copy Number of the Document

It usually happens that a book is acquired in multiple copies by a particular library. Academic libraries usually acquire multiple copies of text books. So, all these books will have to be kept together in a given section of the library. To keep all these copies together Ranganathan provided a copy number facet in the formula. It is positioned after the supplement number and its indicator digit is semicolon (;). The first copy will have no copy number and the second copy will be indicated as ;1, the third copy will be indicated as ;2 and so on. For example, a book published in Urdu on Indian history published in 1987 has 10 copies. All of them will have the class number V44 or 954 and their book numbers will be:

168M7	1st copy
168M7;1	2nd copy
168M7;2	3rd copy
....	....
168M7;9	10th copy

3.3.7 [: g] Criticism/Evaluation Number

This is analogous to the Energy Posteriorising Common Isolate (PCI) of the Colon Classification, though here it is applied to the book number and not to the class number. There are some non-classical or semi-classical books having a semblance of a classic. It is imperative to keep a book and its various commentaries or evaluations together. This is done by adding ':g' to the last facet of the booknumber. For example, if a book published in 1980 has its commentary published in 1983, their book number will be as follows:

M0	For original book
M0:g	First commentary published in any year

It will keep the parent (host) book and its sequel/ commentaries together.

3.3.7.1 [EVN] Accession Part of the Evaluation Number

This acts exactly as [A] does for [Y] facet. The [EVN] is only to distinguish one commentary from the other, and is done by adding 1, 2, 3, etc., to ':g' for the 2nd, 3rd and 4th commentary, respectively. So, for the above book

M0: g1	2nd commentary
M0: g2	3rd commentary
M0: g3	4th commentary
M0: g4	5th commentary, and so on.

3.4. PROBLEMS

So far so good. However, this facet formula is not without problems. For example, it is not able to keep together all the books of the same author on one subject. This is a minor problem compared to another problem of keeping together the different editions of a book.

3.4.1. Keeping together different editions of a book

Since different editions are published in different years, each edition will have the book number based on the year of its publication, and hence will get separated. For example, let us say, a book first published in 2008 was issued in 2nd edition in 2014. Their book numbers respectively will be: P8 and Q4. Obviously, these 'two' books will get separated by many intervening books published between 2008 and 2014. Hence the problem. But Ranganathan had not been oblivious of the problem. At the first instance, Ranganathan did not consider it necessary to keep the different editions of a book together. It would serve no purpose, he felt. However, to those insisting on keeping together these editions, Ranganathan suggested that an edition may be treated as a copy of the first edition. For example, in the above case the second edition will get the book number:

P8; Q4

So, if this book has another edition, say, in 2020 it will have the book number:

P8;R0

Thus the three editions will have the book numbers:

P8	1st edition (2008)
P8;Q4	2nd edition (2014)
P8;R0	3rd edition (2020)

Hence the three editions will get juxtaposed. This method, however, is not a neat solution to the problem as the latter editions are out of their chronological place. Despite these minor problems, Ranganathan's is still the most developed Book Number yet formulated. One great advantage of Ranganathan's system and for that reason of any chronological Book Number is that these are applicable to all the documents irrespective of the language, script or the cultural or ethnic origin of the author. Chronological tables may be devised locally based on literary warrant.

3.5. COLLECTION NUMBER

In the art of library classification, the first division of books does not take into consideration the subject matter. For convenience of administration, every big library divides its documents into different sections. Every big library is a cluster of parallel libraries, i.e., libraries within a library.

Parallel libraries are called sections. The first consideration is the section to which a book should go. We first determine whether the book under classification is a rare book, manuscript, thesis, textbook, reference book or any special collection book. These sections may be dictated by the utilitarian purpose such as reference or a textbook or for the convenience of managing them such as abnormal sized book, rare books, fragile or very precious books, and so on. Thus in a library there are many mini libraries within a given library.

3.5.1. Notation for collection number

The symbol determining the section of the book preceding the class number is termed as the collection number. Putting the symbol for the collection number seems so simple and obvious that no scheme other than the CC has discussed it in an academic way. Here the collection number has been designed in relation to the book number; in many cases the collection number is denoted by adding some indicator digit to the book number. While in some cases—mostly utility oriented—a separate symbol is added for the collection number. It may be any arbitrary symbol, but usually the initials of the section name:

R Reference

RR Rare book

T Thesis

Tx Text

G Government publication

RP Reports

For departmental libraries Ranganathan suggests the following convention:

BD Mathematics Department

DD Engineering Department

LD Medical College

RD Philosophy Department

YD Sociology Department

ZD Law Department

But for the abnormal books Ranganathan gives the following rules:

Underline the book number for small sized books

Over line the book number for large sized books

Both underline and over line the book number for abnormal books

Encircle the book number for worn out and fragile books.

Since each symbol creates its own section, so no ordinal value of these digits has been fixed. These sections may be located at convenience. The most general collection is not given any collection number — application of the favored category principle. Thus majority of the books will have no Section Number.

The combination of collection number, class number, and the book number when taken together in the above sequence is termed as the **call number**. The equation is:

Call Number = Collection Number + Class Number + Book Number

It is the call number which determines the specific and unique place of a document in the library. It means every document has a unique call number in the library. It is called Call Number as in closed libraries in 19th century books were 'called' from the stacks by these numbers.

3.6. USING CC BOOK NUMBERS WITH OTHER SCHEMES

It is not necessary that only the libraries using Colon Classification can use this book number system. Libraries using different schemes such as DDC, UDC, or Bliss'

Bibliographic Classification can use these book numbers with equal ease and effectiveness. But in such cases some adaptation may have to be made. Sometimes what Ranganathan has included in the Book Number is a part of class numbers in other systems. Form of a book a standard subdivision in the DDC; and in UDC language of the book is accounted for in the class numbers. Therefore, in such cases the CC book, numbers will have to be adapted accordingly.

REFERENCES

Ranganathan S.R. (1963). *Colon Classification,* 6th edition. Bombay: Asia. p. 1.9-1.17.

Satija, M.P. (1987). *A Primer on Ranganathan Book Number.* New Delhi: Mittal Publications, pp. Xvii, 87.

"This work explains Ranganathan's book number in all its details, ramifications and intricacies. The text has been illustrated with ample examples. This is a simple and systematic exposition of the theory and practice of book numbers developed by Ranganathan, *International Classification,* 15(2), p. 102 (Cochrane A. Pauline, 1989).

Satija, M.P. (1990). "Book Number and Call Number." In Allen Kent, ed., *Encyclopedia of Library and Information Science.* New York: Marcel Dekker, Vol.45, pp. 18-45.

Satija, M.P. and John P. Comaromi. (1992). *Beyond Classification: Book Numbers.* New Delhi: Ess Ess, pp. 60-78.

Satija, M.P. (2008). *Book Numbers: Indian and Cutter.* New Delhi: Viva Books.

4

Modes of Growth of Subjects in the Universe of Knowledge

STRUCTURE

1. Growth of Knowledge
    1.1 Natural Growth
    1.2 Planned growth
    1.3 Induced growth
2. Modes of knowledge and growth
3. Three modes
    3.1 Specialization trends; 3.1.1 Fission; 3.1.2 Dissection; 3.1.3 Denudation; 3.1.4 Lamination; 3.1.5 Procreation; 3.1.6 Self-procreated; 3.1.7 Analogical mode; 3.1.8 Instrument-based subjects
    3.2 Inter-disciplinary growth; 3.2.1 Loose assemblage; 3.2.2 Fusion
    3.3 Multidisciplinary growth; 3.3.1 Distillation; 3.3.2 Partial comprehensions/agglomerates; 3.3.3 Subject bundles; 3.3.4 Annexation mode

ABSTRACT

Knowledge is seen as a system in a perpetually dynamic continuum. It grows as it is always fragmentary, though quantifying this growth is nearly impossible. Growth, inherent in the nature of knowledge, is natural, planned, and induced. S.R. Ranganathan elucidated the various modes of growth of subjects, viz. Fission, lamination, loose assemblage, fusion, distillation, partial comprehensions, and subject bundles. The present study adds a few more modes of developments of subjects. It describes and fits these modes of growth in the framework of growth by specialization, inter-disciplinary and multi-disciplinary growths. It also examines emergence of online domains such as web directories and focuses on possible modes of formation of such domains. The paper concludes that new modes may emerge in the future in consonance with the new research trends and ever changing social and publication needs.

4.1. GROWTH OF KNOWLEDGE

Every system and entity in this universe is growing and changing. The universe of knowledge is a system; and like every system it grows. Growth of knowledge is both additive, as in humanities, and cumulative, as in sciences (Dogan 2001a, p.11025). S.R. Ranganathan's fifth law of library science, viz. Library is a growing organism, is a simple bibliothecal manifestation of this impeccable law of growth of knowledge. Kevin McGarry aptly equates this growth to biological growth. Today this growth rate is unprecedented and alarming. We are obviously witnessing an information deluge—though it is not easy to quantify the volume of knowledge or its speed of growth (McGarry 1993; Machlup 1979). However, as measured through the quantity of literature, scientific literature grows annually at the rate of 5 to 15% and thus doubles between 5 to 15 years, writes a Director of Chemical Abstract Service (Satija 1984). Here what is called 'big data' generated by e-commerce and social media is not considered. In some areas of soft sciences, such as humanities, knowledge growth is slow, so is the rate of obsolescence. We however see a palpable growth of knowledge in all areas of human thought and endeavors. The growth may be of three types:

4.1.1. Natural Growth

Paul Weiss (1960) and S.R. Ranganathan (1963, p.449) liken knowledge growth to the growth and development of a living organism; so does Kevin McGarry (1993, p.146). Thus knowledge grows without any conscious efforts, as in a forest, provided the environment is not inimical. In every age and society there are curious and restless souls engaged of their own in knowledge creation. This continuous growth makes knowledge a system in a dynamic continuum. Every system needs information feed for its stability and development. This is true even of a homeostasis stage. It means knowledge needs further knowledge for preservation and dissemination of the existing stock of knowledge— thus adding to the existing stock; hence, it grows of its own. Enormity in knowledge creations and need for its communication has given rise to what is called meta-knowledge. Other factors for growth of knowledge are the innate curiosity, the urge to be held in high esteem, and the spirit of adventure and exploration in human beings. Next to food, shelter and security what humans want is to know the unknown. (This is a defect in Maslow's pyramid of human needs that this irresistible urge of human beings has not been given any place in the model). Nevertheless, this quest is known to drive humans to life risking adventures to explore the deep secrets of raw Nature. It is a motivating force to generate and store knowledge. Weiss (1960) is apt to say that "[a] key agent in the growth of knowledge has always been the human mind, imaginative, critical and integrative." Another natural reason is inherent in the fragmentary nature of knowledge. By nature, knowledge is never complete or final. It is an inexhaustible resource. For example, any research inquiry is always open ended. This is too obvious from the fact that every worthwhile piece of research raises more questions than it answers. Ironically advancing knowledge holds a mirror to some areas of our ignorance (Smirensky 1994). Paradoxically, more knowledgeable we are more ignorant we feel. Best knowledge is the knowledge of our own ignorance. Hence, knowledge is always incomplete, whatsoever may be added to its huge and inestimable repertoire. It is always moving towards its ever advancing frontiers. Hence, it has an infinitely innate capacity to grow forever and ever (Weiss, 1960). This growth is both quantitative and qualitative. Qualitative growth leads to refinement and precision or corrects our existing world view. It also fills existing gaps in our knowledge. Quantitative growth opens new frontiers and advances its boundaries in all directions.

4.1.2. Planned growth

No society, no nation can achieve success in economic, cultural, technological and educational welfare activities if the production and consumption of knowledge is not up to a certain optimum level (Satija 2013). Knowledge is a resource for all-round development. Since the Industrial Revolution knowledge based innovations have been prized by every society for leading ultimately to economic growth, which further fuels new social and political ideas for welfare, dignity of life and individual justice to mankind (Al-

Hawamdeh 2005). Every new piece of knowledge translates into wealth creation to enrich life on this planet and brings all sorts of social benefits. Every addition to knowledge is addition to human power. It is essentially the true capital of economy. Knowledge production, as a major economic sector, is now a reality (Cornforth 1955, p.206). Alvin Toffler (1980, p.172) is apt to say that: "Information has become perhaps the world's fastest growing and most important business." Therefore, there are planned and organized national and international efforts for its growth. India's National Knowledge Commission (NKC 2005-2008) is a shining example of national plans for development and harnessing knowledge for overall social development. Research is publicly-financed for new ideas, both basic and applied. Population pressure, rising standards of living and quickly eroding natural resources to sustain economic growth make it imperative to supplement natural resources by artificial ones, and to explore new kinds of natural but renewable resources. This requires further research to make life secure and ensure continued growth on this planet. This gives rise to an abundant growth in cultivated knowledge. Indeed the growth of knowledge is exponential, and needs to be so. Within a decade, the number of universities in India have increased four-fold, and colleges many more—as one indicator of the growth of knowledge.

4.1.3. Induced growth

Induced growth of knowledge lies half way between the natural and planned methods. Knowledge is not a commodity in the sense that it is decimated by consumption. We can eat our knowledge cake and multiply it too at the same time. In fact, the more we consume the more it grows and multiplies. Gaining or communicating knowledge further facilitates the growth of knowledge. Fritz Machlup equates knowledge dissemination to its growth (1962, p.4). Widespread education, social awareness, more leisure time, magical advances in information and educational technology, super fast means of communication, generous financial support from governments, organized research, an increase in number and variety of information media, and growth in library and information services are some of the congenial factors which induce the growth of knowledge. Immense pressure on the academicians to "publish or perish," personal rivalries and corporate wars for priority claims and new patents, are some other such factors. Post World War II the Cold War, especially since the launch of Sputnik, generated lot of research-based knowledge in defense and social welfare among nations and their political blocks across the Atlantic (Bhattacharya 2012). Close interaction between scholars, specialization trends, team work and interdisciplinary studies have also induced the growth of knowledge. In fact all of these are both the cause and effect of the continued growth of knowledge.

4.2. MODES OF KNOWLEDGE GROWTH

Knowledge is essentially a cerebral construct though social in character; and only the socially available or public knowledge is knowledge *ipso facto*. Factors and means to procreate knowledge are numerous and varied. Nature is the ultimate source, and human beings are the only agents to unearth knowledge. Non-human creatures do not have this creative facility. Research is one process to increase the fund of knowledge. Intuition, imagination and apperception are transcendental ways to conceive knowledge, whereas experimental, empirical, and speculative methods are available to all. Studies on the nature of knowledge have given rise to a body of knowledge called social epistemology (Shera 1962).

In spite of the increased importance of epistemological studies in philosophy, psychology, metaphysics, sociology, research methodology, cybernetics, artificial intelligence, and of course information science, surprisingly there have been very few studies on the mode of topology of growth of subjects. "We do not take enough notice of what contemporary philosophers and scientists have to say about the nature of knowledge," aptly warned Foskett (1980, p.3). Knowledge is a librarian's stock-in-trade, and the study of its nature is of as much importance to us as the study of anatomy to a surgeon (Machlup 1962, pp.33-34). Its implications in information management are all pervasive and too numerous (McGarry 1993). In information science, S.R. Ranganathan (1892-1972) is a pioneer in the studies on the modes of knowledge growth and on the science of knowledge. Initially the research in this area started in 1944,but got an impetus in the year 1948 when Ranganathan got introduced a paper "Development and structure of the universe of subjects" in the postgraduate library science curriculum of the University of Delhi. But his announced book on the subject was never published (Ranganathan, 1947; Ranganathan, 1949; Ranganathan, 1967, AC1; Parkhi, 1972, pp.102-104). However, he had an abiding interest in the field and always obtained fresh results (Kemp 1976, p.11; Ranganathan 1968). The work has been continued by his colleagues at the Documentation Research and Training Centre at Bangalore (Neelameghan 1973a; Neelameghan 1973b; Gopinath and Seetharama 1979) and elsewhere (Puranik 1952; Vickery 1952; Kabir et al. 1996). The late Jesse H. Shera (1903-1982) lauded this as Ranganathan's "intellectual contribution to the underlying philosophy of librarianship" (1962, pp.106-7).

4.3. THREE MODES

All the specific modes that Ranganathan discovered, and a few more for the growth of knowledge can summarily be discussed under three general modes: growth by specialization, interdisciplinary, and multidisciplinary growth. In fact Ranganathan studied growth of knowledge not qua knowledge but in form of subjects and especially the basic classes. He defines main class as the first division of the entire mass of knowledge into manageable block of interrelated and coherent ideas for study and communication. He further warns, "Generally speaking a main class cannot be represented either as a subclass of another or as a combination of two or more of the main classes." Ranganathan categorized all the subjects in the universe of knowledge into three categories namely, basic, compound and complex. Main classes are a kind of basic subjects (Parkhi 1972, p.110). Compound subjects, virtually infinite in number, are basic subjects with a focus such as agriculture of wheat, or rural sociology. Complex subjects are two phased subjects such as psychology for nurses. However, he divides main classes which he terms them as basic subjects (BS) into the following categories: Primary (BS) and Nonprimary (BS) (Satija 2011, pp.10-11).

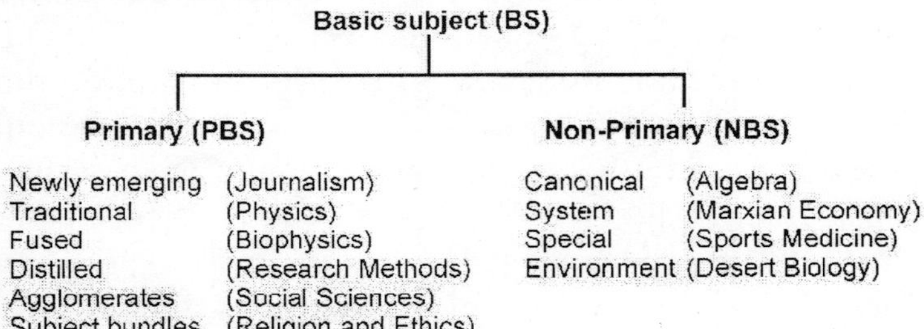

4.3.1. Specialization trends

In the beginning growth of knowledge was mostly additive. When too much growth and vast expansions make a subject unwieldy then the only way left to study and perpetuate it is by fragmentation. In many disciplines of knowledge there is an increasing tendency to specialize; to know more and more about less and less. "Fragmentation and specialization are two faces of the same coin" (Dogan 2001b, p.14851). A specialist is one who knows more and more about less and less till he knows everything about a minuscule part. McGarry (1993, p.141) aptly writes: "Societies cannot afford to work on the principle that everybody can do anything. The basis for efficiency lies in planned specialization of function, so management experts tell us. This principle is the same whether it is in industrial management or in the world of learning. 'Medicine' reflects this specialization function to even greater extent, and the same theory pervades social planning. The common welfare is seemed where each person performs a specialized service for benefit of others, and in turn can rely on their specialized services." Division of labor in the society is a simple outcome of expansion and sophistication. Specialists emerge, as if spontaneously, when a community becomes large. For example, every large religion fragments into sects, and a large community into ideological groups (Kemp 1976, p.103). Similarly in academic fields a narrower area is made the focus of sharp and intensive studies. Today scientists are no more scientists but only physicists, chemists, biologists and so on. This trend does not stop here, still narrower or super specialization has become the order of the day. One hardly knows a physicist today except as nuclear physicist, theoretical physicist, and low-temperature physicist and the like. Generalists are so rare that they have become specialists in themselves. Specialized subjects emerge by the following modes:

4.3.1.1. Fission

As the term from nuclear physics suggests it is successive ceaseless breaking of the subject into smaller fragments as in a nuclear chain reaction. It happens through the following two ways depending upon the time taken and the size to which the fragments are broken.

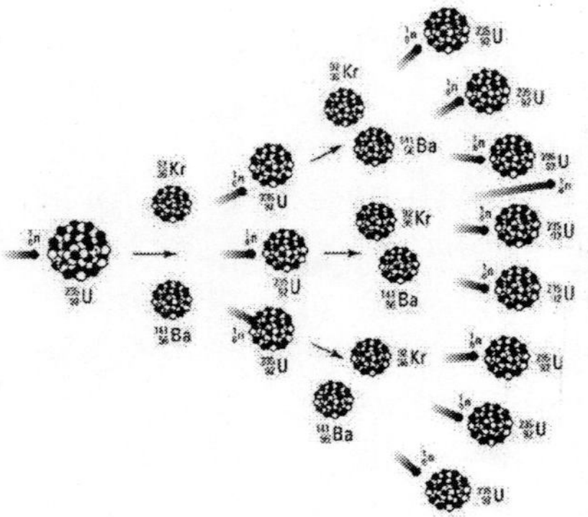

4.3.1.2. Dissection

One time splitting of a subject into an immediate array of its subordinate fragments of equal ranks is called dissection. Cutting a whole loaf of bread into slices (of more and less equal thickness) is dissection. Division of physics into its traditional branches such as properties of matter, heat, light, sound, electricity is an example of dissection. Division of the earth into its constituent seven continents is another example of dissection, so is the political division of a country in to its provinces. Generated divisions have a common genus, are mutually exclusive, exhaustive and equally ranked. In simple words, all segments form an array of cognate classes/entities. Dissection process is horizontal and instantaneous in action. Sometimes earlier Ranganathan had termed dissection by fission itself (Ranganathan 1972).

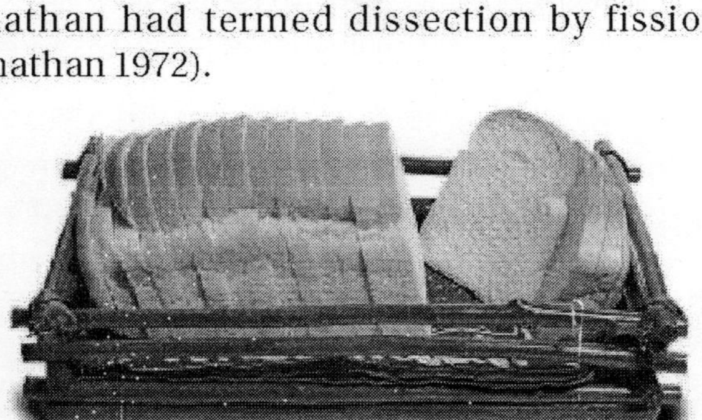

4.3.1.3. Denudation

Long drawn and repeated dissection of a single entity becomes denudation. It is stripping a subject, like pealing an onion, of its successive layers to reach the bottom of the bottomless. Sciences, physical sciences, chemistry, organic chemistry, aromatic compounds, benzenoids, benzene and so on illustrate the denudation at work. It works vertically downwards and generates a chain of entities in successive subordination. Its action is prolonged. In the process extension (breadth) of the subject decreases while its intension (depth) increases in the process. It may be noted that dissection and denudation both are relative terms differing only in degree (Ranganathan 1967, section PD4). Denudation is dissection applied repeatedly on one entity. Therefore, denudation includes dissection. This process is at work especially since the scientific revolution of 17th century when all experimental sciences were termed by a common term "Natural Philosophy" and once all social sciences were called sociology (Dewey 1876).

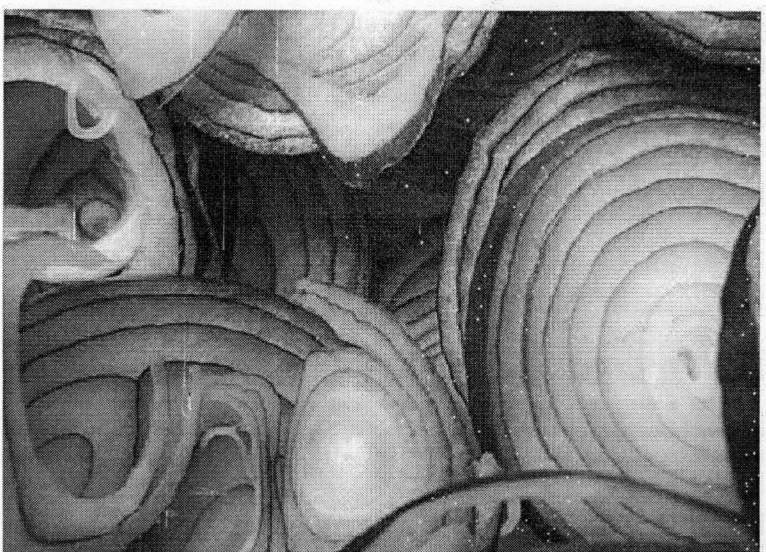

4.3.1.4. Lamination

A main class is a large, diffused but somewhat coherent, limited area of knowledge. When its area of study is further limited by specifying topics, it becomes a compound subject from a basic subject. Lamination is the process of placing one or more isolates on the parent basic subject. English language, linguistic grammar, and English grammar are three examples of laminated subjects from the main class linguistics. These have been obtained by placing the laminae of "English," "grammar," and "English grammar" respectively on the basic subject "Linguistics." These are termed as compound subjects in Ranganathan's terminology. Number of laminae placed on a subject could be as large as feasible. Number of such laminae is a direct measure of the specialization of that topic. Laminated or compound subjects are most populous in this universe of subjects—virtually these are infinite. A faceted classification such as the CC, UDC or BC-2 makes the structure of a compound subject quite clear whereas in the enumerative classification like the early DDC or the Library of Congress Classification compound subjects can neither take many laminae nor their structure is visible. In fact it is another kind of specialization—by qualifying and specifying a fissioned subject.

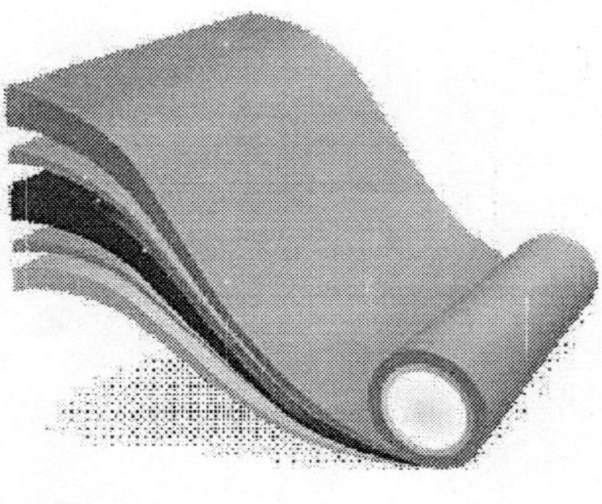

4.3.1.5. Procreation

If knowledge grows organically then some of it might

be procreated by copulation of two subjects. One such subject is linguistics, which is a knowledge field of recent and rapid growth says McGarry. He further writes (1993, p.146):Claiming descent from a union of philosophy and philology, it became a widely taught subject in the early 1960s. It claimed territory in the scientific study of human language and this claim was supported by the increasing need to investigate language and communication in relation to human needs and human behavior. A group of brilliant theoreticians created a new and broader picture for students and scholars. The discipline soon began to diversify and fuse with other disciplines. The results are specialist studies such as psycholinguistics, sociolinguistics, and neuro-linguistics.

4.3.1.6. Self-procreated

Furthering the analogy of knowledge bio-organism some organism like the bi-sexuals are self-procreated. Applied mathematics, applied physics, applied optics, applied chemistry, human biology are a few of numerous such subjects being taught as independent disciplines. Every knowledge is applied, they say. Every mature knowledge is theoretical. Indeed a theory is the most applied knowledge. These subjects are not applied in the sense of technology, as applied chemistry is not chemical technology.

4.3.1.7. Analogical mode

Some subjects find parallels in other disciplines. For example Darwin's theory of the evolution of species and survival of the fittest found echoes in social institutions and processes. Society, its organs and institutions evolve, grow and even mutate into other forms. Such studies are aptly described by the term "social Darwinism." Social Darwinism has been used to illuminate and explicate many social phenomena and problems. Social physics, social entropy, political dynamics and knowledge engineering are some of the examples of such subjects.

4.3.1.8. Instrument-based subjects

Some subjects are based on a machine and have grown into full discipline by gathering around a machine or device. An example is Microscopy or Microbiology which has risen from the Microscope. But the most outstanding example is of the all pervasive discipline of Computer Science and engineering and of late mobile based applications. It has encompassed and influenced every strata of society. Such subjects are growing and even fragmenting, for example, Internet studies is emerging as independent subject with many branches such as digital divide, Internet sociology.

4.3.2. Inter-disciplinary growth

The trend of specialization got so perverse that the scholars became isolated and distant from one another. Subjects became too jargon ridden to be easily communicated to other scholars. McGarry (1993, p.164) argues: "This tendency, though it makes for greater efficiency, can lead to communication problem, to individual researchers loosing sense of the 'whole.' In practical terms it can lead to costly duplication of efforts. It can even lead to duplication of efforts within the same profession". Reporting on the proceedings of a World Conference on interdisciplinarity, Judge (1995, p.82) reports:"However there was a clear concern that the fragmentation of the disciplines was failing to serve society in the face of a complex of global problems and conflicting initiatives."

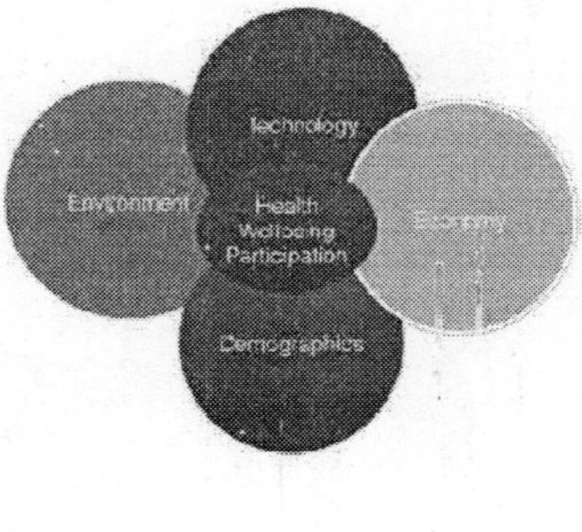

This trend has happily been counter-balanced by interdisciplinary studies, set in especially after the last World War (Puranik 1952). Team and relay research, close cooperation among scholars, availability of subject consultants have led the scholars to join hands for interdisciplinary studies. Knowledge advances through the juxtaposition of subjects. It has been aptly said that subjects criss-cross in boundaries and neat demarcations are now gone. There is experimental inter- and cross breeding to produce new species of subjects. Then there are subjects like "physical education" which feed on the other subjects in the environment. Inter-disciplinary subjects may be defined as a subject of interest to scholars from different disciplines or vice-versa. Ranganathan isolated the following modes of their formation.

4.3.2.1. Loose assemblage

Loose assemblage is a combination of two or more subjects or their parts in a sort of temporary, casual or incidental way involving any relation viz, influencing, comparison, biasing, difference, tool, or any undefined one. These subjects are from different disciplines. For example, "statistics for librarians," "psychology for nurses," or "influence of computers on library operations" are some such subjects taken at random. In such cases a subject is studied in light of the other and here their encounter or assemblage is temporary, *ad hoc* or loose, and reversible. Inevitably these subjects are of inter-disciplinary interest. We can have limitless number of subjects by this process. Subjects formed by loose assemblage are termed as complex subjects by Ranganathan. Each constituent of a complex subject is termed as a phase. Phase relation is counted among Ranganathan's brilliant devices for subject analysis and depth classification of inter-disciplinary subjects. Some of its methods such as the tool and bias phase have been borrowed by other systems such as the *Dewey Decimal Classification,* Broad System of Ordering and Bliss' Bibliographic Classification-2 (Slavic 2008).

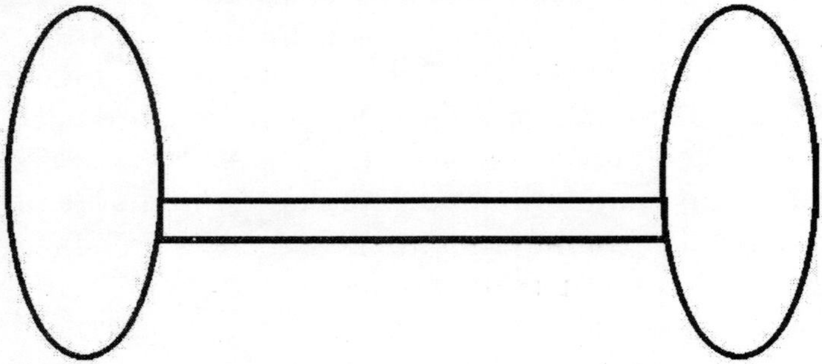

4.3.2.2. Fusion

Fusion is an advanced stage of loose assemblage. When loose assemblage solidifies into a permanent relation and the different constituents are irreversibly joined to form an entirely new subject with its own special isolates and literary warrant, it is called a fused subject or a subject born by fusion. Here the friendship of loose assemblage is upgraded to marriage or permanent bonding. Fused subjects transcend complex classes to become basic subjects. Biophysics biochemistry, chemical physics, political sociology, Internet banking, geopolitics, agricultural economics and plethora of 'e-' subjects such as e-commerce, e-lerning, e-publishing, e-governance are a few random examples of homogeneous and irreversibly combined complex classes—called fused main subjects. Fusion as a mode of formation of subjects has been isolated as recently as 1968, though the phenomenon is much older (Ranganathan 1962). In fact, earlier loose assemblage included fusion. Later in 1968 the loose assemblage and fusion were viewed as two different modes of formation of subjects.

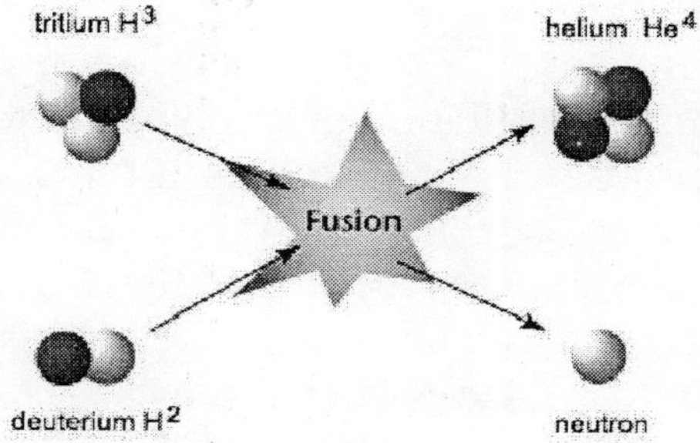

4.3.3. Multidisciplinary growth

During the last year of his life in association with colleagues at the Documentation Research and Training Centre (DRTC) at the Indian Statistical Institute, Bangalore (established in 1962), Ranganathan isolated three more modes of formation of subjects. These are all multidisciplinary in nature in accordance with the latest trends in research. Area or mission oriented or marginalized social groups, such as Indology, dalit studies, women studies, early childhood studies being the latest fashion in research are a major cause for the outbreak of such subjects which are mostly of applied nature. Team work and interaction of pure and applied research and political necessity of regions or minority communities also give birth to such subjects. These modes are as described below.

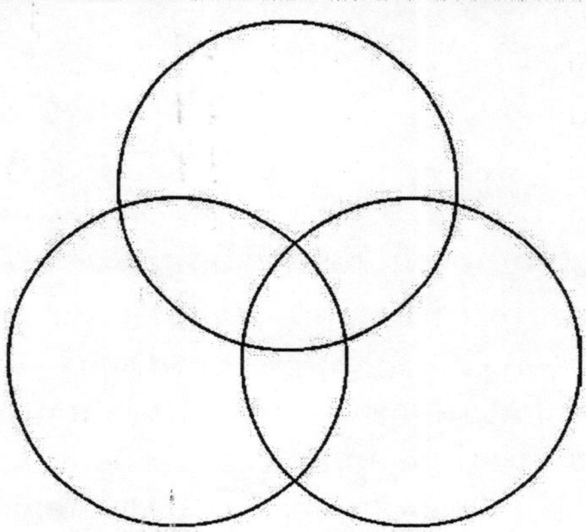

4.3.3.1. Distillation

When relatively not so fully developed a technique finds applications in different disciplines as a result it gets more developed and accumulates a body of its own literature "distilled" out of its different applications. When such a technique acquires sufficient literature then it gets the status of a new main class in itself, and it is termed as distilled main (basic) class. Such main classes are slow in formation. Museology, management science, career-ology, archeology, seminar technique and research methodology are some of the examples of distilled main classes in the Colon Classification (Ranganathan 1987, section DE13, 66). These are new entries to the array of main classes. These are born multidisciplinary in the sense that such subjects have been nurtured on the experience of different disciplines or they inherit the genes of different subjects to make a new organism, which is mostly applied in nature.

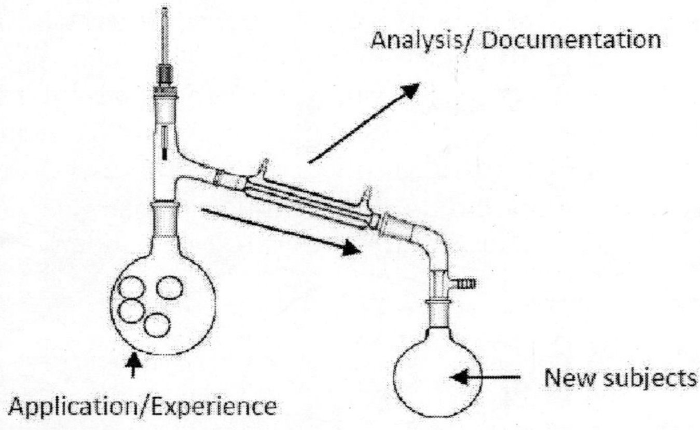

4.3.3.2. Partial comprehensions/agglomerates

Out of courtesy to tradition, and many a time out of necessity, some basic subjects coordinate in rank have appeared coupled together. These are neither loosely assembled nor fused. So in their intra-relations these are somewhat autonomous subjects. Plant sciences (botany, agriculture, horticulture, forestry taken together) mathematical and physical sciences, humanities, religion and philosophy, religion and ethics, geography and history are some examples of partially comprehensive classes of subjects. Usually the constituents of a partially comprehensive class are consecutive main classes held under an umbrella. These are also of generic nature, e.g., social sciences, life sciences. In the Colon Classification these are now existing at many hierarchical levels. Agglomerates may be viewed as bringing together of fissioned subjects. This phenomenon is already viewed by Kedrov (1974, p.3) who writes: "The integration of sciences is today effected to an ever greater degree through their further differentiation." "What is now partial comprehension might have been a main subject in the very early days, before fission advanced sufficiently," says Ranganathan (Ranganathan, 1972). Such subjects are usually embodied in periodical publications, and encyclopedias. Partial comprehensive subjects are also termed as agglomerates in new terminology (Gopinath and Seetharama 1979, section 42j). Partially comprehensive subjects do not have their direct isolates. Though their subdivisions in the form of main classes are there like in a "bunch of bananas" held together by some commonality; they are only good autonomous neighbors having a common distant forefather, but now not interacting much.

4.3.3.3. Subject bundles

As per Ranganathan and Gopinath, the subject bundles comprehend subjects drawn from different disciplines pursued by a team of different specialists (Ranganathan 1987, section DF1, 68). The Gulbenkian Commission accepting the emergence and social relevance of such subjects has now recommended (italics original): *The expansion of institutions, within or allied to the universities, which would bring together scholars for a year's work in common around specific urgent themes.* They already exist, of course, but in far too limited a number. One possible model is the ZiF (Zentrum für interdisziplinäre Forschung) at Bielefeld University in Germany, which has done this since the 1970s. Recent topics for the year have included body and soul, sociological and biological models of change, utopias.

Such subjects are related and either find application in other subjects, or work in unison with other subjects towards a common goal. They are not inert to one another. Usually these are area or mission oriented studies; and mostly such subjects are of applied nature. These may be in the form of a project undertaken by a widely based research team. Such projects fall in the domain of "big" science. Every expert or his group has a demarcated area of work at the initial stages. Some of the subject bundles enumerated in the CC-7 (Colon Classification Ed. 7) are: surface science, social science, material science, earth science, hydro science, ocean science, deep sea science, atmosphere science, defence science (Ranganathan 1987). Tennese Valley Project, Antarctic expeditions, Gandhiana, Indology, Sinology, Middle East studies are some practical examples of subject bundles. These are also called subject clusters (Gopinath and Seetharama, 1979, section 42R, 124). These subjects are beginning to have literary warrant. One actual publication cited by Ranganathan and Gopinath

(Ranganathan 1987) is: *Indian Ocean expedition: Recent progress in surface sciences,* 1964.

For such subjects Whitley (1984, pp.206-7) uses the term fragmented adhocracies which are polycentric in nature. These subjects are weakly bound. "Research is rather divergent and ... limited in its interconnectedness." Professionalization of social sciences has also given a fillip to such studies. Ranganathan erroneously thinks that partial comprehensions and subject bundles are the fruits of new developments in book production (Ranganathan 1969, p. 204). In other words he thinks such subjects have been procreated more by the publishers than the researchers and educationists. In our view, it cannot be so. It is the research trends or social needs which exercise formative influence on the publishing industry, and not vice-versa. Research trends are catapulted by social needs. For example, subject bundles have come into being because of social necessity and availability of huge funds. Publishers make value additions editorially only, and follow the intellectual lead given by author, editors and researchers.

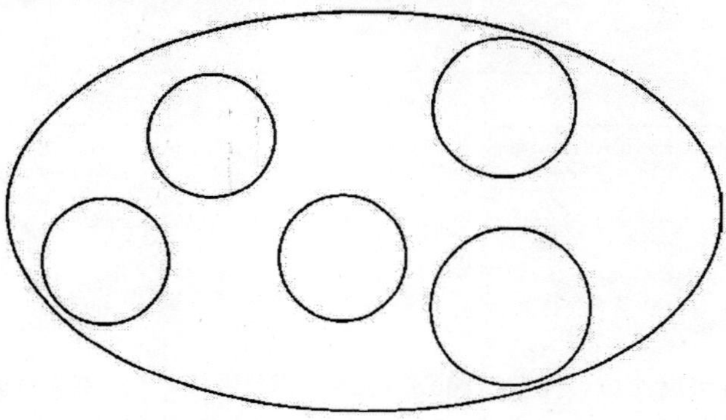

4.3.3.4. Annexation mode

Geography is a good example of all subject "areas that grow by accretion or colonization...it has annexed many loosely defended positions in the social and human sciences" writes McGarry (1993, 146). This imperialist tendency of geography is visible in its branches such as commercial geography, medical geography, political geography and many more. Take another example of Physical education, including sports and aerobics, which draw its sustenance from physical, bio and social sciences. Knowledge and research methods from the hard sciences and mathematics have strongly influenced developments in exercise physiology, kinaesthetic and sport biomechanics. Physiology, sociology, history and philosophy formed the foundation for development of exercise physiology kinematics, sport psychology, motor learning. Sport sociology, sport history and sport philosophy have obviously drawn from social sciences and humanities. The rehabilitation sciences particularly physio-therapy have exercised an indelible influence on sport medicine and adapted physical activity. In sport management the influence of business management, law, communication and marketing is evident (Wuest and Bucher 2006, p.14).

4.3.4. Summary of the diagram of modes of growth of subjects

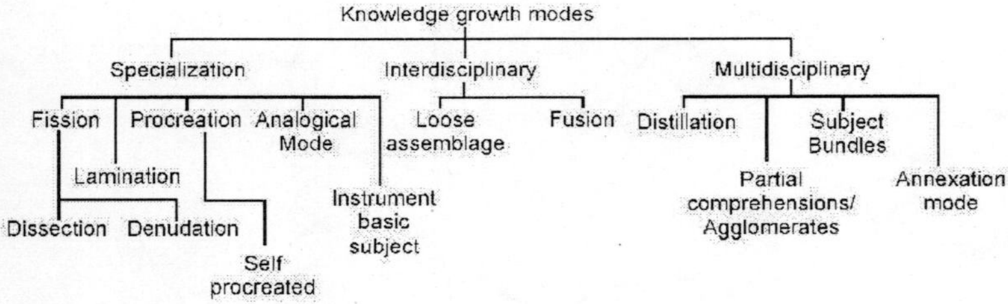

4.4. LIMITATIONS: INTERNET SUBJECTS GROWTH TRENDS

In the preceding sections we discussed so far the various trends and modes of growth of subjects. It is important to note that these modes of formation are based upon the information resources that are physically in the library and those that are meant to be used in the academics mostly. Hence this study can be seen as a study in a more controlled environment mostly drawing on Ranganathan's theory. The growth study becomes a real challenge when we consider the Internet subjects which is chaotic and uncontrolled. There is an information deluge and is not easy to quantify the volume of knowledge, the number of subjects or domains or speed of growth. Having stated this, we do accept there is need for such a study and identification of various modes of formation of Internet subjects. It becomes primarily important to ensure better organization and representation of information resources on the Web. Some of the examples of Internet subjects are: social networking, social organization, online gaming, email, virtual conferencing and communication, e-commerce, webisode, webometrics and so on. The incidence of interdisciplinary (and even multidisciplinary) subjects is greater as collaboration is facilitated by Internet. Transdisciplinary mode is when a subject like ethnography emerges due to work in interdisciplinary domains converging at higher levels of generalization. Barabasi et al (2000) opined that in the era of multidisciplinary and interdisciplinary science despite some randomness, fundamental laws and organizing principles can explain topological feature of diverse system such as Internet.

4.5. RELEVANCE AND USE

Binwal (1992, p.197) aptly writes: "Modes of formation of subjects represent a typology of relations and act as guiding ideas in recognizing and formulating relations among concepts constituting a subject." Implications of such studies for hospitality in library classification have been explained and elaborated by Husain (1989). Beghtol (1998) has reported some attempts to revise major library classification systems to accommodate multidisciplinary works more appropriately to reorient classification research towards pluralistic needs of multidisciplinary knowledge. Importance of such studies to the LIS community in general cannot be gainsaid for its own sake. Knowledge is librarian's stock in trade (Satija, 1992, p.40). A good shepherd knows his sheep.

4.6. SUMMING UP

Ranganathan and McGarry mostly discovered above modes by impliedly empirical studies based on the published literature. Ranganathan was more speculative and intuitive. It may be easily visualized from the emergence of recent academic subjects that these modes of growth are not exclusive or working singularly. There may be two modes at work simultaneously. Take the new subject of early childhood studies where fission and agglomeration are together at work. Specialization with cooperation across the disciplines seems the present trend as exhibited by the recently completed Genome project (HGP 2003). Recombination of specialties across disciplinary borders is viewed by Dogan (2001b, p.14853). Obviously such results are never final. Subjects will continue to be fragmented, aligned and re-aligned in different ways. The more we understand the nature of knowledge more may be the modes that can be visualized. This 'so various, so beautiful, and ever new' universe of knowledge will continue to throw forth new subjects formed by yet unforeseen modes. The report of the Gulbenkian Commission (Wallerstein et al. 1997, p.103) clearly mentions: "We are at a point when it [existing disciplinary structure] has been questioned and when competing studies are trying to come into existence." This is what was said long back by the invincible T.S. Eliot (1888-1965) in his poem East Coker II (1944):

The knowledge imposes a pattern, and falsifies,
For the pattern is new in every moment
And every moment is a new and shocking
Valuation of all we have been.

REFERENCES

Al-Hawamdeh, Suliman. (2005). *Knowledge management: cultivating knowledge professionals.* Oxford, UK: Chandos.

Barabási, Albert-László, Albert, Réka and Jeong, Hawoong. (2000). "Scale-free characteristics of random networks: the topology of the World Wide Web." *Physica A: statisticalmechanics and its applications* 281: 69-77.

Beghtol, Clare. (1998). "Knowledge domains: multidisciplinarity and bibliographic classification systems." *Knowledge organization* 25: 1-12.

Bhattacharya, Nikhil. (2012). "The evolution of knowledge in the university." *The information society* 28: 208-227.

Binwal, J.C. (1992). "Ranganathan and the universe of knowledge." *International classification* 19: 195-200.

Cornforth, Maurice. (1955). *The theory of knowledge.* Calcutta: National Book Agency.

Dewey, Melvil. (1876). *A classification and subject index for cataloguing as arranging the books and pamphlets of a library.* Amherst, Massachusetts.

Dogan, Mattei. (2001a). "Paradigms in social sciences." In Neil J. Smelster and Paul B. Balters, eds., *International encyclopedia of the social and behavioral sciences,* vol. 16. Amsterdam: Elsevier Science, pp. 11023-11027.

Dogan, Mattei. (2001b). "Specialization and recombination of specialties in social sciences." In Neil J. Smelster and Paul B. Balters, eds., *International encyclopedia of the social and behavioral sciences,* vol. 16. Amsterdam: Elsevier Science, pp.14851-5.

Eliot, T.S. (1944). *The four quartets.* London: Faber.

Foskett, Douglas J. (1980). "System theory and relevance to documentary classification." *International classification* 7: 2-5.

Gopinath, M.A. and S. Seetharama. (1979). "Interdisciplinary subjects and their classification." In A. Neelameghan, ed., *Ordering systems for global information networks.* Bangalore: FIDICR and Sarada Ranganathan Endowment, pp. 121-135.

HGP. (2003). *All about the human genome project (HGP).* Available http://www.genome.gov/10001772.

Husain, Shabhat. (1989). "A theoretical basis for the accommodation of new subjects in Colon Classification. 7th ed." *International classification* 16: 82-8.

Judge, Anthony J.N. (1995). "Transdisciplinarity through structured dialogue." *Knowledge organization* 22: 82-88.

Kabir, H. and Jyothirmayi, S. (1996). "Basic subjects in colon classification from editions one to seven: a critical study." *Library science with a slant to documentation and information studies* 33: 1-28.

Kedrov, B.M. (1974). "Concerning the synthesis of sciences." *International classification* 1: 3-11.

Kemp, D Alasdair. (1976). *The nature of knowledge: an introduction for librarians.* London: Clive Bingley.

Machlup, Fritz. (1962). *The production and distribution of knowledge in the United States.* Princeton: Princeton University.

Machlup, Fritz. (1979). "Stock and flows of knowledge." *Kyklos* 32: 400-11.

McGarry, Kevin. (1993). *The changing context of information.* 2nd ed. London: LA Publishing.

Neelameghan, A. (1973a). "Basic subjects and their arrangements." *Library science with a slant to documentation* 10: 207-21.

Neelameghan, A. (1973b). "Primary basic subjects by fission." *Library science with a slant to documentation* 10: 162-163.

Parkhi, R.S. (1972). *Library Classification:: Evolution of a Dynamic Theory.* Delhi: Vikas

Puranik, K.D. (1952). "Field of knowledge and its repercussion on classification." *Abgila* 2: 19-23.

Ranganathan, S.R. (1947). "Classification and international documentation" *Review of Documentation* 14: 154-177.

Ranganathan, S.R. (1949). "Self-perpetuating scheme of classification" *Journal of Documentation* 4: 223-244.

Ranganathan, S.R. (1962). "Application to India." In Jesse Hauk Shera, ed., *Sociological foundations of librarianship.* Bombay: Asia.

Ranganathan, S.R. (1963). *Five laws of library science.* 2nd ed. Bombay: Asia.

Ranganathan, S.R. (1967). *Prolegomena to library classification.* 3rd ed., assisted by M. A. Gopinath. Bombay: Asia.

Ranganathan, S.R. (1968). "Basic subjects and their kinds." *Library science with a slant to documentation* 5: 97-134.

Ranganathan, S.R. (1969). "Colon classification, 7th ed.: a preview (1971)." *Library science with a slant to documentation* 6: 193-242.

Ranganathan, S.R. (1972). "Impact of growth in the universe of subjects on classification." In S.R. Ranganathan and Bernard Ira Palmer, eds., *Ranganathan memorial issue.* Copenhagen: Danish Centre for Documentation.

Ranganathan, S.R. (1987). *Colon classification.* 7th ed., rev. and ed. by M.A. Gopinath. Bangalore: Sarada Ranganathan Endowment.

Satija, M.P. (1979). "Extension of two phased subjects." *Herald of library science* 18(4): 344-348.

Satija, M.P. (1984). "On quantifying knowledge." *Herald of library science* 23: 23-30.

Satija, M.P. (1992). "Book review of Meadows (1991): knowledge and communication: essays on the information chain." *International classification* 19: 39–41.

Satija, M.P. (2011). *A guide to the theory and practice of colon classification.* New Delhi: Ess Ess.

Satija, M.P. (2013). "Information: nature, importance and function." *Annals of library and information studies* 60: 128-33.

Shera, Jesse Hauk. (1962). *Sociological foundations of librarianship.* Bombay: Asia.

Slavic, Aida. (2008). "Faceted classification: management and use." *Axiomathes* 18: 257-71.

Toffler, Alvin. (1980). *The third wave.* New York: William Morrow.

Vickery, Brian C. (1952). "The changing structure of knowledge." *Annals of library science,* 1: 137-47.

Wallerstein, I., et. al (1997). *Open the social sciences: report of the gulbenkian commission on restructuring the social sciences.* New Delhi: Vistaar Publications.

Weiss, Paul. (1960). "Knowledge: a growth process." *Science* 131(3415): 1716-9.

Whitley, Richard. (1984). *The intellectual and social organization of the sciences.* Oxford: Clarendon Press.

Wuest, Deborah A. and Charles A. Bucher. (2006). F*oundations of physical education, exercise science and sport.* Boston: McGraw Hill.

FURTHER READINGS

Documentation Research and Training Centre. (1966) "Universe of knowledge: Depth classification: Documentation list" *DRTC Annual Seminar* 4.

Jayarajan, P. (1972). "The schedule of main subjects proposed for edition7 of the Colon Classification" *Library Resources & Technical Services* 16: 359-363.

Neelameghan, A. (1973). "Basic subjects." *Library Science with a slant to Documentation* 10: 149-157

Neelameghan, A. (1973). "Basic subjects: A select bibliography." *Library Science with a slant to Documentation* 10: 261-265.

Neelameghan, A. (1973). "Basic subjects: Agglomerate basic subjects (from Colon Classification)." *Library Science with a slant to Documentation* 10: 202-206.

Neelameghan, A. (1973). "Basic subjects and their arrangement: a summary." *Library Science with a slant to Documentation* 10: 207-221.

Neelameghan, A. (1973). "Primary basic subjects by clustering." *Library Science with a slant to Documentation* 10: 180-188.

Neelameghan, A. (1973). "Non primary basic subjects." *Library Science with a slant to Documentation* 10: 189-201

Neelameghan, A. (1973). "Primary basic subjects by distillation." *Library Science with a slant to Documentation* 10: 166-172.

Neelameghan, A. (1973). "Primary basic subjects by fission." *Library Science with a slant to Documentation* 10: 158-165.

Neelameghan, A. (1973). "Primary basic subjects by fusion." *Library Science with a slant to Documentation* 10: 173-179

Neelameghan, A. (1974). "Interdisciplinary research and classification problems: A case study." *Library Science with a slant to Documentation* 11: 1-14

Ranganathan, S.R. (1972). *Impact of growth of the universe of subjects on classification.* FID/CR Report 12. Copenhagen: Denmark Centre for Documentation.

Meadows, A.J., Ed. (1991): *Knowledge and communication: essays on the information chain.* London: Library Association Publishing.

5

Mapping of Social Sciences in the Colon Classification

STRUCTURE

ABSTRACT

Defines knowledge as sum total of ideas, emotions, beliefs, and experiences conserved by the society. Enumerates its properties as being social, ever growing, multidimensional and fragmentary. Explains in brief social epistemology. Lists the growth of knowledge by specialization, interdisciplinary and multidisciplinary modes. Views classifications as impermanent maps of knowledge which change with society and time. Explains the four principles of the mapping of knowledge as given by D.W. Langridge (1925-2001), namely, ideological, social purpose, taxonomic, and disciplinary. Defines the field and scope of social sciences and briefly introduces the Colon Classification, its method, structure and kind of subjects therein. Further outlines and critically evaluates the order of basic subjects as divided into major disciplines of sciences, humanities, and social sciences. Lastly, it dwells minutely on the order of social sciences main classes, namely, education, geography, history, political science, economics, sociology and law. Ranganathan claimed this order to be of increasing artificiality of their laws. It refutes Ranganathan's concept of artificiality of social laws. This chapter by analysis argues the order of CC-6 (1960) main classes to be of serial dependency as given by August Comte and already practiced by the Library of Congress Classification.

5.1. INTRODUCTION

Knowledge has been defined as the sum total of known ideas, facts, fiction, myths, experiences and expressed emotions conserved by the society at large. In simple words, what is known to the society and is held in its collective memory is knowledge. Knowledge is essentially public. Tacit knowledge is formed with public knowledge and experience. Private knowledge is not knowledge *per se.* In other words, the society is the preserver and conservator of knowledge. The knowledge is knower, i.e., the human, dependent. Human being is the creator and consumer of knowledge. There cannot be any knowledge without a knower. Knowledge is created to solve problems facing mankind which leads to new systems, products, services, values and ultimately the outlook and perceptions about the world and cosmos.

5.2. CHARACTERISTICS OF KNOWLEDGE

All assorted chunks of knowledge can be unified into a single big fragment. There is unity in knowledge, says J.H. Shera (1970, p. 106). In other words, the entire body of knowledge is a living system having its definite properties:

- Knowledge is not independent, it is dependent upon the knower, the sensory being. It is subjective, and resides in the mind.
- It is generated, used and preserved by human society. Thus it is social in character.
- Knowledge is never complete. It is growing, dynamic, multidimensional and changing. It changes with time and society, and changes as it grows. What we know is a tip of the iceberg. Finality in knowledge can never be reached. Thus knowledge is always fragmentary. At any point of time what is known to the mankind is little *vis-a-vis* the yet to be known.
- Thus it is inexhaustible, i.e., never ending. In other words it tends to be infinite.
- Technology, social advancements, knowledge creation and use are mutually dependent.
- Knowledge originates from the environment, both physical and social. Man is the knower, the nature,

including society, is the ultimate source of knowledge. Our sense organs are organic tools to perceive information and data (Satija 2004). Brain transforms them into knowledge.

- Knowledge is socio-biological. Information is generated when the knower interacts with the nature through the sense organs. Information thus gained is integrated with the previously conserved knowledge for its use and validation (Foskett 1974, p. 202). Thus knowledge is socio-biological in nature.
- Society is the producer and consumer of knowledge, while knowledge in turn is the prime mover of society. Thus society and knowledge are locked in mutual influence on one another. It is not possible to isolate the one way influence. Knowledge grows as society grows; whereas society changes, develops and progresses as new knowledge is generated. It is the society which decides which kind of knowledge it is going to have; in which direction, and in how much quantity; society determines the value scales for the different categories of knowledge. Therefore, thrust areas in research to develop new knowledge essentially depend on the changing values and priorities of a society. The prevailing philosophy, material culture, economic and technological needs, cosmic vision, sense of history and values held by the society influence the status and structure of the stock of knowledge in its possession. This is known as social epistemology.

5.3. IMPORTANCE OF KNOWLEDGE STUDIES FOR LIBRARIANS

Knowledge is both recorded and oral. Tribal and illiterate societies orally perpetuate their knowledge. Librarians deal only with recorded knowledge i.e., documents. Knowledge is stock-in-trade of the librarians and information professionals. Therefore, quite obviously the study of the knowledge, its characteristics and structure is important to librarians. Study of the nature of knowledge is as important to the library and information professionals as is the study of anatomy important to a surgeon, says Jesse Shera. Hence librarians need to know the sources, properties and structure of knowledge. Only then librarians will be able to collect, organize, preserve, retrieve and disseminate it effectively.

5.4. MODES OF GROWTH OF KNOWLEDGE

Knowledge is growing constantly. New subjects are ceaselessly emerging. S.R. Ranganathan (1967, pp. 382-391) identified many modes of growth of subjects of various kinds. These are:

A By Specialization

- A1 By denudation (Vertical split)
- A2 By dissection (Horizontal division)
- A3 By lamination (Imposition of concepts)

B Interdisciplinary mode

- B1 By loose assemblage (Combination)
- B2 By fusion (Permanent combination)

C Multidisciplinary mode

- C1 By distillation (Sublimated essence of many subjects: Management sciences)
- C2 By agglomeration (Collection of neighbourly subjects: Social Sciences)
- C3 By subject bundles (Missions oriented aggregation: Antarctica Expedition)

The modes of formation of a subject cast a considerable influence on its structure (Satija, et al. 2014).

5.5. CLASSIFICATION

A classification is a structure; a map. Knowledge classification is a cognitive map of knowledge (Iyer 1995, pp. 12-29). But no classification is absolute or value free. It reflects boundaries and structure of knowledge as perceived by its designer, and is not universal in application (Sahadath 2013). The designer in turn is invariably influenced by the intellectual or social milieu of time and place. As said earlier, knowledge is social, fragmentary and dynamic, so it is aptly said that there is no finality of knowledge. If so, then a map can neither be stable nor universally acceptable. Consequently there cannot be any consensus on its structure and inter-relations of subjects. Inevitably the knowledge is depicted and mapped differently in different classifications – and there is nothing right or wrong about it (Gnoli 2006). There is no universal pattern of all knowledge that could be all things to all users. Nevertheless, organization of knowledge that a classification does, acts as a force towards integration and synthesis of knowledge. Classification is utilitarian in purpose. And mostly that purpose is immediate (Satija 1998).

5.5.1. Mapping of the universe of knowledge

Ever growing and changing knowledge is thus ever new. New subjects constantly emerge, old subjects change their status, structure and boundaries. Therefore, individual subjects change their structure; and relationships between subjects are seen in different ways. In fact knowledge has no inherent structure. It is imposed by the society on it. Every age and society has a distinct view of knowledge. For example, in the middle ages theology was considered the queen of sciences and other subjects were valued according to their capacity to serve her. Natural sciences considered as an idle man's task were not valued much then. Even during the times of Melvil Dewey in late 19th century philosophy and theology occupied a very respectable position which is evident from the fact that 1/5th of space in the Dewey's universe of knowledge is occupied jointly by these two classes (Miksa 1998, p. 67). Today the scales are tilted towards the study of natural sciences and their economic and technical implications. Sciences rule the roost and have been given the status of a national religion in some secular countries. Empirical and experimental modes of investigation are considered reliable methods to discover new knowledge and solve problems. These days authority, faith and intuition as sources of knowledge are looked upon with suspicion. Thus, the status a subject commands in a society is never stable. Some subjects once important and at the center stage of society are now relegated to a peripheral position. Once it was industrial production which was important. Today the cyberspace, environmental studies, human/animal rights, management, biotechnology and research on non-conventional sources of energy are pervasive (Satija and Martínez-Ávila 2017).

5.5.1.1. Classifications are Impermanent

As said earlier, with the emergence of new knowledge the status and position of existing subjects undergo a change. Subject equations are always in a flux. For example, many subjects such as public health, international law, geopolitics, demography which had status of compound or complex subjects in the 6th edition of the Colon Classification have gained the status of basic subjects in its 7th edition (1987) (Satija 1990). Many similar examples can be tendered from regular revisions of the DDC. Thus knowledge structure is always changing. Classification essentially represents knowledge, and is its map. It is a tool to analyze, organize and notionally represent knowledge. Therefore, as the knowledge advances by multidimensional expansions and filling gaps, we need new classifications, or adjust and modify the earlier ones. We have not only to revise classifications, but have to invent new classificatory techniques to organize new species of knowledge. S.R. Ranganathan commended the DDC as the best classification for the 19th century literature. At the same time he thought it quite unsuitable to classify 20th century knowledge especially of the post world wars period. Thus 20th century needed new classification system and techniques and the 21st century may well need new techniques particularly for organizing the Internet. To visualize structure of knowledge we need to limit ourselves to one epoch within one culture to find some firm basis for a unified knowledge.

5.5.2. Principles for mapping the universe of knowledge

D.W. Langridge (1925-2001 identifies four principles for mapping of the universe of knowledge (Langridge 1976, pp. 1-7). These, however, are not mutually exclusive.

5.5.2.1. Ideological principle

These are based on some school of thought, or some ideologically held principles. Earlier examples are Christian schemes of the middle ages. Latest example is the Russian classification system BBK which had made Marxism-Leninism as the center of the universe of knowledge. To some extent every scheme is based on some ideology. As said earlier, no classification scheme can be value free or independent of the time and culture of its origin. Every scheme is biased towards the values and culture of the society of its origin. That is why the Dewey Decimal Classification has to be modified and adapted to classify African and Asian subjects (Comaromi and Satija 1985).

5.5.2.2. Principle of social purpose

In the Vedas (1500 BC) the division of knowledge into

categories of *Dharm* (normative principles), *Arth* (social sciences), *Kam* (pure sciences and arts) and *Moksh* (spiritual knowledge) is an example of this principle. This is a broad classification which arranges knowledge in an order of decreasing current social utility and in the increasing potential for future use. This is a theoretical classification which has never been the basis of a library classification or any detailed knowledge classification. Ranganathan was bit influenced by it but he never used it as the basis of his Colon Classification.

5.5.2.3. Scientific order

Based on some natural and logical order of subjects, its principles were first crystallized by the famous American classification author, E.C. Richardson (1860-1939) in his famous book, *Classification: Theoretical and Practical* (1912). C.A. Cutter (1837-1903) used the evolutionary order of main classes in his Expansive Classification (1893). Cutter was of the opinion that nature has an order which should be reflected in organization of knowledge in libraries. His system is based upon the assumption, "Order of sciences is the order of things, and order of things is the order of their complexity" (Maltby 1975, pp. 122-135). This obviously betrays the influence of the theory of origin of species as given by the naturalist Charles Darwin (1809-1882). Entities in nature have evolved from atomic to molecular and to molar forms. These principles were used to some extent by J.D. Brown (1862-1914) in his Subject Classification (1906) and H.E. Bliss (1870-1955) in his Bibliographic Classification (1935). The arrangement of classes in the Library of Congress Classification (1904+) is also based on this principle. The internal arrangement of entities in botany and zoology in the DDC and CC is predominantly taxonomic. But its full implications were explored by the Classification Research Group (CRG) London (established in 1955) when the Group attempted to solve the problems of general classification schemes and tried to design a new system of library classification. The vague evolutionary order was more deeply explored and precisely defined in the theory of Integrative Levels by J.E.L. Farradane (1906-1989) and later propagated by D.J. Foskett (1918-2005). The objective of this theory was to "identify all the entities or objects of knowledge in existence, and to order them by means of a theory and thus provide a structure of knowledge". Obviously this theory applies mostly to natural objects which have physically evolved. It is also applicable to social entitles which obviously are always in a state of slow social evolution, growth and change.

5.5.2.4. Principle arrangement by disciplines

A discipline is a major and cohesive chunk of knowledge formed by a single mode, or has similar objects of study. A major trend setting contribution of Melvil Dewey (1851-1931) was to divide knowledge by discipline. The DDC (Glossary) defines a discipline as "An organized field of study or branch of learning dealing with specific kinds of subjects and/or subjects considered from specific points of view". Disciplines differentiate knowledge into number of logically distinct domains characterized by the possession of cohesive types of concepts, structure and method of creation and verification of new knowledge. Division by discipline offers comparatively better solution to the problems of information retrieval to meet the needs of present day library users. First exposition of this method is from the *Advancement of Learning* (1605) by a famous English philosopher, man of letters, and scientist, Francis Bacon (1561-1626). He deeply examined the then prevailing state of knowledge and means of its progress. He suggested that there are three kinds (major disciplines) of knowledge based upon three faculties of mind, namely Memory, Imagination and Reason. This produces correspondingly three major disciplines: History, Arts, and Sciences.

However, it is debatable whether these disciplines are autonomous, mutually exclusive and fuse to make an integrated whole of knowledge. Neuro sciences have discovered many more functions of human brain. Anyhow, the present age is the age of division by discipline in unison with the trends pursued by scholars and reflected by the university academic organization (McGarry 1993, pp. 140-153).

5.6. SOCIAL SCIENCES

Social science is a discipline of academic study and research which started in the late eighteenth century with the exhortations like "Best study of mankind is man". Later day protagonists have adopted it as "Proper study of mankind is human groups and institutions". Indeed knowledge of human nature, the object of social sciences, is the essence of learning and living. Influenced by the modern methods of research (applied successfully in natural sciences) and driven by industrialization, urbanization, menaces of growing population and depletion of natural resources and threat of war, the social sciences have grown thick and fast since the early 20th century. Formally these are defined as study of humans and their relations with one another, and in particular the study of various groups linking other groups, individuals, persons and entities in the environment. A social group is any aggregate of human beings who are brought into kinship and other relationships with one another. Social scientists agree that their studies extend the whole range of human relationships between groups of people and inter human-environmental relationships. Social sciences make a comprehensive study of the functions and mechanism of human society and its affiliates. It lays emphasis on distribution of power, wealth, socialization and mechanism to ensure security and justice for all. Scope and complexity of social sciences are on the increase (Broadus 1981, pp. 265-281).

5.7. COLON CLASSIFICATION (CC)

Colon Classification (1st ed. 1933) by S.R. Ranganathan (1892-1972) is a thoroughly faceted and theory based classification. It is now in its 7th edition published in 1987, though the sixth edition (1960) continues to be popular. Ranganathan was very particular about the order of main classes and of facets in a class number. For him the order is the essence of classification. He formulated some postulates and principles for ordering classes in arrays and chains, and facets in the facet formula. Contrary to expectation the order of main classes in the CC is not Vedic, though a weak influence of this system can be seen.

5.7.1. Division of knowledge in the CC

Existence of time honored main and canonical classes makes the CC look steeped in disciplinary tradition. Ranganathan identified three types of subjects in the universe of knowledge: Basic, Compound and Complex, analogous to chemical substances. Basic subjects are unitary subjects, such as Physics, Economics, Music, Law and Library Science. Compound subjects are basic subjects specified by subdivisions or additional facets, e.g., Velocity of light, Transport economics, Guitar music, or Law of marriage, and Libraries in India. Compound subjects are virtually infinite in number. Complex subjects are mostly interdisciplinary in nature, e.g., mathematics for engineers, psychology for nurses, or Comparative Law. Ranganathan postulated that every subject, be it of any type or level, has a basic subject which forms the first facet in constructing a class number. Ranganathan further divided basic subjects into: Main basic subjects and Non-Main Basic subjects and further divided them into ten species. On the basis of their modes of formation the following ten types of basic subjects have been identified.

1. Main Basic Subjects
   1.1 Traditional (Law, Physics)
   1.2 Newly emerging (Library & Information Science)
   1.3 Fused (Geopolitics)
   1.4 Distilled (Research methodology)
   1.5 Subject bundles (Apollo mission)
   1.6 Agglomerates (Social sciences)
2. Non-main basic subjects
   2.1 Canonical classes (Macro economics)
   2.2 System constituents (Marxian economy)
   2.3 Environment constituents (War economy)
   2.4 Special constituents (Gerontology; Cooperative economics)

His broader main class order is:

Sciences A/M Δ(delta) Mysticism & Spiritual Experience, Humanities N/S and Social Sciences T/Z

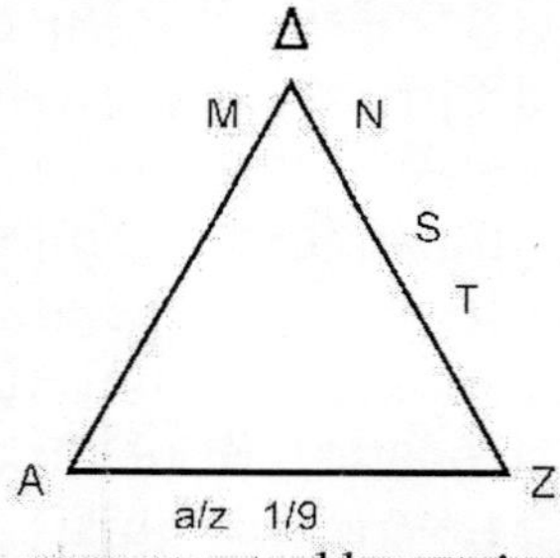

These can be represented by a triangle as given above.

Ranganathan was of the considered view that study of natural sciences had evolved first which was followed by humanities. Though the society is old but the social sciences are the last to come into being on the academic horizon. Keeping in view the social and academic trends Ranganathan devoted half of the total main classes to science and technology. The other side of the triangle has been divided between humanities and social sciences.

Sciences A to M are in the order of their increasing concreteness. B mathematics is most abstract of the sciences; C physics is more concrete than B mathematics and less concrete than D Engineering, and so on. M useful arts having classes such as Home economics, Textile arts, Carpentry, Smithy, Games and sports is the most concrete of the sciences. Within sciences Ranganathan follows the serial system i.e., theory and practices of a subject alternate one another – as first given by Auguste Comte (1798-1857). For example, B mathematics has many applications in C Physics which in turn forms the theory of D Engineering. F (Chemical) Technology follows E Chemistry; and J Agriculture follows I Botany. In this way theory and its applications have been brought together, which have been separated in the DDC. The Humanities N/S have been arranged in the order of their increasing richness of contents. That N Arts, even O Literature have no subject, only form. Social sciences T/Z have been arranged in the order of their increasing artificiality: For Ranganathan Z Law is the most artificial of all the social sciences. Main class Δ (delta) Mysticism and Spiritual experience positioned between M and N, and placed at the vertex of the triangle has been given top position in the mapping of knowledge. It is at the cross roads of sciences and humanities. Ranganathan was of the opinion that mystic and spiritual knowledge is the source of all kinds of knowledge: its sum and summary. Spirituality in Hinduism is regarded as highest knowledge of God and self—*sarva vidya pratishtha*. Hence, its highest position. Δ (delta) is the confluence of two different streams of knowledge, the sciences and humanities, the two different cultures of C.P. Snow (1905-1980). Ranganathan learned from the Veda that spiritual experience is the fountain head of all knowledge, thus refuted C.P. Snow's two cultures theory. Inter-disciplinary knowledge such as socio-biology and inter breeding of subjects have already given death blow to Snow's convictions.

The classification philosopher H.E. Bliss (1870-1955) endeavored to discover a permanent order of main classes based upon scientific and educational consensus. In fact no consensus can ever be permanent. Ranganathan based his order instead on concrete and objectively stated principles. These principles are helpful in placing ever emerging new main classes at their logical places in the array of main classes. Number of basic subjects has increased to about eight hundred in CC-7 (1987) without any problem of placing them at their rightful place in the lengthy array of basic subjects (Ranganathan 1987, pp. 49-51).

5.7.2. Main classes and their order

Knowledge is librarian's merchandise. Understanding its nature and modes of growth is vital to a classificationist. Ranganathan's research in social epistemology has been lauded as everlasting "intellectual contribution to the underlying philosophy of librarianship" by late Dean Jesse H. Shera. Ranganathan laid great emphasis on the order of knowledge and consequently on the arrangement of basic subjects in his CC. For him the essence of library classification lay in a filiatory sequence of subjects and documents. A classification must depict the structure of knowledge. As said earlier, first division of knowledge in the CC is into traditional disciplines, which he arranges in the order of their evolution as academic studies, namely, Science and Technology, Humanities and Social Sciences

Now the disciplines are divided into sub disciplines, namely,

B*Z Physical Sciences

G*Z Bio Sciences

K*Z Animal Sciences

L*Z Medical Sciences

MZ*Z Humanities and Social Sciences

S*Z Behavioural Sciences

T*Z Social Sciences

Within each discipline the CC has an order of main classes meticulously based on objectively stated principles (Satija 2001, pp. 199-210). An overview of main classes in the CC is as follows:

A/B Science/Mathematics

C/D Physics/Engineering

E/F Chemistry/Chemical technology

G/H Biology/Geology

I/J/K Botany/Agriculture/Zoology

L Medicine

M/N Useful Arts/Fine Arts

Δ Spiritual experience & Mysticism

O/P Literature/Language

Q/R Religion/Philosophy

S/T Psychology/Education

U/V Geography/History

W/X Political Science/Economics

Y/Z Sociology/Law

These main classes are in fact preceded by Generalalia and Form classes denoted by a/z, and newly emerging classes 1/9, e.g.,

a	Bibliography	1	Universe of knowledge
k	General encyclopedias	2	Library science
m	General Periodicals	3	Book science
p	Conference Proceedings	4	Mass communication
w	Biographies	5	Management science
z	Generalia classes		

Sciences (including technologies), in classes A to M, have been arranged in order of their increasing concreteness: B, Mathematics, is the most abstract of the sciences, while M, Useful arts (which includes crafts and applied technologies) is the most concrete in the group. Within A/M, theory and practice alternate: theory always precedes its practice or applications. For example, B, Mathematics, precedes C, Physics, which in turn precedes D, Engineering. E, Chemistry precedes F, Chemical technology. Similarly I, Botany is followed by J, Agriculture. This internal arrangement is based on the principle of dependency, first promulgated by Auguste Comte (1798-1857). Unlike Dewey, Ranganathan preferred to collocate the theory with the practice of a subject. Indeed the Library of Congress Classification (1899/1940+) followed this principle earlier to him. In the humanities, which are spread over main classes N to S. This arrangement is in order of increasing richness of subject contents. The order of social sciences, in main classes T to Z, is of increasing artificiality of their laws: Z Laws being legislative and subject to frequent modifications are considered most artificial of the social laws.

In an article published prior to the release of CC, R.S. Parkhi (1933) commended its arrangement of main classes as logical and evolutionary. Elucidating his viewpoint, he described the Generalia class as the complete microscopic view of knowledge that precedes the entire universe of knowledge. B Mathematics pervades every science. Physical sciences C-F study the matter and forces, which constitute this primal universe. G, Biology is vital science. Classes H-K are in evolutionary order of life on our planet. Classes L-P are application subjects for the well being and prosperity of humankind. Classes from Q, Religion to T, Education are for the moral and social development of individuals beyond animal existence, which in fact depend upon the correct applications of classes L-P, which in turn depend on classes A-K, the physical and the animal world.

5.8. SOCIAL SCIENCES IN THE COLON CLASSIFICATION

As with knowledge in general, position and boundaries of social sciences vary from classification system to classification system. As said earlier, the social sciences have been placed as the last discipline of knowledge in the CC denoted by the main classes T to Z. This evaluation is based on CC-6 (1960) which is the popular edition of the system.

On the face of it there seems no obvious order of the social sciences in the CC. The S Psychology, the bordering class, has been included in the humanities which by majority accounts is a behavioral science close to the hard sciences. Ranganathan claims that the social sciences have been arranged in the order of the increasing artificiality of their laws. It means that the laws of T Educations are more natural as compared to the laws of geography and history. That sounds true as theories of learning are based on psychology and medical sciences. But that does not mean the laws of geography and history are artificial or man-made. It also implies that laws of Z Laws are the most artificial ones. If so, Ranganthan has failed to make the fine distinction between the legislative laws enacted by parliaments and the normative principles that emerge and evolve for conducting a society. Such patterns of behavior or urges are inherent in individual humans and their groups. Laws enacted by a legislative body may be artificial, *ad hoc*, and suited to the ruling group, and subject to frequent amendments, but its normative principles such as law of natural justice, law of tradition, law of precedence are as good as the laws of, say economics, namely, laws of consumption, utility, marketing. Economic man is a predictable entity. In brief law has its own norms and philosophy. There seems no convincing rationale in the arrangement of social sciences. In fact it is not appropriate to call the laws of social sciences as artificial. For example, economics laws are not artificial but based on long observation of human nature and behavior.

T Education is the process of socialization, hence precedes all other social sciences. Of the duo U-V Geography/History, geography is poly-disciplinary and has vital impact on history and culture. In the CC most confusing and hazy boundary is between V history and W Political Science. It seems Ranganathan has confined W Political Science to political theories and kinds of state, whereas practical politics, governmental functioning, elections, political parties, functions of a given state or its organs, and foreign policies of all sorts are placed in V History. It is so much so that public administration also goes in V History, which perhaps no scholar will accept it as its right place. Bureaucracy and politics complement each other to run a society and its government. Economy functions in an organized society and state, depends upon latter's kind. Indeed politics and economy are inseparable. Continuing the rationale, Y sociology is the study of society and its communities. Society gets its moorings from the government by which it is governed, whatever be its kind and sophistication, whereas economy gives a society some definite shape and name as Hunting society or Information society. Any organized society forms its cultural and legislative laws to keep it integrated and moving. Hence the justification of keeping Z law at the end. Laws overarch every action and thought of a civilized society and its members and institutions. From the above it is clear that the underlying rationale is the Principle of dependency as enshrined in the wall-picture principle.

Contents of the CC look dated and senile. Statistics has been reduced merely to numerals keeping every sort of it with the subject itself. For example demography is placed in Y Sociology, while mortality statistics must go to L Medicine. Insurance, a welfare measure, has been placed in Economics, which also includes commerce and management including a depth schedule for industrial relations. Military science and police administration are not fully developed, so is the case with public administration, which makes an insignificant part of V History. Anthropology is a part of sociology and is not fully developed. Military science is a part of M Useful arts, but has no schedule of personality or energy isolates. No distinction seems to have been made between military science, its administration on the one hand and its history on the other. In Y Sociology, there is no specific number for various social theories, though by the use of chronological device number for such systems can be constructed. Above all, terminology is dated, which can cause a great problem in chain indexing and information retrieval.

5.9. CONCLUSION

Broadly speaking, the organization of social sciences in the Colon Classification is weak and inadequate. Logic of ordering of the social sciences may not be strong, Also it needs new and updated schedules to reflect current knowledge. Nevertheless, the Colon Classification has a powerful armory of adjunct basic subjects (i.e., canonical classes, systems, specials or environmental basic subjects), devices for hospitality for intercalation of new subjects, and phase relations to help in the precise and in depth information retrieval.

REFERENCES

Broadus, R.N. (1981). *Selecting Materials for Libraries*, 2nd ed. New York: The H.W. Wilson.

Comaromi, John P. and M.P. Satija. (1985). "History of the Indianization of the Dewey Decimal Classification." *Libri* 35(1): 1-20.

Foskett, D.J. (1974). *Classification and Indexing in Social Sciences*, 2nd ed. London: Butterworths.

Gnoli, Claudio. (2006). "Phylogenetic classification." *Knowledge Organization*, 33(3): 138-152.

Iyer, H. (1995). *Classificatory Structures: Concepts, Relations and Representation.* Frankfurt: Indeks Verlag.

Langridge, D.W. (1976). *Classification and Indexing in the Humanities.* London: Butterworth.

Maltby, A. (1975). *Sayers' Manual of Classification for Libraries*, 5th ed. London: Andre Deutsch.

McGarry, K. (1993). *Changing Context of Information*, 2nd ed. London: Library Association.

Miksa, Francis (1998). *The DDC, The Universe of Knowledge, and the Post-Modern Library*. Albany, N.Y.: Forest Press/OCLC.

Parkhi, R.S. (1933). "Colon scheme of library classification." *Modern Librarian*, 3(2): 85-88.

Ranganathan, S.R. (1967). *Prolegomena to Library Classification*, 3rd ed. Bombay: Asia.

Ranganathan, S.R. (1987). *Colon Classification*, 7th ed. Ed. M.A. Gopinath. Bangalore: Sarada Ranganathan Endowment.

Sahadath, Catelynne. (2013). "Classifying the Margins: Using Alternative Classification Schemes to Empower Diverse and Marginalized Users." *Feliciter* 59(3): 14-17.

Satija, M.P. (1990). "A critical introduction to the 7th edition (1987) of the Colon Classification." *Cataloguing and Classification Quarterly*, 12(2): 135-138.

Satija, M.P. (2001). "Relationships in Ranganthan's Colon Classification." In *Relationships in organization of knowledge*, eds., Carol A. Bean and Rebecca Green. Dordrecht, The Netherlands: Kluwer, pp. 199-210.

Satija, M.P. (2004). "Man as an information processor." *SRELS Journal of Information Management*, 41(2): 151-160.

Satija, Mohinder P., Devika P. Madalli and Biswanath Dutta. (2014). "Modes of Growth of Subjects." *Knowledge Organization* 41(3): 195-204

Satija, M. P. and Daniel Martínez-Ávila. (2017) "Mapping of the universe of knowledge in different classification schemes." *International Journal of Knowledge Content Development & Technology* 7(2): 85-105

Shera, Jesse H. (1970). *Sociological Foundation of Librarianship.* Bombay: Asia.

6

A Plea to Save the National Heritage: Revise the Colon Classification

STRUCTURE

1. Introduction
2. History of the Colon Classification
3. Features of the Colon Classification
4. The extent of the use of Colon Classification
5. Suggestions for resuscitating and revitalizing the system

References

Appendix

ABSTRACT

The chapter presents a case for the revival of Colon Classification (CC). It traces the status of CC in brief and discusses its features. It historically brings to light attempts made at providing a base for continuous improvements in the scheme and bringing it back to life. Measures for the revival of CC are suggested.

6.1. INTRODUCTION

The longevity graph of many library general classification systems is a chequered one. Classification history is littered with many dead systems; many such classification systems have suffered the vagaries of time. Some have stumbled, never to rise up while others have risen and walked steadfastly. Some have been drowned in the deluge of knowledge they could not cope with. A classification system has essentially to keep pace with the times, as a classification is essentially social, and has to keep its head above in the shifting sands of knowledge and social needs. To be relevant it has to keep itself in constant repair and remain oriented to contemporary academic, social and economic needs. Obviously the life and health of a library classification system depends upon its acceptability and use which in turn depends mostly on:

(a) Time of its arrival on the scene: BC, CC arrived late on the scene.

(b) Institutional backup: LCC and DDC have excellent back support.

(c) Status of the designer: Dewey, Cutter and Ranganathan were well known and highly respected in the profession.

(d) Body for its governance and machinery for its regular revision: DDC and LCC have dynamic and stable organizations which maintain best machinery for their upkeep.

(e) Extent to which it serves users' needs: Depends what you expect from a classification system. It could be anything from broader shelf arrangement to minute knowledge mapping and retrieval.

(f) Ease of use by librarians and readers: DDC and LCC are most easy to use.

(g) Use by centralized classification agencies like CIP and

MARC: LCC and DDC are used in MARC records.

(h) Its teaching in the library schools: CC is the highly taught classification in India

(i) Now another factor is its online availability: DDC, LC and UDC are now web based in addition to their print versions.

Ironically technical soundness of a classification matters little.

6.2 HISTORY OF THE COLON CLASSIFICATION

The Colon Classification (CC), when published in 1933, was a latecomer on the scene. Until the sixties it was considered the last general classification system for libraries. The Dewey Decimal Classification (DDC), the Universal Decimal Classification (UDC), and the Library of Congress Classification (LCC) had already established themselves in the library world. The CC was received both with wonder and contempt. It was different in structure and methods. And in many ways superior to already existing systems for meeting the challenges of the rising flood of knowledge since the early 20th century. But it did not find ready acceptance in India and abroad. It was considered different to understand and apply. Unfortunately the law of free market that a good product will drive out an inferior product does not always apply to classification systems. Forces of inertia keep a bad product perpetuated; librarians are reluctant to reclassify their libraries. Foskett (1989), knowing well that reclassification provokes a hostile reaction, asserts:

> Yet experience shows that it can be done, if necessary in stages, without too much expense or upheaval. Experience also shows that authorities appear to be quite happy to spend very large sums of money to provide new and elaborate buildings and to invest very large sum in machines for automation which have to be

> replaced, at even large sums, in a relatively few years. By comparison the labour and cost of reclassification is small; and it should not be forgotten that here we are dealing with progress of information and knowledge and the provision of these is the prime motive for having a library at all.

In the same vein Ranganathan (1967b) noted that we have been classifying for only a little over one hundred years:

> It is fortunate that in the United States people began to classify books only in the middle of the nineteenth century. Suppose libraries had been formed and collections classified in the beginning of the Christian Era. Generation after generation would have asked how it would be possible to change the class number since it seemed that they had to continue with the old system. This would mean that we should still be using the classification system of the first century of the Christian Era, and this would not be tolerable. This answer follows the method of *reductio ad absurdum*.

But for Indian libraries the time was propitious, even though the DDC had already been introduced here by the famous American librarian Asa Don Dickinson (1896-1960). A vast virgin field lay open before the CC. Many Indian libraries are still classifying their collections for the first time, and many new academic libraries are being opened every year. We still need many more libraries than we currently have (National Knowledge Commission 2007). Why it is that new Indian libraries cannot patronize India's own classification system? As early as 1964, when the CC was in full bloom, Jain (1964) noted: "There are in India a few who ridicule or oppose CC, while quite a few are of praise for it and have adopted CC as their scheme of classification."

The CC was designed by S R Ranganathan (1892-1972), the undisputed Father of the Indian Library Science and Movement. He was held in high regards all over the world for his innovations, foresight and dedication. He was enigmatically prolific, a trend-setter and his authority was unquestionable. Any Indian classification system associated with a lesser name perhaps would have gone unnoticed. However, it is also true that he came to be recognized as great only after the merits of his system were recognized abroad, especially in the UK (Wells 1953).

Technically the CC scores high marks because of its intrinsic merit on account of its helpful order at every level and almost infinite hospitality to new subjects. Its theory has been recognized as the general theory of classification, but unfortunately it has virtually no institutional backup. There is no library which works as its laboratory. Ranganathan had the benefit of the Madras University Library during 1924-1944 to test his theories and methods. Even before publication of the first edition, the CC was used to classify the rich and varied collection of the Madras University Library. Lessons learned during this period were incorporated into the first edition, and later ruminations on its theoretical basis were crystallized in the first edition of the *Prolegomena to Library Classification* (1937) which proved to be his *magnum opus* and a classic of the professional literature which has guided and inspired many a genius in our profession.

In 1945, Ranganathan single-handedly classified the entire library of the Banaras Hindu University (BHU), and from 1947 onwards he supervised the reclassification with the CC of the Delhi University library. No doubt, such experiences helped the development of the CC, but these institutional backings were only incidental. There has been no permanent or statutory institution to experiment with and test the use of the CC and to give the needed feedback for its revision. The DRTC library is too small and specialised to work as a laboratory for the CC. Furthermore, there has not been any institution to provide organizational support the way the LC and OCLC do for the DDC, or as the FID had been doing for the UDC (The closed down FID has now been replaced by the UDC Consortium). The CC had not even that support which the Classification Research Group (CRG) had given to the Bibliographic Classification (2nd edition) (BC-2) which was being revised under the competent leadership of Jack Mills (1918-2010). In the 1980s and 1990s the discussions in the CRG meetings were mostly devoted to the revision of the BC-2.

In the constitution of the Documentation and Training Centre (DRTC) there is no mention of supporting and promoting the CC (Ranganathan 1965). As long as Ranganathan was alive, the DRTC faculty worked as a research team on the CC in the guise of the advance documentation work. The results were published in the DRTC Annual Seminars and in the journal *Library Science with a Slant to Documentation* [from 1964 onward]. This work also continued to some extent after Ranganathan's death though the team suddenly felt rudderless, and soon shifted interest to broader areas of library and information science. On whom Ranganathan had pinned high hopes did nothing to perpetuate CC. They had their own priorities. Indeed DRTC has no legal or moral concern to back the CC. The Sarada Ranganathan Endowment for Library Science (SRELS, established in 1963), the legal heir to Ranganathan's material property and legacy, is not in itself a research institution, although it is now the copyright owner of Ranganathan's books, including the CC. However, its backing is not of much consequence towards the acceptance of the CC. The Endowment twice did endeavor to revise the CC under the leadership of late Professor A Neelameghan (1924-2014) who had been a towering personality among the DRTC faculty and a favorite of Ranganathan. But the efforts came too late after his retirement from many international assignments abroad. Moreover, that lacked planning and resources; it was too late and too little to be of any consequence (Satija and Singh 2013).

An analogous and central question is about the formal machinery for revising the CC. Ranganathan was all alone in his task. The CC never had any editorial board, nor did he ever associate anyone with it in any formal way. No one has been acknowledged in the sixth edition. Ranganathan always projected the CC to be a self-perpetuating scheme, which it is not. If he meant the use of devices for creating new isolates and keep the CC working then it is experienced that free use of these devices leads to cumbersome and unwieldy class numbers with loss of uniformity across the libraries. No social institution or man's creation can be self-perpetuating in this sense. Revising a classification scheme is vital:

- to incorporate new main classes at their logical places,
- to elaborate topics in light of their literary warrant,
- to relocate some old topics to more appropriate places,
- to delete obsolete classes,
- to replace obsolete terms with current ones, and above all,
- to attune the classification system with the contemporary structure of knowledge in harmony with the current perceptions of scholars.

For Foskett (1989) the objective of revising a classification scheme "is to give library users an opportunity to see a spectrum of the universe of information displayed in an order that makes sense, which enables them to discover how the experts in each field think it best or arrange their information". Revisions are also necessary to incorporate and display new relations among subjects and their combinations. That is to conform the system to the perceived current structure of knowledge. Revisions should incorporate research based innovations in designing classification systems and also on users' approaches to the library classifications, and their expectations from them. Regular revisions are absolutely necessary to give the scheme an updated terminology and a contemporary outlook.

Revision is in fact a double-edged sword that cuts both ways. If you revise (drastically) you die, and if you do not revise you surely die (Satija 2013). In this regard the comments of McIlwaine (1995), the first full time editor of the UDC, are very apt and interesting:

> Whatever we do, we will get criticism. If you do not revise outdated parts of a classification it is immediately decried as being out of touch with modern developments. If you do revise it, you immediately receive a welter of complaints from long-established users who do not wish to change their classification practices.

For constant revision we need a formal, well-conceived policy and sound machinery. In the case of the CC, the revision policy and process have been opaque. Different editions were published when Ranganathan had time or had any substantial change to incorporate, especially in the notational plane. The new editions were published at an uneven pace: 2nd (1939), 3rd (1950), 4th (1952), 5th (1957), 6th (1960), 6th revised (1963) and 7th (1987). As a result many librarians thought it to be at experimental stages rather than to be a ripe and stable system. Different CC editions incorporated varying degrees of changes. Drastic changes always make switching to new editions difficult – Ranganathan's method of osmosis notwithstanding. That is why different libraries are still using different editions, making it difficult to have coordination among them (Singh and Satija 1998).

Ranganathan always promoted team research (Satija 1993b). In spite of the contributions of a close group of disciples in the form of the Library Research Circle (Delhi) in 1950s, the DRTC faculty, and Ranganathan's spirited students like Professor P N Kaula, the CC has always been considered as a one man show. Many of the colleagues and students were slavish to him, mostly because of his towering personality and peerless intellect. For many Indian colleagues, he was a czar or a hoary father not to be argued with. Some critics were even considered as enemies.

There never has been a formal editorial board for the CC. Ranganathan (1967b) once announced in a seminar on classification in the USA:

> At the request of Peter Jayasinge of Asia Publishing House [Ranganathan's publisher in the 1960s] a self-perpetuating Ranganathan Colon Classification Board has been formed. Its function is to stay up-to-date and bring out new editions of the Colon Classification, the Basic Versions as well as the fascicules containing the Depth versions for diverse subject areas. It will also bring out new editions of such of the other books of Ranganathan as deserve to be so treated. The board will be an auxiliary of the Sarada Ranganathan Endowment for Library Science (1963).

But nothing has been heard of this board: when and where it was constituted, and with whom? Perhaps it was never born! Ranganathan's students and admirers, who valued the CC and wished to see the CC perpetuated, tried here and there to form such a board. Late Professor P. N. Kaula (1924-2009) recounts that in 1957, with the concurrence of Ranganathan, he approached Dr. Lal C.

Verman, then the Director General of the Indian Standards Institution (now renamed, Bureau of Indian Standards), to take up the future revisions of the CC and the Ranganathan Cataloguing Code. But Dr. Verman in turn suggested that they approach the Indian National Scientific Documentation Centre (INSDOC, New Delhi) [Now merged to form NISCAIR], in view of the expertise available there and the professional information services provided by it. Perhaps he was right. Since in those days Ranganathan was associated with INSDOC as chairman of its technical committees, so he himself did not think it appropriate to be involved in pursuing the idea with INSDOC. A committee was appointed in 1960 for this purpose. In the meantime (in 1962) Documentation Research and Training Center (DRTC), Bengaluru was established with Ranganathan as its honorary director, and he thought, perhaps erroneously, that the DRTC was the right institution for the purpose. So the committee became defunct. One problem with the DRTC is that it does not have the requisite large library to base and test a classification system on literary warrant. All these fruitless efforts made by Ranganathan to establish a permanent governing body for the CC have been documented by Ranganathan in a paper which makes a comparative study of CC with the DDC, UDC and LCC (Ranganathan1968) (See the Appendix).

The issue was again taken up by Kaula after Ranganathan's death in 1972. He raised it while addressing the staff of the Jawaharlal Nehru University Library, New Delhi. Kaula (1973) also mentioned that a committee was appointed to explore the possibility of revising the CC. But again nothing came out of this endeavor too.

In a seminar on "Classification and Knowledge Organization" organized by the Indian ISKO chapter in January 1994, Professor Kaula again voiced his concern for revision of the CC and sought some institutional backing for it. He again suggested INSDOC for the purpose. Mr A. R. Sethi, then the Deputy Librarian, offered the Jawaharlal University Library, New Delhi, to serve as the laboratory in social sciences classification for the CC. Although this suggestion was welcomed, so far it has not been followed up (Singh and Prasad 1994). Nor does there seem any likelihood of this now. In fact no editorial committee was named; the Sarada Ranganathan Endowment has been inflexible to lose its copyright hold. Perhaps they believed, rightly, that such resolutions are never to be taken seriously. These never materialize.

Jones had raised his concern in May 1966 in a letter to the editor of the *Library Association Record*. Projecting the scientific value of the CC and the need for its perpetuation, he wrote (Jones 1966):

> Would it not therefore be a good idea if in full consultation with Dr. Ranganathan, a Permanent International Committee were established consisting of men and women well-versed in either practical or theoretical classification (and preferably in both) with the purpose of revising and republishing the Colon scheme, whenever the committee considered this desirable?

Ranganathan has endorsed this proposal in his *Prolegomena* and elsewhere (Ranganathan 1968), and in his heart of heart he wished (now)erstwhile FID to step in to take the CC in its fold for further research and maintenance (Ranganathan 1967a). It was too much to expect from the FID which was beleaguered to maintain its own UDC. Such a proposal was only silently mooted without submitting that to any forum or organization. It is difficult to say what made Ranganathan leave the CC a virtual orphan without any heir to bring new editions after his death. Otherwise so tenderly careful about the profession at large and its organizations,

Ranganathan left the CC to an uncertain fate.

Even his professional heir and Secretary of the Sarada Ranganathan Endowment, late Professor M.A. Gopinath (1940-2012), was alone in his colossal task. In the seventh edition of the CC (1987), the first after Ranganathan's death, there is no sign of any collective work, or outside help. Gopinath was without the benefit of the cooperation and expertise of the individuals and organizations that are sincerely eager to see the Colon alive and thriving (Satija 1993a). An editorial board is a must for any library classification system to survive. Commenting on the revision of the Library of Congress Classification (LCC), Curwen (1978) summed up: "Autocratic, cumbersome, detailed, illogical, pragmatic, practical: it works for the Library of Congress and will probably continue to do so, with a guaranteed built-in mechanism for revision, for as long as book shelving classification is needed, it would seem". Ranganathan himself considers it a very important factor for adopting a classification scheme in a library. Fully cognisant of his failures to find any institutional support for the CC he awarded nil marks to his CC while giving full marks to the DDC, UDC and LCC (Ranganathan 1968).

6.3. FEATURES OF THE COLON CLASSIFICATION

According to Comaromi (1989), the Editor of the DDC20, a library classification is expected to perform three generic functions:

1. Organization of ideas i.e. filiatory sequence representing the structure and map of knowledge (the cognitive function).
2. Organization of document surrogates for information retrieval (the bibliographic function).
3. Arrangement of documents on shelves (the library function for document display and browsing). The DDC till sixteenth edition (1958) fell in this last

category (Custer 1960).

Comaromi further asserted that all these functions are conjoined so much so that a classification which performs a higher function well will perform any lower function equally well, but not the vice-versa. A bibliographic classification will certainly be good at shelf arrangement too, but a shelf classification may not be good at mapping or information retrieval.

The CC has a modern structure and also provides a good shelf arrangement. It is eminently suitable for information retrieval both in manual and online environments. It has a very sound theoretical foundation based upon normative principles, canons, principles and postulates and on the modes of growth of knowledge. Ranganathan is credited with making classification an objective science. But sound theory alone is not sufficient. Melvil Dewey knew it very well when in 1931 he wrote that the existence of the DDC depends on constant sales of new editions and that the practical needs of users must always be a major consideration (Curwen 1978). It is something which was rehashed by Mr. Benjamin A Custer (1960) the editor of the DDC from editions 16 to 19. Melvil Dewey sacrificed theory on the altar of pragmatism. It paid dividends to the DDC in terms of popularity.

The extent to which the CC serves library and information centers is controversial. For some, it is too theoretical, for others it is very practical, though complicated. In the West many erroneously consider it a classification designed for Indian subjects - especially the Indology classics; while many Indian librarians consider it as a theoretical and experimental classification due to its frequent revisions in 1950s. Accordingly, its acceptability by the users is mixed. To many librarians the CC is intellectually stimulating. The pattern woven by it on the shelves is logical, pedagogical and aesthetical - famously termed as APUPA pattern. But many are put off by its too highly mixed notation and are bogged down by its devices, facet and phase analysis and raft of rules for number synthesis. The majority of the librarians of Ranganathan's generation and the one following him never learned or understood it easily. Some had personal apathy with the system and its creator. Indeed the system appeared complex because of its details, frightening notation and jargon, as well as its number-building methods.

However, charges of complexity are a bit overblown. The famous J. Mills (1918-2010), in the early 1950s, wrote that "once the basic rules and disciplines of Colon are grasped (not a difficult matter), the scheme becomes extremely easy to apply - easier than Bliss [BC-1], because [being] more purely logical and leaving few decisions to the classifier" (Mills 1951). In the same vein Langridge (1985), a famous member of CRG and an ardent admirer of Ranganathan, challenged all those who dubbed CC as a complicated system. Having taught classification for a long time, this author can vouch for that students are more at ease with Colon number-building than with the DDC; they feel a sense of achievement on building a complicated class number.

It is also true that Ranganathan never fully understood the value of simplicity of notation to gain acceptance from the users. He used to cite an airplane engine analogy that a passenger need not worry about the complexity of the airplane engine. That analogy may distantly be true in a closed-access library. For online information retrieval or for arrangement of entries in a bibliography, the complexity of notation is not a hindrance. Perhaps it is an inevitable price for coextensive class numbers, for a logical sequence, for hospitality, and for high recall and precision ratios. The CC is at a disadvantage because of its non-use by any centralized classification/cataloging agency. The only solace is that the CC class numbers are given in the bibliographic entries of the Indian National Bibliography, which otherwise is arranged by DDC numbers.

Marketing and public relations of the CC are extremely poor. Many mediocre systems are popular and thriving because of their marketing networks and techniques. Colon has been under attack both at home and abroad from motivated critics. But nothing effective has been done to counter the attacks of its detractors and attend to the genuine difficulties of its users. The CC has been projected as India's *de facto* national classification system, yet nothing substantial has been done to promote its honor. There is no forum for CC users, and there is nobody to whom one can turn to in case of difficulties. Those who were supposed to promote CC and take care of its users never responded to queries from the users despite repeated requests. Their callous attitude did considerable harm to its progress and popularity. Books explaining the system are no better than student guides to help them pass examinations, and these books ignore the practical difficulties of librarians. Reliability of some of such books is doubtful. There is no official manual to apply the CC; notes and instructions in the schedules are not adequate to ensure intended interpretations and uniformity of its application. Inter-classifier consistency is very much deficient despite claims to the contrary.

6.4. THE EXTENT OF THE USE OF COLON CLASSIFICATION

No serious and wide ranging study of the use of the CC in computerized information retrieval or organizing the Web has been made, yet by all accounts a faceted classification is eminently suitable for such applications. Also, no exact and authentic figures are available on the extent of use of the CC in libraries for shelf arrangement. Ranganathan (1967b), in a seminar at Rutgers University, described the extent of the CC use as follows:

> The Colon Classification is in use in the universities of ten constituent states of India. Almost all the public libraries and the college libraries in the state of Madras and Maharashtra use it. It is also in use in some public libraries in other states. Some of the legislative libraries and libraries of government departments are also using it.

Indeed it was an exaggerated claim.

Dahlberg (1977) quotes late Dr. Gopinath on the issue as follows: "The CC sixth edition has been used in about 2500 libraries in India, mostly in public libraries, but also in nearly 20 universities, 2000 special and 1000 college libraries."

However, according to the ILA Directory (1951) of the Indian Library Association, out of the 363 libraries listed therein, only 31 (8.5%) libraries used the CC. The majority (55%) of these 31 libraries were academic. According to the IASLIC Directory (1962) of the Indian Association of Special Libraries and Information Centres, which listed 173 libraries, only 23 (13.3%) were using the CC. The use of the CC even ranked behind the use of the DDC and UDC in Indian libraries. A Delhi library directory (1973) shows the use of the system in 10.5% of the Delhi libraries. According to Dr. Pushpa Dhyani's doctoral research survey of Delhi and Rajasthan libraries, the use of CC is up to 24% of the libraries, the majority being academic (Satija 1986).

Till recently the CC was being taught in all the Indian library schools at every level. Abroad, especially in the UK and Europe, its theoretical principles have been taught as a model of faceted classification, however, this place is being taken over by the BC-2, which is admittedly based upon theories of Ranganathan (Bury 1986; Williamson 1994). The DDC, UDC, and numerous specialized systems have also employed Ranganathan theories and techniques in their revisions. Numerous specialized classifications have been designed on the Ranganathan model by the CRG members and others (Vickery 1960). But regretfully the CC has not adopted the organizational and marketing techniques of these successful systems.

6.5. SUGGESTIONS FOR RESUSCITATING AND REVITALIZING THE SYSTEM

If the trend continues, the future generations may know of the CC beauties and ingenuities only through Mills' BC-2, and the CC may become a mere name. Thus, the future of the CC is predictably bleak, and it is a foreboding to us all to rise to the occasion. The CC needs to be resuscitated, as it is a precious national heritage and can be an important force for the management of libraries and organizing the World Wide Web. A revitalized CC can be a symbol and evidence of India's intellectual power. Accordingly, some suggestions to revive it are, that:

1. A Colon Classification association be formed by those who want to save this national heritage.
2. Some institutional support be sought for the system; some national library organization or institution must be responsible for the upkeep and propagation of the CC. Government of India must step in and form a broad-based editorial board to revive and modernize the CC. In the Sixth IASLIC conference held at Trivadrum in December 1965 it was recommended in the proceedings that "An Editorial board on the lines of Decimal Classification, Universal Decimal and Library of Congress Editorial Boards be constituted to ensure continuity and up-to-dateness of the Colon Classification" (IASLIC Conference 1966). In the Indian ISKO seminar (1994), "Professor Kaula advocated that still more people should cooperate in

the revision work of CC. Prof. Gopinath had agreed to the proposal of having a wide based editorial board (Singh and Prasad 1994).

3. A new revised edition be brought out by updating and correcting the errors of the CC-7 (1987). The CC-6 and CC-7 should be merged and system be bit simplified and standardized.
4. A CC website be created and a bulletin and blog be started to keep in touch with the CC users, researchers and enthusiasts.
5. A directory of CC users be compiled. The IASLIC Conference (1965) had also recommended a survey of the CC users (IASLIC Conference 1966).
6. The use of the CC in online systems be studied, and the CC be brought out in a web based version.
7. Occasional conferences and refresher courses on the CC, faceted classifications and subject indexing be organized regularly.
8. An official manual on the use of the CC schedules (on the lines of the DDC manual) be prepared and published. This will be a device "Whereby the CC classificationists and classifiers can understand each other" (Jain 1964).
9. The above named organization would keep a watch on the correct use of the CC and help raise the level of teaching the system. It would also work as a clearinghouse for CC literature and publicizing innovations.
10. Public relations of the CC with the library professionals and users be spruced up; librarians and the public at large should be educated about the high and peerless qualities of the CC.

We are left with no other option but to act. In

perpetuating the Colon Classification, the Indian Library profession has much at stake.

REFERENCES

Bury, S. (1986). "Ranganathan's theories embedded in both Colon Classification and second edition of Bliss Bibliographic Classification." *Herald of Library Science* 25(1): 1-13.

Comaromi, J.P. (1989). "Comparison of major classification schemes." In A. Nitecki and T. Fell, eds., *Proceedings: International Conference on Library Classification and its Functions.* University of Alberta; Edmonton, Canada.

Curwen, A.G. (1978). "Revision of classification schemes: Policies and practice." *Journal of Librarianship* 10(1): 19-38.

Custer, B.A. (1960). "Mr Phillips." *Library Association Record* 62: 406-407.

Dahlberg, I. (1977). "Major developments in classification." *Advances in Librarianship* 7. Academic Press; New York.

Foskett, D.J. (1989). "Classifications and information languages: Thoughts on revising a bibliographical classification scheme." *International Forum for Information and Documentation* 14(1): 3-7.

Jain, H.C. (1964). "Colon Classification: A review article." *Library Association Record* 66(8): 348.

Jones, M.F. (1966). "Colon, revise or die." *Library Association Record* 68(5): 186.

Kaula, P.N. (1976). "Editors preface to M. F. Jones: Colon, revise or die." *Herald of Library Science* 15(3-4): 345-346.

Langridge, D.W. (1985). ·The unique value of Colon Classification.· In Rajagopalan, T.S., ed., *Ranganathan's Philosophy: Assessment, Impact and Relevance.* Vikas; New Delhi, pp. 600-601.

McIlwaine, I.C. (1995). "UDC centenary: The present state and future prospects." *Knowledge Organization* 22(2): 64-69.

Mills, J. (1951). "The Bliss and Colon Classifications." *Library Association Record* 53(5): 146-153.

National Knowledge Commission. (2007). *Libraries: Gateways to knowledge-A Roadmap for Revitalization.* New Delhi, 2007. Available at: http://knowledgecommissionarchive.nic.in/downloads/documents/NKC_Library.pdf (Accessed on 14 November 2015)

Ranganathan S.R. (1965). *DRTC and its role in documentation.* Paper A, DRTC Annual Seminar, 3: 3-25.

Ranganathan, S.R. (1967a). *Prolegomena to library classification,* 3rd edn. Asia; Bombay, pp. 583-590.

Ranganathan, S.R. (1967b). *A DescriptiveAccount of Colon Classification.* Asia; Bombay.

Ranganathan, S.R. (1968). "Choice of scheme for classification." *Library Science with a slant to Documentation* 5(1): 1-69.

IASLIC Conference. (1966). "Recommendations of the 6th (1965) IASLIC Conference, Trivandrum." *IASLIC Bulletin* 11(1): 50.

Satija, M.P. (1986). "Use of Colon Classification." *International Classification* 13(2): 88-92.

Satija, M.P. (1993a). *Editor's Introduction to Colon Classification,* 7th edn. Sterling; New Delhi.

Satija, M.P. (1993b). "Ranganathan and team research." *Herald of Library Science* 32(1-2): 84-94.

Satija, M.P. (2013). *The theory and practice of the Dewey Decimal Classification.* Chandos; Oxford; UK.

Satija, M.P. and J. Singh. (2013). "Colon Classification: a requiem." *DESIDOC Journal of Library & Information Technology* 33(4): 265-276.

Singh, S. and K.N. Prasad. (1994). "Indian ISKO Chapter: Seminar on classification and knowledge representation." *Knowledge Organization* 21(1): 38.

Singh, S. and M.P. Satija. (1998). "Indian classification systems: An analysis." *Library Science with a Slant to Documentation* 35(3): 165-178.

Vickery, B.C. (1960). *Faceted classification: A guide to construction and use of special schemes.* ASLIB; London.

Wells, A.J. (1953). "Our debt to India." In Chandrasekharan K, ed., *Library Science in India,* ILA; New Delhi, pp. 55-63.

Williamson, N. (1994). "Subject analysis systems." In P. Johnson, ed., *Guide to Technical Services Resources,* ALA; Chicago.

APPENDIX

A catalog of Ranganathan's efforts for formulating a governing body for his CC as extracted from his paper: Ranganathan, S.R. (1968). "Choice of scheme for classification." *Library Science with a slant to Documentation* 5(1): 1-69.

Colon Classification

With regard to a permanent organisation for future development, CC is in the same plight as BC. Here is an account of the past attempts and of the future hopes in this matter.

Madras Library Association

In 1939, the Madras Library Association started its annual Memoirs. The intension was to give an Annexure in each annual volume giving an account of the additions and changes made in CC during the year. It was also intended that librarians should be invited to state in its pages the problems they had come across during the year. World War II started; and the Memoirs had to be discontinued after three issues. In 1945, I had to leave Madras to work in North India. Thus ended the first attempt.

University of Delhi

In 1947, I joined the University of Delhi. Sir Maurice Gwyer, its then Vice-Chancellor, had great ambitions for that University. He wanted that it should be the home of all All-India Learned Bodies. In particular, he was keen that it should develop Library Science in full measure. For this purpose, he told me that he was endeavouring to establish a Regius Professorship in Library Science in the University. He was soliciting help for this from some of the Indian princes and business magnates. But when these things were only in the stage of negotiation, the absorption of the Indian States into the Indian Union was set on foot. Therefore, no further progress was possible. Sir Maurice had told me quite often that one of the functions of the Department of Library Science with the Regius Professor at its head would be to have full charge of the future development of CC.

Insdoc

In 1950, Sir S S Bhatnagar, Sir K S Krishnan, and myself

promoted the establishment of the Insdoc. Sir S S Bhatnagar was the Director-General of the Council of Scientific and Industrial Research (CSIR); Sir K S Krishnan took administrative charge of the Insdoc; and I became the Chairman of the Technical Committees. In 1951, the first two proposed that the Insdoc should take charge of the future development of CC. It was an attractive proposition. However, we thought that we should wait and see, as much would depend upon the Head of the Insdoc. Therefore, this proposal was not pursued. This appears to have been for good. For, recent events show that CC has fallen out of favour with the Insdoc even as DC had fallen out of favour with the Library of Congress about 67 years ago (See Sec 72). It is hoped that this will be temporary.

Indian Standards Institution

In 1952 an idea was developed that the Indian Standards Institution might take charge and sponsor the development of CC This was suggested on the analogy of the British Standards Institution having charge of UDC. However, this idea was not pursued seriously.

Madras University

In 1956, at the suggestion of my wife Sarada, and with the concurrence of my son R Yogeswar, an Endowment of Rs. 100.000 was given to the University of Madras for use in establishing the Sarada Ranganathan Professorship of Library Science. With the aid of the University Grants Commission and the other resources of the University, a Department of Library Science was established in the University in 1961 with the Sarada Ranganathan Professor at its head. At the request of the Vice-Chancellor as to what all could be done by the Professor and the Department, I gave a memorandum of suggestions. One suggestion was that the Department should take charge of the future development of CC. This would be appropriate as during its first 20 years, CC developed in the Madras University Library. But, the University has not yet taken up this matter.

Asia Publishing House

About 1962, the subject of the future development of CC came up for discussion between the Asia Publishing House and myself. We considered the possibility of persuading either the Indian Standards Institution or the Union Ministry of Education to take over the future development of CC But Peter Jayasinghe of the Asia Publishing House said in effect "Is it wise to give this academic work to a Department of the Government? After all, you will have to yourself find out your successor to take charge of CC. He in his turn will have to find out his successor. The Asia Publishing House will always be guided by your decision and that of your successors in this matter. Can you not leave it in our hands?"

Sarada Ranganathan Endowment for Library Science

In 1961, the Sarada Ranganathan Endowment for Library Science was established. Its funds are vested in the Treasurer for Charitable Endowments, India. Its affairs are managed by a self-perpetuating Board of Trustees. To provide a source of income for this Endowment, the copyright of all my books including the Colon Classification and of some other books in the Ranganathan Series in Library Science has been assigned to this Endowment. This made Peter Jayasinghe to make another proposal.

He suggested the formation of a self-perpetuating Ranganathan Colon Classification Board. The Board would have a panel of probable authors from whom it will choose the editor and the reviser for my respective books including the Colon classification. All these books would continue to appear as volumes in the Ranganathan Series in Library Science. The Board would be an auxiliary of the Endowment. This proposal has not yet taken a final shape.

Documentation Research and Training Centre

In 1962, the Documentation Research and Training Centre (DRTC) was established in Bangalore with me as the first Honorary Professor. Since then, the development of CC is being informally looked after by DRTC. From 1964, the DRTC and the Sarada Ranganathan Endowment for Library Science are jointly sponsoring the quarterly *Library science with a slant to documentation*. The DRTC is also having its Annual Seminar and its Proceedings are published every year since 1963. These two periodicals contain the current developments in CC. Between themselves, these two periodicals have so far published 73 articles and depth schedules for diverse subjects. There are also 25 unpublished depth schedules for other subjects, worked out by the students and some visiting research workers of DRTC. The DRTC is fortunate in having a band of competent, devoted, and enthusiastic permanent staff for teaching and research and also a circle of research workers informally attached to it: All the articles and depth schedules are directly or indirectly due to them. This informal development has prompted a new hope for the future. At the instance of the far-seeing Professor P C Mahalanobis, the Indian Statistical Institute founded the DRTC and has been generously maintaining it. It is a small residential institution. It works in the spirit of the All Souls College of Oxford and the Institute for Fundamental Research in Princeton. According to the Chairman of the FID/CR (= Classification Research Committee of the International Federation for Documentation): "It is well known, however, that the Documentation Research and Training Centre (DRTC), which was founded at Bangalore in 1962, has become not only an Asiatic but a world center for classification research. Many significant research reports have been issued by this institute, partly in the quarterly *Library science with a slant to documentation* since 1964, and partly in the Proceedings of the Annual DRTC Seminar since 1963."

A Call for an International Organisation

M F Jones of UK has suggested the need for an international organisation to maintain CC up-to-date. The following are his words:

"New particles of knowledge may conceivably arise; new methods of combining these particles may also occur; and changes in the notation may become necessary; here are three good reasons for continuing to revise the Colon scheme (as its founder has already done on five separate occasions). Furthermore, the "depth" schedules have not reached edition one yet, let alone revision.

Would it not therefore be a good idea if, in full consultation with Dr Ranganathan, a permanent International Committee is established, consisting of men and women well versed in either practical or theoretical classification (and preferably in both) with the purpose of revising and re-publishing the Colon scheme whenever the Committee considered this desirable? Provided the Committee's concern was not lavishly to worship Dr Ranganathan, no harm would be done; and the original product of one man's mind over 33 years could be developed into whatever may be its logical conclusions."

7

Classification and Indexing in India: A State-of-the-Art

STRUCTURE

1. Modern Library Classifications
2. Colon Classification
3. Features of the Colon Classification
4. Ordering Knowledge
5. Shelf Order
6. Theory of the CC
7. Contribution of the CC
8. Contributions of DRTC and Sarada Ranganathan Endowment
9. India's Contribution to Subject Cataloging
10. POPSI and Classaurus
11. Book Numbers
12. India's Contribution to Classification Terminology
13. Classification Practices in India
14. Classification: Teaching, Research and Literature
15. Doctoral and Other Degrees Research

16. Literature
17. Textbooks
18. Classification Organizations, Conferences
19. Continued Impact of Ranganathan
20. Conclusion
21. References

ABSTRACT

States the features, structure and mechanism of Ranganathan's Colon Classification (1933-1987). Explains its revolutionary method of facet analysis so eagerly adopted by all classification systems. Further states India's contribution to subject cataloging, book numbers and the research carried out in the DRTC, Bengaluru. Also describes the current state of classification theory and practice in India in terms of teaching in library schools, publications, doctoral research, and use of different systems of classification in Indian libraries. Bibliometrically proves the continuing relevance and influence of Ranganathan on traditional classification systems and web retrieval methods. States Ranganathan's theories are seminal in designing databases, expert systems and multilingual knowledge representation, web engineering and information architecture in the 21st century.

7.1. MODERN LIBRARY CLASSIFICATIONS

Knowledge and its classification were the main stay of India's ancient glorious civilization as evident in Vedas (4th Century BCE). Here we only dwell on the knowledge organization activities inaugurated by Dr. S.R. Ranganathan since early 20th century. With the advent of western classification systems and the Indian libraries becoming rich with books in European languages in all subjects in the 19th Century, the libraries felt that the Indian systems of classification were inadequate for the classification and arrangement of books on the shelves, at least they did not serve the purpose of British officers in India and westernized educated Indians. By the early 20th century, the Dewey Decimal Classification (1876) had spread its wings on the libraries the world over. The scheme being very simple and of pure notation, many libraries in India adopted it. In 1915 an American librarian, Asa Don Dickinson (1876-1960), introduced the DDC in the library of the University of Punjab, Lahore (now, in Pakistan), He also designed his own Table of Author Numbers in his *Punjab Library Primer* (1915) which was considered to be the first book on librarianship in India. Another American, W S Borden, a student of Melvil Dewey, was invited in 1911 to Baroda by its ruling prince to set up a network of libraries to support adult education in the state. Borden also devised a classification system based on Dewey to suit subjects and books in Indian libraries (Guha 1932).

7.2. COLON CLASSIFICATION

As already said modern classification methods had been introduced in India at least a decade before the coming of S.R. Ranganathan to the scene in 1924. He is aptly called the father of the Indian library movement. The real story of classification in India began in 1924-1925, paradoxically on the English soil. Ranganathan, then a student at the School of Librarianship, University College London, was very much impressed by his classification teacher, W.C.B. Sayers (1881-1960). While doing classification with the Dewey Decimal Classification 11th edition (1921), he was always puzzled that he could assign more than one correct class number to a given book. In most cases, a class number could take only one aspect of the knowledge contents of the document and ignored many other subject aspects treated in the document. He soon diagnosed that as the case of a one-dimensional tool trying to cope with multidimensional knowledge. His idea of a classification was that of translating faithfully the specific subject of the book into an artificial language of ordinal numbers called notation. Discarding the methodological approach of the DDC in listing top down all the possible subjects and their subdivisions in the universe of knowledge, he hit on the solution in a faceted approach which also implied bottom-up approach. That approach was to analyze the constituent concepts of the subject of the document into some recurring broader abstract categories of knowledge and then string together those concepts according to some rules of synthesis. The idea that he conceived was developed with the moral support of his classification teacher W C B Sayers. The tentative schedules organized into some main classes and further into some broader facets and ultimate isolates were fully developed in 1928 and applied for eight years on about 60,000 books before being published in 1933 as *Colon Classification* by the Madras Library Association of which Ranganathan was the executive secretary. So far its seven editions have been published from 1933 to 1987. CC is a faceted classification. It has also been called 'Analytico-Synthetic Classification' as the classification numbers are obtained by the analysis of the subject into various facets of five fundamental categories, PMEST followed by the synthesis of these facets in well-argued and formulated citation order (Satija 2017).

7.3. FEATURES OF THE COLON CLASSIFICATION

A library classification is expected to perform three functions:

1. Organization of ideas i.e. filiatory sequence representing the structure and map of knowledge (the cognitive function).
2. Organization of document surrogates (the bibliographic function) for information retrieval.
3. Arrangement of documents on shelves (the library function for display and browsing).

All these functions are conjoined so much so that a classification which performs a higher function well will perform any lower function equally well, but not the vice-versa. The CC has a modern structure and also provides a good shelf arrangement as Ranganathan always laid stress on order. It has a very sound theoretical foundation based upon canons, postulates and principles, and on the modes of growth of knowledge. Ranganathan liberated classification from the shackles of flair gifted to only few. He turned it into a science.

7.4. ORDERING KNOWLEDGE

The sequence of subjects in various main classes of CC is of alternating pure and applied subjects. It resembles with that of the Philosophical Serial System of Andre Marie Ampere (1776-1836) and also of the divisions of Auguste Comte (1798-1857). The main class order of science subjects A/M begins with the abstract discipline of B Mathematics and goes to M Useful Arts with progression from abstract to concrete and from the primary to the integrative levels. The discipline of Spiritual Experience and Mysticism Δ (Delta) is at the top forming a peak from which all disciplines emerge and confluence into. It is a fountainhead of all knowledge. Then there starts the descent on the right side of the peak with N Fine Arts which emanate mostly from the intuition followed by the other subjects of Humanities with greater intellection and lesser intuition. The order in humanities N/S is the increasing richness of contents. The Social Sciences T/Z are in an order of increasing deviation from the naturalness culminating into the most artificial Law Z. Form main classes a/z such as Bibliography, Serials Encyclopaedia, and emerging interdisciplinary main classes 1/9 such as the Universe of Knowledge, Library science, Journalism form the base of this triangle.

7.5. SHELF ORDER

On the shelves or in a classified bibliographic database, however, the order of subjects is from general to specific, that is, from abstract to concrete. Overall order within a class comes out to be:

General treated generally

General treated specially

Special treated generally

Special treated specially

This order is achieved by logically fixing the ordinal value of semantic and indicator digits of notation and dividing common isolates into two categories: anterior and posterior. This results in a very ingenious arrangement called APUPA pattern — which is a self-learning or pedagogical order of documents on the shelves.

7.6. THEORY OF THE CC

The system was conceived intuitively. The theory underpinning the scheme then lying unconsciously in his mind was crystallized in his *magnum opus* and still a classic, *Prolegomena to library classification* (1st ed. 1937, 2nd ed. 1957; 3rd ed. 1967). All this mechanism has been built into a dynamic and coherent theory of library classification described in a hierarchical system of 55 canons, 22 principles, 13 postulates besides the all supreme five normative principles called the "Five Laws of library science", first published in 1931(Indian Statistical Institute,2012). His famous Five Laws of Library science, the highest normative principles are the rock bottom of all his theories including those on knowledge organization. All these principles knit hierarchically with systematic expositions have gained the status of a general theory of classification. It will be no exaggeration to call it as the mathematics of classification which has inspired and guided many generations of librarians. Apart from this Ranganathan wrote about half a dozen books, scores of reports and hundreds of papers exclusively on many aspects of classification. About 30% of the total literature on and by Ranganathan pertains to classification alone (Das Gupta 1967). Rightly or wrongly classification is considered his main forte.

The unique features of the CC are the separation of the whole designing work in Idea, Verbal, and Notational Planes. Semantic and syntactic relations are enshrined in his well thought order of main classes, Principles of Helpful Sequence in arrays, PMEST facet formula fitted with rounds and levels of facets, and other principles, such as the famous wall-picture principle for citation order of facets and numerous devices for improvising class numbers for non-existent isolates and potential subjects. Devices endow the system with infinite hospitality and make it self-perpetuating. Miksa (1998) aptly says that Ranganathan "treated library classification as a single unified structure of ideas which followed from a cohesive set of basic principles." For this, Ranganathan evolved apt principles and forged precise tools. In line with Pierce Butler (1886-1953) Ranganathan was among the few pioneer advocates of the use of scientific method to library services. His postulates are based on intuition. He was of the opinion that practice of a discipline precedes its theory.

7.7. CONTRIBUTION OF THE CC

The theory of the CC is, in fact, considered as the theory of classification in general is taught in many library schools the world over. The contribution of the CC lies in its facet analysis technique, the debatable concept of "Five and only Five Fundamental Categories", and a raft of practical postulates for ordering and almost infinite hospitality to new subjects. It provides scientific and concrete guidelines for construction of any new classification system. Canons and principles are also the bench marks to evaluate any classification system. He made objective and mechanized the science and art of designing classification systems. Many depth and special classification systems have been designed using the CC methods (Vickery 1960). It can be used to design other indexing vocabularies such as thesauri or depth classification for micro subjects. The Classification Research Group, (CRG, London) declared in its manifesto the faceted classification as the basis of all information retrieval as back as 1955 (Broughton 2006). The world has expressed its debt to Ranganathan for the development of the faceted system and use of scientific method to library science (Langridge 1985; Broughton 2018). Its facet analysis is immensely helpful in query formulation for better recall and precision of output. Some of the search engines or Web directories are invariably using Ranganathan's approach with good result in retrieval on the Web. One wonders if Ranganathan anticipated the WWW and search engines (Glassel 1998). Advances in classification theory and practice in the online environment very much depend on facet analysis. It is no surprise that even the classical systems such as the DDC, UDC and the BC of Bliss/Mills have adopted Ranganathan's methods in their revision to make them more effective and relevant. His impact is obvious and continues unabated. It is now being studied globally while discussing the theoretical basis of classification, indexing and the knowledge organization and representation in the e-networks and knowledge bases.

7.8. CONTRIBUTIONS OF DRTC AND SARADA RANGANATHAN ENDOWMENT

Ranganathan's work has been furthered by the Documentation Research and Training Centre (DRTC) established in 1962 at Bangalore as a unit of the Indian Statistical Institute, with Ranganathan as the founder head.

Ranganathan envisioned DRTC as a world class centre of fundamental research especially in classification and advanced documentation work (Ranganathan 1965). It is therefore no surprise that the very first article in the newly started DRTC journal published a ground breaking article on the methodology of designing depth classification schemes (Ranganathan 1964). Another aim of Ranganathan, who was 70 at that time, was to train his successors. The foremost among the DRTC founding faculty and personally loyal to Ranganathan were Professors A. Neelameghan (1924-2014), G. Bhattacharyya (1936-2006), and M.A. Gopinath (1940-2013). The DRTC is an institute devoted to training manpower and to conduct research in broader areas of information work and services. The early work of the Centre focused on classification, and its major work in that area is:

- Teaching and research on the methodology of designing of depth schedules for special subjects to classify micro subjects. The methodology has been summed up in a research monograph (Gopinath 1986). More than 150 depth schedules ranging from fountain pen technology to library cataloging and food technology have been designed, and a few of them have been incorporated in the 7th edition of the CC.
- Research on modes of formation of new subjects continues. This includes the system view of the Universe of Knowledge, and its implications for the revision of classification schemes. Research in this area seems to have come a full circle with a paper on modes of growth of subjects by this author in collaboration with two of DRTC faculty being adjudged the best paper of 2014 in the ISKO journal *Knowledge Organization* (Satija et al. 2014).

- Developing typology and checklist of component ideas involved in facet analysis.
- Further research on classification has specifically centered on the Colon Classification, with a new edition released in 1987 under the editorship of M.A. Gopinath, then Professor and Head of the DRTC. Published by the Sarada Ranganathan Endowment the CC-7 brings in too many and far reaching changes than these could be coped up with by the libraries using it. The changes consist in postulating more than 700 new basic subjects and discovering new varieties of common isolates and subcategories of the fundamental category Matter. The Endowment has built a bibliographic database on Ranganathan.

7.9. INDIA'S CONTRIBUTION TO SUBJECT CATALOGING

To relieve the subject catalogers from the tortuous hit and miss method of locating subject headings from a pre-fabricated list, Ranganathan in his book *Theory of library catalogue* (1938) introduced the now very famous and ingenious method, then called chain procedure, now it is Chain Indexing. It is more or less a mechanical, simple and economical method for deriving subject headings from the class number; thus it is equally applicable to all languages. Its successful application in the British National Bibliography from 1950 to 1970 attested to its value. Since then it has been used in many national bibliographies and current awareness services such as the British Technology Index. Even many classification systems such as BC-2 and the Russian BBK have used this technique for making indexes to the schedules. All the CC classified libraries invariably use it to provide the alphabetical index to the classified part of the catalog. As is obvious from the BNB experience the chain indexing is equally applicable to all the classification systems which are hierarchical in nature. With a little modification it can be applied in a dictionary catalog, too. Despite its inherent problems, it has stood the test of time for more than seven decades. Further improvements in chain indexing are afoot. It is heartening to note that research and progress in automation of chain indexing was reported at the 5th International Study Conference on Classification Research held in Toronto in June 1991 (Williamson 1991). By every account chain indexing is an enduring contribution of the stature of facet analysis.

7.10. POPSI AND CLASSAURUS

To overcome some of the problems of the chain indexing, especially of vanishing chain, and entries being out of context, in 1980s DRTC, especially G. Bhattacharyya, invented a cyclic method of indexing named Postulate Based Permuted Subject Indexing (POPSI). The POPSI entries are all verbal, divided into two parts called main part and complementary to the main part. Every heading provides the full context of the document. It is based on the extensive comparative study of the structure of different subject indexing languages. Its postulates are based on Ranganathan's theory of classification. Bhattacharyya's considerable work centres on the deep structure of subject indexing languages (SILs) which provide the underlying principles for POPSI which is available in many versions. Complementary to it is the Classaurus which is a standard tool for vocabulary control. Classaurus is a faceted, hierarchical and systematic classification incorporating all the necessary features of a thesaurus. As indicated by its name it emerges from a thesaurus and a (faceted) classification. Though very slim in volume it can also serve as a thesaurus; for that reason it can be used with any indexing system. By assigning it notation it can be made to work as a classification scheme. Many DRTC students have designed Classauri for different subjects as student projects. Professor G. Bhattacharyya proposed to rewrite POPSI,

Classaurus and the general theory of SILs after retirement in 1999, but could not for apparently for lack of research support and death in 2006.

7.11. BOOK NUMBERS

Going beyond the subject groupings, book numbers, call them author marks, are critical to shelf arrangement and for precise location of books in a library. Apart from subject classification, India has contributed considerably for devising effective and efficient book numbering systems. Asa Don Dickinson devised an exclusive author table based on cutter methods for Indian names in his celebrated book *Punjab Library Primer*, so has done the National Library of India at Kolkata. But it was Ranganathan who devised a comprehensive and sound chronological system based on arrangement of books by the year of publication. It was of course based on chronological system devised by W S Biscoe (1853-1933) and endorsed by his mentor Melvil Dewey. But Ranganathan's system is much more systematic and comprehensive in its approach. He made it an integral part of his Colon Classification, and also gave a canon of Book Numbers to make it mandatory for every classification system and every library to make it an integral part of call number. The broader formula for book numbers is [L][F][Y].[V]-[S];[C]:[g] -standing for language, form, year of publication, volume, supplement, copy and commentary respectively on the book. It helps to keep together a book and its associated commentaries and supplements. In practice this mechanically and mnemonic system turns out very brief book numbers. By all accounts it is the most systematic book numbering system ever devised (Satija 2015).

7.12. INDIA'S CONTRIBUTION TO CLASSIFICATION TERMINOLOGY

From the very beginning, Ranganathan fully

understood the need and importance of the availability and use of a standard terminology for the library and information science profession. He was an apostle of standardization. To communicate his new ideas, he very often coined new terms for all branches of the discipline. His terminology especially in classification has got lot of currency. He did noteworthy work as the founder chairperson of the Documentation Section EC: 2 of the Bureau of Indian Standards and as a member of ISO /TC 46. He created numerous standard sources of LIS terms published as separate ISI glossaries, and in the media of books and journal articles. J. Herbert Coblans (1972) considers it as a contribution to the English language itself. In the wake of Ranganathan's work and appeals to fellow librarians, about half a dozen Indian glossaries of LIS terms in English have been created in addition to many bilingual glossaries in English and Indian vernaculars (Satija 1991).

7.13. CLASSIFICATION PRACTICES IN INDIA

As a visible vacuum in our classification literature, there is no exclusive directory or other source to infer the quantitative or qualitative use of different classification systems in India. Nor is it easy to compile one for many different but obvious reasons for a vast country like India. Different libraries use different classification systems; some still use homemade substandard methods, and many still use none at all. Many of the libraries are beginning to classify their collections for the first time. Many of the newly opened libraries resort to Dewey as if by default. Expectedly the DDC, CC, and the UDC are the most popular general classification systems in India. Though no reliable data are available, nevertheless some indirect and fragmentary sources can be tapped to shed some clues to the extent of use of different classification systems. Some excerpts are cited below from a study made by this author based on secondary sources (Satija 1986). From an all India library directory compiled by the Indian Library Association (1951) the use of different systems was inferred as follows: DDC 38.3%, CC 8.5%, UDC 2%, Brown's and Cutter's system 0.5%, other methods 37%; and 13.5% of the libraries did not answer this question. Another small directory compiled by the Indian Association of Special Libraries and Information Centres (IASLIC 1962) indicated the use of the different systems as follows: DDC 43.9%, UDC 20.2%, CC. 13.3%, other systems 1.8%, homemade systems 10.4%; the remaining 10.4% of the libraries did not respond. It clearly shows that in special libraries the UDC is popular. Dr. P. Dhyani (1989), who made a sample survey of classification practices in 339 Indian libraries presents the following picture: DDC 175 (51.6%), CC 81 (23.9%), UDC 51 (15.0%), LCC 2 (0.6%), Special schemes 15 (4.4%) while 15(4.4%) used no scheme at all. These studies offer only a rough estimate of the comparative popularity of different systems. Despite the CC projected as India's national classification system, the DDC is the most widely used system in all types of libraries in all parts of India. India's national library at Calcutta and more than 95% of the 970 university libraries using the DDC are no exception. India is the largest user of the DDC in the Orient (Vann, 1967). The Indian National Bibliography (INB) (1955+) modeled on the BNB is classified by the DDC, although every entry also provides the Colon class number to help libraries using the CC. To cope with the inherent WASPish bias most of the big libraries have modified, extended and adapted it to suit them locally. There is hardly any large library in India which has not done so. The long and interesting history of such adaptations is a lesson on the socio-cultural bearings of any classification system (Comaromi and Satija 1985). Every classification is social and holds mirror to time and place of its birth.

7.14. CLASSIFICATION: TEACHING, RESEARCH AND LITERATURE

Under the still overwhelming influence of Ranganathan, the theory and practice of library classification constitute an essential and weighty component of library science curricula in all the 100+ library science schools in India. Ranganathan made classification and cataloguing as core of the library education curricula. It is about 40-50% of the total curricula at the B.Lib. Sc. level. All the library schools offering M.Lib.I.Sc. place emphasis varying from 25% to 5% of the total curricula contents depending upon the extent of their 'modernization'. The national average of classification content in M.Lib.I Sc. curricula can be placed at 10%. As if by an unstated law, the schools laying more emphasis on information science and technology give less weightage to classification studies. Nevertheless, classification *per se* studies have remained firm and steadfast in India even when they suffered a setback in the West in the early 1980s with the coming of OPACs. In theory, it is Ranganathan's theory of classification which dominates the syllabi with a marginal touch of historical or comparative studies of other systems. Classification curriculum of any library school reads like a synopsis of Ranganathan's work. In classification practical, the CC and DDC are taught at the B.Lib. Sc. and CC and UDC are taught at the M.Lib.I. Sc. level. It can safely be said that India has the largest number of schools in the world teaching the theory and practice of classification. In India it has been the most popular system for writing and research as evident from the largest ever classification bibliography listing 1371 references all on the CC (Satija and Amrik Singh 1994)

7.15. DOCTORAL AND OTHER DEGREES RESEARCH

Consequence of intensive teaching, classification

issues and problems are not less popular with academic researchers. It is not any coincidence that the first two doctoral degrees in library science were awarded on classification problems. Doctoral research work done on classification and indexing mostly by the DRTC senior faculty members (now retired) under the guidance of M.R. Kumbhar at the Karnatak University, Dharward, is interesting and valuable. These are: A general theory of subject indexing language by G. Bhattacharyya, Criteria for recognition of fundamental categories by M.A. Gopinath, Development of terminology in the field of library classification by K.N. Prasad, A matrix for compatibility of schemes for classification by S.Seetharama, and A computer-based software for generating subject indexes by F.J. Devadason. Yet Kumbhar had no influence on the classification work of the DRTC (Kumbhar 1983). The other topics of research in the area are POPSI by D. Chandran (1985), Analytico-Synthetic Classification by R. Vohra (1984), Classification practices by P. Dhyani (1981), Common Isolates by A.Y. Asundi (1982), and Use of Classification systems in Delhi Libraries by Dipti Gulati (2014). In a bibliographical study of LIS dissertations in India from 1957 to 1985 it was revealed that out of the total of 44 Ph.Ds 8 (18%) were on classification alone - which is the highest percentage for any single area. Similarly, the percentage of M.Lib. Sc. dissertations is 6.6% (Kumar 1987).

7.16. LITERATURE

Classification literature forms a sizable chunk of the total LIS literature in India. In a bibliography (Gupta 1991) of the total of 2,957 entries from 1970 to 1990, 617 (21 %) pertain to classification alone. Another study of classification literature published in India from 1971-1980 found total of 220 entries of all sorts. Of these 44 articles were contributed by foreign authors (Sewa Singh 1986). In a depth analysis of Indian classification literature published from 1932 (beginning) to 1980 the authors found 814 entries: periodical articles 624, conference papers107, textbooks 68 and theses 15. They further revealed that "Classification research in India is mostly based on the contributions of S.R. Ranganathan" (Kaula and Prasad 1981). But in the recent years there has been a sharp decline. Indian Library science Abstracts from 2000-2005 listed only 140 entries on classification and indexing out of the total of 3110 making it merely 4.47 per cent. Most of the literature on classification is on and by Ranganathan, with other systems taking a back seat. In a systematic study of classification literature published internationally in the first decade of the 21st century the author found five Indian authors among the total of 48 who have contributed more than five papers during the period of analysis (Kumbhar 2012, p. 184) Most of the post-Ranganathan literature is descriptive, repetitive, pedestarian and un-innovative. Though all the Indian library science journals welcome articles on classification, the *Herald of Library Science* (1962-2009) and *Library Science with a Slant to Documentation* (1964+) were the core journals for this purpose. The former has ceased publication now, while the latter has changed name to reflect its widened scope

7.17. TEXTBOOKS

In textbooks, too, Ranganathan ruled the roost. Some textbooks on classification have been written, especially in theory, to elucidate or simplify his work. It is interesting to note that his books, even after more than half century of their publication, are attracting more citations than his papers (Das and Mishra 2015).With the passage of time, some other areas such as comparative studies, general theory of classification, book numbers, and some monographs on the CC, DDC, and UDC number building have been written. Inevitably the CC, with about a dozen books on its practical aspects, is the most favourite topic of the Indian authors, although many librarians and students at large continue to complain of its complexity. Apart from Ranganathan, whose books belong to the richest writings on our science, many Indian authors have written extensively on classification. The foremost names include P.N. Kaula, Krishnan Kumar, A.A.N. Raju, P.S.G. Kumar, P. Dhyani, R. Kumbhar, Shahbahat Husain and M.P. Satija. Quantity is impressive, though apart from Ranganathan all the Indian books on classification are pedestrian.

7.18. CLASSIFICATION ORGANIZATIONS, CONFERENCES

Ranganathan had an immense faith in collective work; he was an ardent advocate and exponent of team and relay research. He used to say that the days of solo research are over. He inspired and helped the establishment of library associations in India. Being a crusader, it was incumbent upon him to train and take people along to spread his message and to create a library awakening, and above all to do team research. In the early 1950s a Delhi based Library Research Circle functioned actively under the chairmanship of Ranganathan. In a way, it was CRG's counterpart with which it always exchanged notes. This group of volunteers did considerable work published in the pages of the ILA organ ABGila (1949-1953), or in the annual ILA conference proceedings. It is a glorious chapter of Indian library history now (Parthasarthy 1952). Library science study circles have existed here and there but not worth mentioning on classification. The various library associations have subject interest groups (SIGs), but they exist in papers. The Indian Association of Teachers of Library and Information Science (IATLIS) in the early 1980s formed the Classification Society of India as its affiliate with P.N. Kaula its President and M.A. Gopinath its Secretary. After one or two inconsequential meetings and two irregular issues of bulletin it has remained defunct. Now nobody remembers it. The Indian chapter of the International Society for Knowledge Organization

(ISKO) had more than 30 members in 1990s, which was then about 10% of the total ISKO membership from about 40 countries. Two Indians, Krishnan Kumar and M.A. Gopinath were members of its Scientific Advisory Board. India was well represented at the first and highly successful ISKO Conference held in Germany in August, 1990. ISKO reposed its confidence and trust in the classification profession in India by agreeing to hold its 2nd Conference from August 26-28, 1992 at Chennai then Madras.

Ranganathan helped the foundation of FID/CA in 1951 (later FID/CR), served it with distinction, and made its foundations strong and deep. From 1973 to 1980, the FID/CR Secretariat was shifted to India with A. Neelameghan its chairman. In addition to issuing various regular reports on research in classification it started a regular FID/CR Newsletter, which was still published regularly in the columns of *International Classification.* In 1975, the 3rd International Study Conference on Classification Research held in Bombay on "Global Ordering Systems" was highly acclaimed internationally. At the International Conference on Ranganathan's philosophy held in New Delhi in 1985 the largest session was on classification. "On that occasion the FID/CR availed itself of the opportunity to hold its second regional conference on "Classification and Communication" (Krishnan Kumar, 1985). Earlier Indian librarians have actively participated in international conferences on classification and related areas. However, classification research and problems are no more forming topics of Indian library conferences. Last conference on classification held in India was the ISKO Annual conference which not only attracted wide international participation, but also hogged lot of appreciation (Smiraglia 2013).

7.19. CONTINUED IMPACT OF RANGANATHAN

Apart from two very comprehensive bibliographies on

Ranganathan one by Das Gupta (1967) and other by Satija and Amrik Singh (1994), there are numerous bibliometric studies on Indian library literature. In all such studies Ranganathan dominates the scene with his enduring contributions. However four important studies, two before the Google era (Lancaster et al. 1992) and two very recent ones studying Ranganathan's presence in databases (Smiraglia (2014), Das and Mishra (2015) attest his continuing relevance and international popularity). Lancaster's team made citation analysis of Ranganthan's writing from 1956 to 1990 to report that his influence continues intact. "Citations to the *Prolegomena*... (95), *Colon Classification* (69) and *Five Laws*... (28) account for more than a third of the total citations (690)". They further observed, "Facet analysis and subject structuring get substantial references, including computer generation of thesaurus, deep structure indexing systems and expert systems design." Impressed by his depth and breadth of his contribution they concluded that hardly anyone can match his diversity of contributions to LIS field. (For the second such study see page 49 of this book) Smiraglia (2014), employing domain analysis technique to the references of the last three decades in the database of the *Web of Science* (WoS), shows Ranganathan's legacy in the 21st century is leading the knowledge organization (KO) domain to a new territory. He empirically reviews and maps Ranganathan's influence on research in KO to demonstrate with evidence that facet analysis is "fuelling its popularity in K O systems and web engineering". His research shows Ranganathan's ideas form starting discussion to the current era of progress in K O. His legacy is an integral part of the 21st century research in this widening domain. Das and Mishra almost came out with similar results finding Prolegomena, CC and Five laws as the most popular and highly cited works in the Google Scholar, Web of Science and Scopus databases.

Quantitatively they reported citations: Prolegomena 748 (GS), 127 (WoS), Five Laws 671 (GS), 87 (WoS), and the CC 559 (GS), 177 (WoS). His other books such as *Elements of Library Classification* (1940s), *Philosophy of library Classification* (1950s), and *Classification and communication* (1950) also continue to be considerably cited all over the world. Relevant journal articles in these databases discuss the theories of facet analysis and faceted classification systems. They found out "Many authors also discuss Ranganathan's theoretical framework in today's context, analysing his influence in designing modern ICT-enabled information systems and retrieval techniques". Citations also indicate his theories are contextual in semantic web applications, designing search interfaces, organizing and accessing web resources and other specialized databases. This study also documented that his seminal work continues to guide us to formulate multidimensional and multimodal information architecture to design semantic web and ontologies. "Ranganathan's principles can be applied for multilingual knowledge representation, and designing efficient search and retrieval interfaces for the common netizens", they find out further (Das and Mishra 2015, p.298). In view of such studies nothing could be more appropriate than ALA's 1992 tribute describing him as the "Librarian to the world".

7.20. CONCLUSION

India espouses a great civilization of knowledge and culture. Knowledge also implies some classification which in this case is enshrined in Vedas. But this story of library classification begins with the early 2oth century when two US librarians William Borden and Asa Don Dickinson came to India in the early 20th century to organize our libraries on modern lines. The real story of classification and indexing begins with the emergence of S R Ranganathan in the 3rd decade of the previous century. Ranganathan developed his

Colon Classification which was suited to classify the post war literature of complex kind. The CC has a modern structure and it was a paradigm shift in classification theory and applications. It has a very sound theoretical foundation. Ranganathan liberated classification from the shackles of flair gifted to only few. He turned it into a science. The theory underpinning the scheme then lying unconsciously in his mind was crystallized in his magnum opus and still a classic, *Prolegomena to library classification* (1st ed. 1937, 2nd ed. 1957; 3rd ed. 1967). All this mechanism has been built into a dynamic and coherent theory of library classification described in a hierarchical system of 55 canons, 22 principles, 13 postulates besides the all supreme five normative principles called the "Five Laws of library science", first published in 1931. His famous Five Laws of Library Science, the apex normative principles, are the rock bottom of all his theories including those on knowledge organization. All these principles knit hierarchically with systematic expositions have gained the status of a general theory of classification. His impact is obvious and continues unabated. It is now being studied globally while discussing the theoretical basis of classification, indexing and the knowledge organization and representation in the e-infonetworks and knowledge bases. Work of Ranganathan was furthered by the DRTC and Sarada Ranganathan Endowment. India's contribution to subject indexing lies in the famous invention of Chain Indexing and further one in POPSI by late Bhattacharyya. Ranganathan was a stickler for technical terminology and he created many terms for the subject which are documented in the ISI Glossary (ISI2550-1963). Inspired by Ranganathan India held the fort for classification when all over the world it was losing its hold due to overzealous, though misplaced, faith in the power of computers in subject retrieval. Classification teaching, research and publications continue considerably well and Ranganathan still wields a considerable global impact as reflected in Google scholar citation studies.

7.21. REFERENCES

Bhattacharyya, G. (1981) "Some significant results of current classification research in India." *International Forum on Information and Documentation* 6(1): 11-18.

Broughton, V. (2006) "The need for a faceted classification as the basis of all methods of Information retrieval" *Aslib Proceedings* 58(1/2):49-72

Broughtan, V. (2018). *Facet analysis.* London : Facet Publishing.

Coblans, H. (1972) "Ranganathan in the international scene." In: Edward Dudley, ed., *S.R. Ranganathan, 1892-1972.* London: Library Association, 1974, p.29.

Comaromi, John P. and M.P. Satija. 1985. "History of the Indianization of the Dewey Decimal Classification." *Libri* 35(1): 1-20.

Das, Anup K. and Sanjay Mishra (2015) "S R Ranganathan in Google scholar and other citation databases." *Annals of Library & Information Studies* 62(4): 290-298

Das Gupta, A.K. (1967) *An Essay in Personal Bibliography: a Bibliography of the Writings on and by Dr. S.R. Ranganathan.* Bombay: Asia, pp.194-242.

Dhyani, P. (1989) *Classification schemes and Indian libraries,* 2nd ed. New Delhi: Metropolitan, pp.61-67.

Glassel, A (1998). *Was Ranganathan a Yahoo.* Available at: http://scout.wisc.edu/scout/toolkit/enduser/archive/1998/euc9803.

Girja Kumar and Krishnan Kumar (1987). "International conference on Ranganathan's philosophy." *International Forum on Information and Documentation* 12(2): 24-32.

Gopinath, M.A. (1986) *Construction of depth version of Colon Classification: a manual.* New Delhi: Wiley Eastern.

Guha, Satisa Chandra (1932). *Prachya-Yargikaran Paddhati: Being a system of Book Classification developed on orient lines.* Varanasi: Grantha Goshti, pp.44-49.

Gupta, B.M., ed. (1991). *Libraries, archives and information technology: an annotated bibliography.* New Delhi: Aditya Prakashan, pp.130-222. (Handbook of libraries archives and information centres in India; vol. 11).

Indian Statistical Institute. Documentation Research and Training Centre.

(1982). *A report of its activities for two decades, 1962-1982.* Bangalore: DRTC, pp.13-14 (mimeographed).

Indian Statistical Institute. (2012). *Dr. S. R. Ranganathan's Fifty Years of Experience in the Development of Colon Classification.* Bangalore: Indian Statistical Institute, Bangalore Centre. http://WWW.isibang.ac.in/~library/portal/Pages/chp1.pdf (Accessed on1 5 March 2017). Permanent website: http://www.webcitation.org/6ovdax2pD

Kaula, P.N. and H.N. Prasad (1981) "Classification literature in India: analysis and trends." *International Classification* 8(3): 145-149.

Krishnan, Kumar (1985). *FID/CR Regional Conference (2nd: 1985: New Delhi): Classification and Communication.* Delhi: Delhi Library Association,

Kumar, P.S.G., Comp. (1987). *Research in library and information science in India: a bibliography of PhD., M.Phil. and M.L.I.S. Dissertations.* New Delhi: Concept, pp.xii-xv.

Kumbhar, M.R. (1983) "Recent trends in classification research in India." In: P.B. Mangla, et al., eds., *Fifty years of librarianship in India, past, present and future.* Delhi: ILA, pp.401-404.

Kumbhar, R. (2012). "Trends in classification literature: analysis of literature published during 2000 to 2009." *DESIDOC: Journal of Library & Information Technology* 32 (20): 179-185.

Lancaster, F.W. et al. (1992). "Ranganathan's influence examined bibliometrically", *Libri* 42(3): 268-281.

Langridge, D.W. (1985). "The unique value of Colon Classification" In: T S Rajagopalan, ed., *Ranganathan's Philosophy, Assessment, Impact and relevance.* New Delhi: Vikas, pp. 600-601.

Miksa, F. L. (1998). *The DDC, the Universe of Knowledge and the Post-Modern Library.* Albany, NY: Forest Press, p.67.

Neelameghan, A., ed. (1979). *International Study Conference on Classification Research (3rd: 1975: Bombay): Global Ordering Systems.* Bangalore: DRTC.

Parthasarathy, S. (1952). "Memoirs of library research circle, Delhi." *ABGila* 2: 153-159.

Ranganathan, S.R. (1964). "Design of depth classification: Methodology." *Library Science with a Slant for Documentation* 1(1): 1-42

Ranganathan, S.R. (1965). "DRTC and its role in documentation." *DRTC Seminar* 3: Paper A (Mimeographed).

Satija, M.P. (1986). "Use of Colon Classification." *International Classification* 13(2): 88-92.

Satija, M.P. (1991). "Sources of Indian Library and Information Science Terminology." In: *Infoterm Symposium (3rd: 1991: Vienna)*. Papers

Satija, M.P. (1992) "Ranganathan's contribution to LIS terminology." In: *ISKO Conference (2nd: 1992: Madras)*. Papers

Satija, M.P. (2015). *Book Numbers: Indian and Cutter*. New Delhi: Viva Books, 132p.

Satija, M.P. (2017). "Colon Classification" *ISKO Encyclopedia of Knowledge Organization*. Accessible at http://www.isko.org/cyclo/colon_classification; and *Knowledge Organization* 44(4): 291-307.

Satija, M.P. and Amrik Singh (1994). *Bibliography of Colon Classification, 1930-1993*. New Delhi: M.D. Publications, xi, 129p.

Satija, M.P., D. Madalli, and B. Dutta (2014). "Modes of Growth of Subjects." *Knowledge Organization* 41(3): 195-204

Sewa Singh (1984) "An analysis of the contributions to library and information science journals in India, 1971-1982". *International Library Review*, 16: 223-230.

Smiraglia, Richard P. (2013). "ISKO 12's Bookshelf— Evolving Intension: An Editorial." *Knowledge Organization* 40(1): 3-10

Smiraglia, Richard P. (2014) "Prolegomena to a new order: A domain-analytical view of the influence of S.R. Ranganathan on knowledge organization" In: K S Raghavan and A Neelameghan, eds., *Knowledge Organisation: from libraries to Web*. New Delhi: Ess Ess, pp. 7-18

Vann, Sarah K. (1967). "Dewey abroad: the field survey of 1964". *Library Resources & Technical Services* 11: 67.

Vickery, B.C. (1960). *Faceted Classification: A Guide to the Construction and Use of Special Schemes*. London: Aslib, 70p.

Williamson, Nancy (1991). "The ICCR Conference." *International Classification* 18(4): 230.

FURTHER READINGS

Chatterjee, Amitabha. (1992). "Structure of Indian Classification systems of pre-Ranganathan era and their impact on the Colon Classification". In: William, N.J. and Hudson, M., eds., *Classification Research for Knowledge Representation and Organisation*. Elsevier Science Publishers, p.151.

Datta, Bimal Kumar. (1976) "India's contribution to the science of classification". *Iaslic Bulletin* 21(2): 41-48.

Dickinson, Asa Don. (1932). *Punjab-Yargikaran Paddhati: Being a system of Book Classification developed on orient lines,* Varanasi: Grantha Goshti, pp.44-49.

Kaula, P.N. (1980). "India's contribution in cataloguing and classication." In Aman, M.M., ed, *Cataloging and Classification of Non-Western Material: Concerns, Issues and Practices.* Phoenix: Oryx Press, pp235-252

Kaula, P.N. (1980). "Classification in India." *Progress in Library & Information Science* 1: 3-15

Langridge, D.W. (1976). *Classification and indexing in the humanities.* London: Butterworths, pp.1-7.

Neelameghan, A., and K.S. Raghavan. K.S., eds. (2012). *Categories, Contexts and Relations in Knowledge Organization: Proceedings of the Twelfth International ISKO Conference 6-9 August 2012 Mysore, India.* Würzburg, Germany: Ergon.

Raghavan, K.S and A Neelameghan, eds. (2014). *Knowledge Organisation: from libraries to Web.* New Delhi: Ess Ess, 230p.

Satija, M.P. (1992). "Ranganathan and Classification: a Chronology 1924-1992". *International Classification* 19(1): 3-6.

Suman, Aparajita (2014). From Knowledge Abstraction to Management Using Ranganathan's Faceted Schema to Develop Conceptual Frameworks for Digital Libraries. Oxford,U K:Chandos,272p

Sundaram, C. (1942). "India and Library Classification." In: *Shree Iyanki Venkata Ramayya Commemoration Volume,* presented by Sir. R. Reddi, Vice-Chancellor Andhra University at the Fourth Andhra Library Workers' Conference, Guntur on December 13, p. 28.

8

Ranganathan and Classification : A Chronology 1924-2017

STRUCTURE

1. Introduction, Purpose and Sources
2. The Teacher of Mathematics Becomes a Librarian. Madras 1924-1944
3. Experimenting with the CC
4. Towards a Theory of Library Classification
5. University Librarian and Professor of Library Science at BHU
6. Professor of Library Science at the University of Delhi (1947-1955)
7. Ranganathan's two Years in Europe (1955-1957)
8. Years of Lecture Tours and various Visiting Professorship. (1957-1961)
9. Finding a Residence for CC in Bangalore (1962-)
10. Posthumous Events

ABSTRACT

Based on a number of sources given in the introduction the dates of Ranganathan's development in the field of library classification are given together with a short description of their impact and significance. The chronology has been structured according to some epochs of his life. The relevant publications on and by Ranganathan are also listed.

8.1. INTRODUCTION, PURPOSE AND SOURCES

The purpose of this chronology is to catalog Ranganathan's achievements in the discipline of library classification, and consequently to trace the evolution of his thoughts in this area. The chronology was compiled on the basis of several sources: (1) on general chronologies, especially the one by Kate Wood in *S.R. Ranganathan, 1892-1972*, ed. by Edward Dudley, London: Library Assoc. 1973, and the one by P.N. Kaula appended to S.R. Ranganathan's *Autobiogrophy: A librarian looks back*, New Delhi: ABC 1992; (2) on Ranganathan's own books, expecially those reviewed in M.P. Satija: A note on Ranganathan's reprints. International Classification 17 (1990) No.3-4, p.182-183; and (3) on M.A. Gopinath's article on *Ranganathan, Shiyali Ramamrita* in the *Encyclopedia of Library and Information Science*, ed. by Allen Kent et al., New York: Marcel Dekker 1978. Vo.25, pp. 58-86. And lastly on his biography written by his son; Yogeshwar, Ranganathan. *S.R. Ranganathan: Pragmatic Philosopher of Information Science: A Personal Biography*. Mumbai: Bhartiya Vidya Bhavan, 2001. vi, 402p.

8.2. THE TEACHER OF MATHEMATICS BECOMES A LIBRARIAN. MADRAS 1924-1944

Jan. 1924 : Ranganathan joins as librarian of the Madras University.

1924-1925 : Studies at the School of Librarianship, University College, London. W.C.B.Sayers (1881-1960) taught him classification.

1924 (October) : Idea of a faceted classification conceived to cope with the inadequacies of a classification after using the DDC, 11th edition (1922). Spends sometime with Prof W.C.B. Sayers in the cafeteria of the College to discuss his plan of a faceted system.

Dec. 1924 : The Colon Classification (CC) conceived, and its design begun.

8.3. EXPERIMENTING WITH THE CC

1925-1932 : Period of development, experimentation and application of CC.

February /March 1925 : Ranganathan prepared sample schedules for different facets and experimented with synthesized class numbers. In June 1925 he also classified the library of the ship *SS Dumana* on his way back from England to India; and also assigned class numbers to about 30,000 books listed in the printed catalogue of the Madras University Library which he had with him.

1926 : Five fresh graduates were recruited in the Madras University library. Of these K. M. Sivaraman and C. Sundram associate with him in the design of the CC

1926-1932 : CC applied to about 60,000 books of the Madras University Library (MUL). Open access was introduced in the library and reaction of the library users was noted while doing reference service to them.

1927 : The first formal schedules of different main classes completed. Ranganathan consulted the experts such as Professor Edward B. Ross for general layout, mathematics and general science, Prof. M. S. Sabestan in Botany, Dr. B. B. Dey in Chemistry, Prof. S. Kuppuswamy Sastriar for Indology and Sir Sivaswamy Ayyar and Sir S. Vardachariar in Law.

1929 : The School of Library Science of the Madras Library Association (MALA, established in 1928) was set up.

The school taught both the CC and the DDC. Strong features of the CC over the DDC were highlighted. The teaching also provided an opportunity for an academic exposition of CC and its critical evaluation.

1931 : Ranganathan incorporated into the CC new findings gained by observing the readers and the suggestions put forth by them. The schedules were recast or readjusted wherever necessary in the light of experience gained.

1931-1944 : Head of Library School, University of Madras.

1932 : A press copy of the CC was finished with the help of library colleagues who volunteered to help Ranganathan at his residence.

1933 : *Colon Classification,* 1st ed. Madras: Madras Library Association. 3 parts in 1 volume.

8.4. TOWARDS A THEORY OF LIBRARY CLASSIFICATION

1933-1937 : Period of formulating the theory of library classification.

1935 : Henry Evelyn Bliss (1870-1955) writes to Ranganathan and enquires about the theory behind his Colon Classification (1933). Exchange of the copies of CC 1st edition with Bliss' two volumes on KO takes place. Ranganathan starts writing the explicit theory of his Colon Classification. Ranganathan perceives 1935 as the ripe time to work out the theory of classification lying on the back of his mind. Reading of Bliss' KO books is confessed by Ranganathan.

1937 : *Prolegomena to Library Classification,* 1st ed. Madras: Madras Library Association, xvi, 305p.

This book enshrines the theory of classification in general and of the CC in particular. It transformed classification from an art into a science. It is considered

Ranganathan's *magnum opus*.

1934-1944 : Comparative study and teaching of DDC and CC; CC applied to about 4000 micro documents (non-book documents like journal articles) and pamphlets.

1935-1938 : Chain Indexing invented, which was published for the first time in his *Theory of Library Catalogue* (1938). Chain Indexing is a very ingenious method to derive subject headings from the class number. It is considered one of his prominent invention for subject cataloging made famous by the British National Bibliography by using it from 1950-1970 for giving subject index to its weekly publications and their accumulations.

1939 : *Colon Classification*, 2nd ed. Madras: MALA. 154+ 180+ 149p. The book contained many new ideas and listed about 3000 elaborated examples. The book was vetted against the norms formulated in *Prolegomena* (1937). And in turn the Canons and principles got refined while preparing the 2nd ed. of the CC.

1940-1946 : A period of break from classification theory to work on other books of library science such as cataloging, bibliography, classification practice, etc.

1943 : Mr Bernard I Palmer(1910-1979), a teacher of Library Science in England then on War Duty in Madras, came to meet Ranganathan in his library at Madras. He had already read his *Prolegomena* (1937) and was quite keen to meet its author. Soon both of them developed close friendship. On going back to England Palmer who also became Education Officer of the Library Association, London (Now CILIP) introduced Ranganathan to his colleagues especially interested in Classification. Some of these high profile librarians were Derek W. Austin, Eric Coates, Jason E.L. Farradane, Robert Fairthorne, Douglas J. Foskett, Barbara Kyle, Derek Langridge, Jack Mills, Bernard Palmer, Jack Wells, and Brian Campbell Vickery. All members of the CRG were highly impressed by facet analysis, and did lot of work to refine it further. Ranganathan was their mentor and a friend. Palmer was his *de facto* ambassador. It can be easily said Palmer was to Ranganathan what emperor Asoka was to the Lord Buddha.

1944 : The concepts of 'phase', 'facet', 'focus' and the Five Fundamental Categories (FFC) were formulated. Ranganathan also hit on the concept of 'Three Planes of work in classification: Idea Plane, Verbal Plane, and Notational Plane'.

The first attempt to examine the mode of development of the universe of subjects was made.

During the Sixth All India Library Conference (1944: Jaipur) a symposium named "Decimal and Colon Classification in Perspective" was organized. About a dozen papers were presented on the comparative study of the CC and the DDC. The merits of the CC were highlighted.

December 1944 : Ranganathan delivered Extension Lectures on classification at the University of Bombay. These were printed in 1945 as the famous *Elements of Library Classification* (1945). *Library Classification: Fundamentals and Procedure,* with 1008 graded examples and exercises. Madras: MALA, 496p.

This hook was epoch making: It brought to surface several unsolved problems needing fundamental research. It presented a refined account of facet analysis and gave also some inkling of the postulate of the Five Fundamental Categories.

8.5. UNIVERSITY LIBRARIAN AND PROFESSOR OF LIBRARY SCIENCE AT BHU

August 1945-June 1947 : Ranganathan worked in Banaras Hindu University(BHU) for about 20 months as librarian and professor of library science. As this university library had a different kind of collection than the one at

Madras, the work turned out as an educative experience of considerable professional value. The BHU library presented many classification problems at depth level. Ranganathan classified a promiscuous collection of 100,000 books single handed in about 18 months. He reported in Prolegomena, 2nd ed., Sect.774: "Continuous work at such high pressure on such a variety of materials gave a remarkable insight into the structure and development of the universe of knowledge. It impressed upon me the versatility needed in notation. This was indeed an unusual and unexpected experience of immense richness."

1945 : Elements of Library Classification. 1st ed. Poona: N.K. Publishing House. 112p. (cf: Bombay University Lectures, 1944).

8.6. PROFESSOR OF LIBRARY SCIENCE AT THE UNIVERSITY OF DELHI (1947-1955)

June 1947-1955 : On the invitation of Sir Maurice Gwyer, on 17 June 1947 Ranganathan joined the University of Delhi as Professor in Library Science. The Department instituted programmes for Diploma (now B.Lib.I.Sc.) and later 'Degree' (now M.Lib.I.Sc.), and Ph.D. in Library Science - the latter two degrees for the first time in the entire British Commonwealth. The Delhi School provided him the opportunity to continue teaching the CC and the UDC.

The concepts of 'Rounds', 'Levels', and 'Zones' were formulated and the concept of 'Fundamental Categories' was further refined.

October 1947 : Invitation from F. Donker Duyvis, Secretary FID to attend the FID Conference and to prepare a paper on 'Classification and International Documentation'.

1947-1958 : Work on abstract classification, and symbolic meta-language for precision in classification and to depth classification.

1948 : Ranganathan invited to FID Congress held at the Hague to give a presentation on the theory of faceted classification

1948 : Founding of the 'Library Research Circle' (LRC) at Delhi. This informal group used to meet at Ranganathan's residence C-6, Maurice Nagar, University of Delhi on every Sunday afternoon. The group used to discuss practical problems of every sort, especially on library classification. Considerable work was done by this group and the subsequent findings were presented in the All India Library Conferences in 1951 at Indore and in 1953 at Hyderabad. The LRC also exchanged notes with its counterpart in England. Work of the LRC has been described in: Parthasarthy, S. "Memoirs of the Library Research Circle (Delhi)" *Annals of Indian Library Association* vol.2, 1952: 153-159.

Also in 1948, Ranganathan visited the UK for the first time after 1924 and the USA. He met many important people such as Julian Huxley, then the Director of Unesco and Head, All Souls College, as well as representatives of the Carnegie Trust and the Rockefeller Foundation. This helped to discover new directions in classification.

1948 : "... the rigidity imposed by the facet formula given under each main subject of the CC was discovered, and the concept of 'optional facets' evolved". (M. A. Gopinath). A. J. Wells suggested to conceptually describe the CC as 'Analytico- Synesthetic'. Another such name was 'Faceted scheme'

1948 : Classification and International Documentation. 24p. (FID Publ. No. 227)

1949-1953 : A tripartite journal, "Annals", "Bulletin", and "Granthalya" of the ILA (Indian Library Association) (in short: ABGILA) was edited by Ranganathan. In the *ABGILA* many important articles and new findings in classification were published.

April 1950 : Consultant to Unesco for the preparation of a report on the use of machinery in literature search and the subsequent publication of *Classification, Coding and Machinery for Search.* Paris: Unesco. 58p. (UNESCO/NS/SL3).

July 1950 : Golden Jubilee Address to the Classification and Cataloguing Division of the American Library Association, Cleveland, Ohio.

1950 : Then newly established British National Bibliography(BNB) used Ranganathan's Chain Indexing for its subject index. BNB's successful application of the chain indexing also encouraged many other national bibliographies and classified bibliographies to use chain indexing for designing alphabetical subject index for the classified part.

1950 : FID created its committee on the general theory of classification.

1951-1961 : Ranganathan worked as Rapporteur General of the Classification Committee of the Fed. Int. de Doc. (FID/CA, later in 1962 name changed to FID/CR). He regularly drafted its reports chalking out the progress made in the preceding year.

1951 : *General Theory of Classification.* FID /CA Report No.1, 16p.

Classification and Communication. Delhi: University of Delhi. 291p.

Philosophy of Library Classification. Copenhagen: Munksgaard. 132p.

Public Library System and Documentation Problems. Papers presented at 9th All India Library Conference (Indore, 1951. Delhi: Indian Library Association. 223p. The conference also discussed issues relating to classification especially those conceptualized in the deliberations of the Library Research Circle.

1951 : Chatterjee, A.N.: *A Review of Literature on Colon Classification.* ABGILA 2 (1951) No.6, p.167-172. It is an almost exhaustive bibliography of the CC enlisting all references from 1924 to 1950.

1951 : Palmer, B.I., Wells, A.J.: *Fundamentals of Library Classification.* London: Allen and Unwin. 114p. The first whole length interpretation of Ranganathan's theories of classification in the West. The book introduced Ranganathan to the world outside India and won him many admirers and adherents.

1952-1957 : Work of classification separated into three planes of work. This theory was initially stated in Ranganathan's article "Optional Facets in Library Classification (9)", *Annals of Indian Library Association* 2(1952), Sect.720.

1952 : Classification Research Group (CRG) established in London, and this elite group of classification theorists and practitioners treated Ranganathan as their mentor, and did lot of research work on facet analysis and faceted classification

1952 : Principle of inversion discovered and incorporated in the 4th edition of the CC (1952).

1952 : *Colon Classification*, 4th ed. Madras: MALA. 4 parts in 1 volume. 127 + 155 + 50 + 149 p.

This edition introduced many new concepts in the idea plane and techniques in the notational plane. Important among them are: 'Five Fundamental Categories', 'Rounds and Levels'. Introduction of three more connecting symbols, viz. , (Comma for Personality), ; (Semicolon for Matter), . (dot for Space and Time) and : (Colon), exclusively reserved for the Energy Category. This step broke the rigidity of the facet formula and simplified the CC Class Number to a great extent. The concept of 'Anteriorising' and 'Posteriorising Common Isolates' was also introduced, as well as the concept of Partially Comprehensive Main Classes denoted by letters of the Greek alphabet.

1953 : *Depth Classification, Reference Service, and Reference Material*: Papers for discussion at the 10th All India Library Conference, Hyderabad 1953. Delhi: ILA. 444p. (edited by Ranganathan)

1954 : *General Theory of Classification*: FID/CA Report No.4. Copenhagen: FID 1954. (FID Document F50-40) Also published in *Annals of Library Science* 1 (1954): 5-80.

1954 : *Annals of Library Science*. Ranganathan was founder editor of this scholarly journal. It is published quarterly by INSDOC (Now NISCAIR, New Delhi) and continues under the name Annals of Library Science and Information. It published many eminent papers on classification by Ranganathan and his schoolmen. (See M.P. Satija (1985) Ranganathan in the Fleet Street. *Herald of Library Science* 24(3): 166-173).

1954 : UDC accepts the Octave device (now called sectorising digit) for extrapolation in an array.

8.7. RANGANATHAN'S TWO YEARS IN EUROPE (1955-1957)

1955-1956 : Ranganathan stayed in Zürich, Switzerland. Some important European librarians came to consult him to prepare schedules for special classifications, e.g. D.J. Foskett for "Occupational Health", and D.W. Langridge for "Management".

1955 : D.B. Krishna Rao (d.1985) completed his Ph.D dissertation on the depth schedules of agriculture under the supervision of Dr. S.R. Ranganathan and S. Das Gupta (1912-1966). He became the first person to be awarded Ph.D degree in LIS in India perhaps in the entire Commonwealth and Asia.

"Common Isolates in Documentation Work 1: Terminology and Anteriorising Isolates." (FID/CA Report No.4 on General Theory of Classification). *Review of Documentation* 22 (1955): 18-25

"Zones in Array: FID /CA Report No.5 on General Theory of Classification." *Annals of Library Science* 2(1955)No.1, pp. 33-39.

Mixed notation and Zones in an Array: FID/CA Report No.5 on *General Theory of Classification.* The Hague: FID. 14p.

Classification Research Group (London): The need for a faceted classification as the basis of all methods of information retrieval. (UNESCO IAC. Doc. Ter. Pas. Memo 320/5515); also published in *Library Association Record* 57(1955) pp.262-268.

1956-1960 : Postulational approach formulated. Principles of Facet Sequence such as the Wall-Picture principle, or the Cow-Calf principle discovered.

Separation of problems needing fundamental research from those needing routine investigations in building up schedules for common energy matter and personality isolates.

1956 : Common Isolates in Documentation Work (2): Anteriorising Isolates: FID/CA Report No.4 on General Theory of Classification. *Review of Documentation* 23(1956) pp.43-48.

Common Isolates in Documentation Work (3): Time Isolates. (FID/CA Report No.4 on General Theory of Classification. *Rev. of Documentation* 23(1956) pp.70-79 *General Theory of Classification*: Zone Analysis and Efficiency Tables. The Hague: FID. 18p.

1957 : The(First) International Study Conference on Classification Research in 1957 (Dorking, England) provided a forum to discuss his theories on classification with a large and varied group of international experts working in various disciplines. In 1957, the "age of faceted classification" was declared.

The conference conveners stated: "This conference will be a development of all of Dr. Ranganathan's work in the last 20 years, and it will be a means of spreading interest in his work and appreciation of it." Ranganathan delivered the opening address. Facet analysis was accepted as the basis of classification for information retrieval.

The recognition inspired Ranganathan to continue his work to meet the challenges of documentation for information in industry and advanced research.

1957 : Ranganathan made honorary member of the FID. The citation read: "In commemoration and honour of his many important contributions to library science, and his creation of the Colon Classification, as well as his multiple activities in promoting the intellectual and cultural co-operation between the Eastern and Western worlds."

1957 : *Colon Classification,* 5th ed. Madras: MALA. Vol.1. Basic Classification. 148 + 179 + 136p.

Prolegomena to Library Classification, 2nd ed. London: The Library Association. 487p.

Explicitly stated the idea of semantically empty digits and the Sectorizing Device for hospitality in arrays. This concept already existed in a rudimentary form in the 2nd edition of the CC (1939).

1957: *Classification of Commodities and Services*: 7th Report FID/CA on the General Theory of Classification. The Hague: FID. 4p. *Common Isolates in Documentation Work* (4): Space Isolates. FID ICA Report No.4 on General Theory of Classification. *Rev. of Documentation* 24(1957) pp.18-28

8.8. YEARS OF LECTURE TOURS AND VARIOUS VISITING PROFESSORSHIPS. (1957-1961)

1958 : *Classification of Environmented Entity*: FID/CA Report No.8 on General Theory of Classification. *Annals of Library Science* 5(1958) pp.113-121 and *Review of Documentation* 25 (1958) p.122-127, also published as a report by FID, The Hague, 6p.

1958 : The idea of Absolute Syntax of facets mooted at the Conference on "Retrieval of Scientific Information" (Washington).

1959 : The indicator digit for [T] changed to ' that is an inverted comma on the suggestion of P.B. Roy of Calcutta.

Classification and Retrieval: Problems for Pursuit. FID/CA Report No.9 on the General Theory of Classification. The Hague: FID. 13p. Also published in *Annals of Library Science* 6 (1959) pp.33-43

1960 : *Common Property Isolates* (1). FID/CA Report No.10 on the General Theory of Classification. New Delhi: INSDOC. 14p.

Colon Classification, 6th ed. Bombay: Asia. 3 parts in 1. 124+172+ 126 p.

Elements of Library Classification. 2nd Indian ed. Bombay: Asia. 108p.

Vickery, B.C.: *Faceted Classification: A Guide to Construction & Use of Special Schemes*. London: Aslib, 1960. 70p.

This is the first full book on the theory and methodology of designing faceted classification systems

1961 : *Facet Sequence and Telescoping in the Schedule*. FID/CA Report No.11 on the General Theory of Classification.

8.9 FINDING A RESIDENCE FOR CC IN BANGALORE (1962-)

FID/CA changed its name to FID/CR(Committee on Classification Research), and Ranganathan appointed its honorary chairman for life.

1962 : Documentation Research and Training Centre (DRTC) established at Bangalore as a unit of the Indian Statistical Institute Calcutta by the Government of India on the pursuance of Professor P. C. Mahalanobis, F.R.S. who was director of the Indian statistical Institute (ISI),and a very influential person in the Planning Commission of India. The DRTC is a unique institute of library and documentation research and teaching. It provided Ranganathan an opportunity for formal and institutionalized team research. Its work is as fundamental as it is famous. Here, the development of depth schedules for various subjects began to take shape. Every student of the DRTC had to prepare a depth schedule on a new subject as a course work.

1962-1966 : Ranganathan discovers deeper cause for the rigidity of earlier versions. It was by realizing that the facets belong to the compound subject, not to the basic subject (ISI 2012, Sec.7)

1963 : *Elements of Library Classification*, 3rd ed. Bombay: Asia. 168p.

1963 : The guided design of Depth Schedules begins at DRTC.

1963 : Greek letters for new main classes and partial comprehensions were replaced by the digit pairs formed with the help of emptying digits. Only the Greek letter delta continued to be used to denote the main class Mysticism and Spiritual Experience

Colon Classification, 6th ed., reprinted with amendments. Bombay: Asia. 3 parts in 1 volume. 28+ 124+ 172+ 126p

1964 : Ranganathan served as Chairman of the International Study Conference on Classification Research held in Sept.1964 in Elsinore, Denmark.

Classification Research 1957-1963: Trend Report. Copenhagen: Danish Centre for Documentation, 11p.

Library Science with a Slant to Documentation started a quarterly journal founded and edited by Ranganathan, and sponsored by the Sarada Ranganathan Endowment in Library Science. During his last years, it was almost an exclusive vehicle of his ideas and papers. The journal is still known for its rigorous standards. It published many depth schedules of the CC. It was renamed: *Library Science with a Slant to Information*. Presently it is titled *SRELS Journal of Information Management*. The first paper in the first issue of the journal was by Ranganathan on designing depth schedules: "Design of depth schedules: Methodology" *Library Science with a slant to Documentation*, vol.1, no.1: 1-42.

1964 : Period of Applied Research and Development

1965 : *Colon Classification*. New Brunswick, NJ: Rutgers University Press. 300 p. (Rutgers Series on the Systems for the Intellectual Organization of Information, edited by Susan Artandi).

Ranganathan explained the theory and philosophy of Colon Classification in the Seminar on the Systems for the Intellectual Organization of Information Organized by the Rutgers University, New Jersey in November 1964. This explanation by Ranganathan led to attract many adherents and admirers to the CC in the USA.

1967 : *A Descriptive Account of the Colon Classification*. Bombay: Asia. 300p. (Earlier published in the USA under the title "Colon Classification").

Prolegomena to Library Classification, 3rd ed. Assisted by M.A. Gopinath. Bombay: Asia. 640p.

1970 : Ranganathan received the Margaret Mann Citation for 1970. (Since 1951 the Margaret Mann Citation is awarded by the ALCTS Cataloging and Metadata Management Section for outstanding professional achievement in cataloging or classification. Ranganathan seems the only person outside the North America to receive this honor so far).

1970 : A double inverted comma " used as indicator digit for ACIs.

1971 : Colon Classification, 7th ed: A Purview. Bangalore: Sarada Ranganathan Endowment. 52p.

1972 : *Library Classification: Evolution of a Dynamic Theory*. Delhi: Vikas. 222p. (by R.S. Parkhi, but completed by S.R. Ranganathan.

Sept. 1972 : Ranganathan died on 27th Sept. 1972 at Bangalore after a brief illness.

8.10. POSTHUMOUS EVENTS

1972 : *Impact of Growth in the Universe of Subjects on Classification*. FID/CR Report No.12. Copenhagen: Danish Center for Documentation, p. 1-20 (Published as a Ranganathan Memorial Publication).

1975 : 3rd International Conference on Classification Research held at Bombay on Global Ordering systems.

1975 : The FID/CR established a biennial Ranganathan award in his memory for outstanding work in knowledge organization. The first ward was given to Derek Austin in 1976 for his invention of PRECIS which replaced Chain Indexing in the BNB.

1983 : Portrait of Ranganathan included in the ISI "Cathedral of Man"

1985 : International Conference on "Ranganathan's Philosophy: Assessment and Relevance", organized by ILA and others in Nov.1985 at New Delhi.

1987 : *Colon Classification,* 7th ed. Edited by M.A. Gopinath. Vol.1: Basic and depth version. Bangalore: Sarada Ranganathan Endowment, XIV, 332p.

1991-1992 : The Ranganathan Birth Centenary celebrations took place in many countries of the world.

August 1992 : 2nd International ISKO Conference held in Madras, as "the grand finale for commemorating the birth centenary" (Suseela Kumar).

1994 : *Bibliography of Colon Classification, 1930-1993* by M.P. Satija and Amrik Singh. New Delhi: M D Publications, 1994.xi, 129p.

With 1371 entries arranged chronologically it is the largest ever bibliography compiled on any individual library classification system.

2015 (April 23) : A Museum on S. R. Ranganathan at Documentation Research and Training Centre, ISI, Bangalore, inaugurated by Dr. Arun Shourie, Chairman, Indian Statistical Institute (ISI) in presence of Prof. Bimal K. Roy, Director, ISI. The museum apart from his books, research papers and documents houses his physical memorabilia.

2015 (December): *The Annals of Library Science and Information Studies* Vol.62, no. 4 brought out a special issue on Ranganathan. It has many articles on Ranganathan and his classification.

2017 (October 23-25) : Ranganathan revisited : International Conference on Knowledge Organisation Literacy and Information Management. (Organised by the Sarada Ranganathan Endowment at IIT Chennai).

9

His Impact and Continued Relevance : What They Say

STRUCTURE

1. Ranganathan as a Man
2. Ranganathan as a Scientist
3. Ranganathan as a Classificationist

Sources

Appendix-I : ALA Resolution

Appendix-II : Nasser Sharify

9.1. RANGANATHAN AS A MAN

9.1.1

The author combines the culture of India with the scholarship of England...

Library Quarterly, review of the Prolegomena, 1937.

9.1.2

His reputation as a librarian extends far beyond the borders of his own country and his opinion and advice are valued in all lands where librarians are held in honour.

Maurice Gwyer while presenting him for the conferment of honorary doctorate by the University of Delhi in 1948.

9.1.3

Your words are the words of the Anglo-American, but your language is the language of the East and your ideas are universal. You answer the challenge of the future with a challenge. Most of us are not your disciples; all of us are your students. For a generation you have forced librarians to think. We are proud to be in your debt.

Greetings from the American Library Association on his 71st birthday in 1962. (other tributes paid by the American Library Association are enclosed in the Appendix I).

9.1.4

...In his company I learned to think a new, and reached maturity.

Palmer, B.I., 1962. p.57.

9.1.5

Dr. Ranganathan writes and speaks English fluently and idiomatically, but the idiom is not always current in rest of the English-speaking world... Yet, put Ranganathan in front of a European audience and he will explain the most difficult concepts in a way which strikes home to the simplest listener. He will lard his discourse with examples, and the questions and answers will flow on until the chairman of the meeting has to call a halt.

Palmer, B.I. / Kaula, P.N., ed., 1965, Sec. T13.

9.1.6

...every Indian who has any interest in libraries, library science, documentation or any allied fields takes a justifiable pride in being a fellow countryman of Dr. Ranganathan whose talents and genius have contributed so much to the advancement of knowledge in the world.

Verman, Lal C. / Kaula, P.N., ed., 1965, Sec. H21.

9.1.7

All those publications show that he possesses:

1. the quality of being a trained philosopher;
2. the tolerance and wisdom of a countryman of Gandhi of the best sort; and
3. the knowledge and capacity to bring together and unify the thoughts which have directed the present important classifications. Summarizing those three characteristics make together Ranganathan and much more than that.

Donker Duyvis, F. 1966 (While enumerating his contributions to FID/CA).

9.1.8

Ranganathan played a very important role in deciding the policy of the UN library otherwise it would probably have been much more American than an international library.

Coblans, H. / Dudley, E., 1974, pp. 27-28.

9.1.9

Ranganathan had real gift for using words creatively... He used words in a strange but telling way.

Coblans, H. / Dudley, E., 1974, p.28.

9.1.10

Ranganathan made the most significant contribution to librarianship and information studies during this century...not only in his own country but throughout the world.

Downing, Joel / Dudley, E. 1974, p.7.

9.1.11

Much as he appreciated the significance of mysticism, Ranganathan was not himself a mystic. He was an intellectual who absorbed much from the West and outdid us all in the application of scientific method to librarianship.

Langridge, D.W. / Dudley, E., 1974, p.32.

9.1.12

His spiritualism flowered when he divorced himself from the mass of details which were incubating in his mind. It just worked like the mind of a painter, who periodically steps back from the canvas to gain perspective. The integral nature of Ranganathan's theory emerged from occasional intuition; and his intellect strove to make it more explicit to the rational mind of the scientific worker.

Gopinath, M.A., 1978. p. 75.

9.1.13

Ranganathan had a mission. It is only the missionaries who bring great things to life... You must have some fire burning in you and Ranganathan had all these qualities.

Rao, V.K.R.V., 1985, p.vii. (Dr V K R V Rao was an eminent economist and later a successful Finance Minister of India).

9.1.14

The 'monumental accomplishment' was the work of one man [Ranganathan], whose systematization in bibliographic classification surpassed the achievement of any European or American.

Langridge, D.W., 1991, p.14.

9.1.15

Good people die; good ideas do not. A hundred years after his birth Ranganathan's ideas live in us.

Comaromi, John P. / Sharma, R.N., 1992, p.15.

9.1.16

He awoke a nation, his own, and astonished the world with his genius. He expressed his ideas clearly with conviction, but he claimed no finality in his works. He left them open ended, he gave the new generation new path to follow. Ranganathan was a very special human being, perhaps he was a prophet. I was one of those few privileged people who for three weeks sat at the feet of this great man.

Sharify, Nasser / Sharma, R.N., 1992, p.157.

9.1.17

Sayers used to complain that Ranganathan could not distinguish between mountains and molehills; but this is not true. It was simply that mountain or molehill, if a matter needed his attention, it received his undivided attention.

Palmer, B.I. / Dudley, E., 1992, p.14.

9.1.18

He has, I think, an infinite capacity for taking pains, which has been defined as the basic element of a genius. He had also an infinite capacity for communicating with anybody. I think that is the most precious elements of his professionalism that I like to remember.

Foskett, D.J. / Dudley, E., 1992, p. 19.

9.1.19

...On the whole young librarians were always fascinated by his personality and by his teaching methods. This was put rather nicely by the late Barbara Kyle in a poem which she wrote in 1962 (under the pseudonym of Ruth

Archibald). The poem started thus:

Bliss was it in that dawn to be alive
But to be young was Ranganathan

Coblans, H. / Dudley, E., 1992, p.230.

9.1.20

It seems that Ranganathan's name is now frequently used by writers to give their papers some "academic respectability". And this in itself is a sufficient proof of the stature of the man.

Lancaster, F.W., Mary Jo Zeter and Laura Metzler, 1992, p.276.

9.1.21

There is virtually no area of Ranganathan's work and personal life in which this quest for discovering the inner or essential order behind the visible is absent.

Miksa, Francis L., 1998, p.67.

9.1.22

No other bibliographical classification has aroused either the enthusiasm or the severe criticism that have been accorded to Ranganathan's scheme. This mathematician-turned-librarian has shaken what many thought were the foundations of book classification; no matter what our opinions of Colon may be, its influence cannot be ignored... it could be regarded as the greatest stride forward with regard to the principles of bibliographical classification... Yet the full impact of the ideas which Ranganathan has either unearthed, or developed and crystallized, is almost incalculable.

Maltby, Arthur, 2000, p.135.

9.1.23

Ranganathan aimed big—he was looking for the

fundamental laws that underlie experience and it quickly became an obsession. S.R. Ranganathan was the greatest librarian of the 20th Century. No one else even comes close. His ideas influenced every aspect of library science (a term he is credited with coining), and because he was such a complete and systematic thinker, he was gifted in the development of all areas of the field, including theory, practice, and management.

Steckel, Mike, October 7th, 2002.

9.2. RANGANATHAN AS A SCIENTIST

9.2.1

Even those not accepting his conclusions, nor adopting his methods ...will acknowledge the debt under which his industry and erudition has placed them

Sargent, John, 1940.

9.2.2

For the first time practical classification can claim to approximate to a science... Normally, while most students could grasp the theory of classification, when it came to the practice they found it demanding an elusive gift called 'flair'. For 'flair' Ranganathan has substituted reasoned analysis: perhaps flair was a meager or a quasi-intuitive form of the same process. Ranganathan... brings the whole problem from the regions of subconscious perception to those of the intellect. This act makes it at once possible to train any intelligent person to classify, instead of merely demonstrating to the classification-aspirant and then hoping for the best.

Palmer, B.I., 1944.

9.2.3

...No single man has done more to rationalize the theory of library classification than this eminent Indian librarian...

Palmer, B.I., 1962, p.14.

9.2.4

Ranganathan revitalised the whole study of our subject. He gave us doubts about things that seemed fixed and eternal, such as main classes and rules of division, causing us to look again at the theory we thought we had safely learnt once for all. He taught us to look beyond the boundary wall of a universally applied scheme of classification, and to find instead unifying principles. If, in turn he finds his own work being scrutinized and partially outmoded, he will recognise this as a continuation of the process of life, and if he finds new work valid he will accept it.

Palmer, B.I., 1962, p.57.

9.2.5

Like Euclid in mathematics, and Rameau in music, Ranganathan's work must be recognized as the basis for an understanding of the theories, techniques, and procedures in library classification. In his many writings on the subject, he has presented the theory which must underline a classification scheme if it is to provide all the detail, variety, flexibility, and simplicity required for modern information indexing.

Atherton, Pauline, 1965, p.469.

9.2.6

Ranganathan who is certainly our profound thinker in the field of classification, has expounded its scientific and philosophical basis in his *Prolegomena to library classification*. In this work, of which the logical-mathematical treatment follows the *Principia Mathematica* of Whitehead and Russell, he illustrates the 'spiral of scientific method': experimentation, induction, hypothesis, verification, leading to further induction and the formation of deduced laws.

Foskett, D.J. / Shera, 1965, p.xi.

9.2.7

He was striking the most fundamental problems of library classification in ways that they had never been attacked before, and his still remains as the most fertile mind that has yet addressed itself to the problem of bibliographic organization.

Shera, Jesse H., 1965, p.102.

9.2.8

...The great contribution of Ranganathan's methods lies in the theory of librarianship itself. ...Facet analysis derives from Ranganathan's investigations into the way in which knowledge grows, and in his work for the first time, librarianship, as the science of management of knowledge, merges with epistemology. This distinguished Indian philosopher found librarianship little more than a bundle of techniques, a rather simple technology, and he, and his followers, have raised it to an intellectual discipline in its own right. Thus he has laid the theoretical foundations upon which others can build.

Shera, Jesse H. and James Perry / Kaula, P.N., ed., 1965, Sec. B27.

9.2.9

Ranganathan was striking the most fundamental problems of library science in a way that have never been attacked before.

Shera, Jesse H., 1966, pp.1-2.

9.2.10

Ranganathan's early experience as a mathematician

and a teacher as well as a librarian and his sense of limitations of many of the existing schemes of library classification prompted him to reassess the traditional principles of classification and to add new principles which took the increasing and changing demands of library materials and readers in the 20th century.

Batty, C.D., 1967, "Author's note".

9.2.11

Shiyali Ramamrita Ranganathan (1892-1972) of India is the unquestioned giant of 20th-century library science. He tackled all aspects of the profession of librarianship and always added his own individualistic, and sometimes, quirky perception of the subject. He revolutionized the theory and practice of classification. Though his own classification scheme was never widely adopted, its influence can be seen throughout the practice of information retrieval, in the modern revision of the Dewey Decimal Classification scheme, and in such pioneering attempts as the PRECIS subject heading system. If for nothing else, he deserves to be long remembered for his famous "Five laws of library science". The laws are the best summary of what libraries are, or should be about. There is no facet of the practice of librarianship to which those laws cannot be applied. They represent a life time of thought on our profession distilled into universalisms.

Gorman, M., 1980, p.203.

9.2.12

Ranganathan's work was valuable not only because he found the solution to many problems, but particularly because he made explicit so many fundamental ideas.

Langridge, D.W., 1991, p.14.

9.2.13

Ranganathan had the facility for taking hold of ideas

and honing them, giving them a new vocabulary and often rationalizing what was only instinctive in the work of others... He had the facility for identifying principles and standardizing them from what was only partially understood by his predecessors. Standards were among his many enthusiasms and he was responsible for much work in India towards their development.... Many of the principles he propounded were simply a regularization, with strict rules, of more haphazard instinctive approach of his predecessors. These principles are still considered fundamental in the teaching of information work at his old college [University College London]... . Ranganathan's principles remain a solid foundation for subject [access] work of all kinds.

McIlwaine, I.C. / Sharma, R.N., 1992, p.38.

9.2.14

Many principles based on the *Five Laws of Library Science* (1931) and his *Colon Classification* (1933) have been put into application over the years. His philosophies of users service and his theories of the organization of knowledge have been absorbed into the culture of librarianship and information science in the West.

Fazle Kabir, A.F.M. / Sharma, R.N., 1992, p.65.

9.2.15

...It is necessary to acknowledge the increased application of Ranganathan's philosophical principles and his theories of indexing in creation of electronic databases, and in the development of integrated systems. He has given us the instrument for accurate analysis of knowledge and its re-synthesis in linear sequence...

Fazle Kabir, A.F.M. / Sharma, R.N., 1992, p.65.

9.2.16

Ranganathan's approach to classification—that is the

underlying philosophy—and the techniques of facet analysis have been extended to many diverse areas of applications.

Kwasnik, Barbara H. / Sharma, R.N., 1992, p.103.

9.2.17

The proper study of order is order… It is fitting then to note that the *Colon Classification* is a triumph of, for and by the orderly mind… The reduction of all knowledge to five categories was a daring postulation, and he discovered within their progression a natural order.

Stiles, William G. / Sharma, R.N., 1992, p.141.

9.2.18

Ranganathan cautioned us never to assess any enquiry in reference work as trivial. The degree of its importance rests only in the need of the person addressing the question. He demonstrated that he practiced what he preached when, during the question period, a student asked him, semi-facetiously, if he could offer any advice as to how we might easily pass our forthcoming examinations. There was some squirming on the podium, and embarrassment, but unperturbed Dr. Ranganathan replied that it was a good question, and he would be delighted to respond…

Stiles, William G. / Sharma, R.N., 1992, p.142.

9.2.19

It is ironic in that within the information science sector one sees a lively interest in Ranganathan's theories, due to the distancing of his categories from literary warrant. The multitudes of workers in search of the ultimate in 'smart' machinery must eventually come round to an appreciation of general classification and ultimately by that route to Ranganathan and his categories. It must come to that eventually, because that is the way mind works, that's the way it is.

Stiles, William G. / Sharma, R.N., 1992, p.148.

9.2.20

His disciples have observed that as a scientist he has been the first to introduce scientific method in librarianship, applying Newtonian approach of 'What', 'Why', and 'how'. He has adopted Aristotelian approach of analytical thinking. Like Aristotle he predicted five 'relations' or 'facets' in any 'subject': personality, matter, energy, space and time.

Sharify, Nasser / Sharma, R.N., 1992, p.152.

9.2.21

...Standing four-square on the remarkable work of this remarkable man and with the aid of the new technology, we now see the possibility of adequately assessing, for the first time, the relative roles of all the parts that go to make up a total subject retrieval system.

Wells, A.J. / Dudley, E., 1992, p.13.

9.2.22

Ranganathan's was a life of 80 years – a life of unequal productivity in every field of documentation and librarianship.

Coblans, H. / Dudley, E., 1992, p.22.

9.2.23

Ranganathan's books and writings have a systematic rigour and are cast in the logical framework of a system. On the other hand his speaking and teaching were in the form of Socratic dialogue and thus less dogmatic.

Coblans, H. / Dudley, E., 1992, p.23.

9.2.24

There was a remarkable integrity of life and work, of practice, research and teaching. Librarianship was seen as a whole in its place in society; for classification in particular he constructed the only complete and coherent body of theory and practice. In the whole of library history it was an achievement without equal.

Langridge, D.W. / Dudley, E., 1992, p.27.

9.2.25

I believe Ranganathan, more than any other scholar of our discipline, has striven to establish classification upon a scientific foundation.

Svenonius, Elaine, 1992, p.176.

9.2.26

His search for a 'universal' model to organize and classify information that appears in recorded form, has in our discipline represented a passing from macro areas to micro units in discovering the contents and corpus of subject domains. His theory and application of scientific principles in analyzing and synthesizing a specific subject and to individualize it out of millions, can be seen as a phenomena similar to those research interest that have guided other scientific areas too. For example in physics, where the atom was split and the Bohr-Rutherford model of the constituents of the atom served as theoretical basis for the explanation of its properties; and in Biology, where RNA and DNA were observed in cells, and research got a step closer to the understanding of the micro world of genetics.

Ingwersen, Peter and Irene Wormell, 1992, p.187.

9.2.27

Ranganathan represents a milestone in the development of intellectual processes involved in the organization and classification of recorded knowledge. His approach of analysis and synthesis in classification will always be valid, because his application of this scientific principles is not likely to change or appear obsolete at any point of time.

Ingwersen, Peter and Irene Wormell, 1992, p.187.

9.2.28

The most striking single characteristic of all of Ranganathan's work and especially of his work in library classification is that he treated library classification as a single unified structure of ideas which flowed from a cohesive set of basic principles.

Miksa, Francis L, 1998, p.67.

9.2.29

Ranganathan, is by common consent, the greatest figure of librarianship in the twentieth century. A mathematician by training, he brought to the study of library science (a term he invented) a belief in the scientific method and rational examination of social phenomena. Though best known for his considerable contributions to the theory of classification and subject retrieval, he studied all aspects of librarianship and, based on that study, formulated his famous *Five Laws of Library Science*... based on his scientific training... and his rigorous objective analysis.

Gorman, M., 2000, pp.18-19.

9.2.30

...it is worth noting that the full extent of Ranganarthan's distinctive and radical thinking in his numerous books and papers and the significance of his paradigm shift in classification theory which he inaugurated has not yet been fully mined.

Newton, Robert / Marcella and Maltby (eds.), 2000, p.51.

9.3. RANGANATHAN AS A CLASSIFICATIONIST

9.3.1

For the first time practical classification can claim to approximate to a science... Normally, while most students could grasp the theory of classification, when it came to the practice they found it demanded an elusive gift called 'flair'. For 'flair' Ranganathan has substituted reasoned analysis: perhaps flair was a meager or a quasi-intuitive form of the same process. Ranganathan brings the whole process from the regions of subconscious perceptions to those of the intellect. This act makes it at once possible to train any intelligent person to classify, instead of merely demonstrating to the classification–aspirant and then hoping for the best... . Too often the subject is lost in the welter of relationships, and the task of deciding to which class a subject belongs can be quite a major task when it rests on flair. And as A's flair is not always B's flair, anomalies creep in which can vitiate the work of classifier: a work which aims at reducing conflicts to minimum.

Palmer, B.I., 1944.

9.3.2

The significance of Ranganathan's fundamental concepts is that we can use a similar process of abstraction of a generalised rule in classification.

Palmer, B.I and Wells, A.J., 1951, p.43.

9.3.3

The analytic and synthetic methods associated with CC have influenced recent classification study greatly, even to fascination...have introduced ideas of value; one of them, the Octave Device, adopted by the International Federation for Documentation for use in the UDC, is probably important

Sayers, W.C.B., 1955.

9.3.4

...Now there is hardly a classifier who has not felt his influence.

Sayers, W.C.B., 1957, Preface.

9.3.5

Ranganathan aims to uncover the internal structure of the principles of development of scientific library and bibliographic classification, providing... a correct deeply thought out organisation of recorded knowledge in all its divisions... Bypassing it and ignoring it, while developing new current scientific library classification, is impossible.

Shamurin, E.I., 1959.

9.3.6

Dr. S.R. Ranganathan has done so much to establish classification theory as a fundamental study... [that] pervades modern classificatory thought. He has discovered and made explicit the phenomena of classification: he has devised expressive names for them: he has systematised the study of classification into principles, rules and canons...which have worked a revolution in our subject, and changed it from a dull theory with apparently little relevance to practice into an incisive intellectual tool which could be used to analyse existing schemes or to help in the construction of new ones.

Palmer, B.I., 1962, p.46.

9.3.7

...Schemes which are produced today inevitably reflect the work he has done.

Palmer, B.I., 1962. p.55.

9.3.8

Scientific approach to classification is his most enduring contribution to librarianship.

Vickery, B.C. / Kaula, P.N., 1965, Sec. C66.

9.3.9

One of the most significant of Ranganathan's contribution in this area has been his insistence that subject cataloguing and classification are two aspects of the same operation.

Foskett, D.J. / Shera, Jesse H., 1965, p.xvi.

9.3.10

The Colon Classification must be recognized as a milestone in the development of the intellectual process involved in the organization of the information that appears in recorded form.

Shaw, Ralph R. / Kaula, P.N., ed., 1965, Sec. B41.

9.3.11

Ranganathan is probably the only man who can challenge Bliss on his own terms -and he has done so. Whatever one may think of the *Colon Classification*, certainly its distinguished creator has surpassed all others in his grasp of the fundamental problems of organizing the intellectual content of graphic records. In his facet analysis and its American counterpart, semantic factoring, the role of classification in bibliographic organization achieves a new and greater significance than it ever had as applied to book arrangement or even as exemplified in the classified catalogue.

Shera, Jesse H., 1965, p.134.

9.3.12

In England the Classification Research Group, which

can certainly trace its origins to the pioneering work of Ranganathan, has, in a surprisingly brief time, made rather remarkable progress in reviving research in classification.

Shera, Jesse H., 1965, p.139.

9.3.13

A second major advance toward a possible solution to the problem of library classification came when Ranganathan developed the philosophic orientation to his Colon scheme. That he was fully aware of the limitations that inhere in any classification of bibliographic units is evident to anyone who has read with care his *Prolegomena*.

Shera, Jesse H., 1965, p.101.

9.3.14

His great contribution to classification, and the one that is far in advance of the thinking of his contemporaries, is his implicit rejection of the physical book as the constituent unit in the classification and his substitution of the thought—or subject-unit. The distinctive property of the Colon Classification, then, is its emphasis upon the basic ways in which a subject may be characterized and its attempt to ignore the traditional hierarchical grouping of such characteristics.

Shera, Jesse H. 1965, pp.101-102.

9.3.15

Of all librarians, only S.R. Ranganathan has attempted to build a bibliographic classification upon epistemological principles. By demonstrating the ways in which knowledge grows—by "denudation, dissection, lamination, and loose assemblage" —he has clearly shown the relation between bibliographic classification and the patterns of man's cognitive growth.

Shera, Jesse H. and James Perry / Kaula, P.N., ed., 1965, Sec. B261.

9.3.16

Nowhere in the world can anyone seriously discuss or think about problems of recorded knowledge, whether on the most elementary or the most sophisticated levels, without taking into account the development of the theory of synthetic classification that is inherent in the CC and in the work of all those who have worked on the development of the CC.

Shaw, Ralph R. / Kaula, P.N., ed., 1965, Sec. B42.

9.3.17

The most successful method of making classification systems that is available today is that of facet analysis. It is, thanks to Dr. Ranganathan, that this powerful tool has been fashioned to the point where it has been used in many specialist systems as well as in the Colon Classification itself.

Foskett, D.J. / Kaula, P.N., ed., 1965, Sec. D21.

9.3.18

It is... a considerable tribute to the universality of Ranganathan's thinking on classification that his ideas have recently found application on a comparatively large scale in connection with classification of European music.

Coates, E.J. / Kaula, P.N., ed., 1965, Sec. D31. (E.J. Coates was the founder editor of the *British catalogue of music*)

9.3.19

His contribution to the whole field of classification has been far reaching and the students of today may get an inspiration from his work that will guide them to further discoveries in classification. Dr. Ranganathan has been a force that cannot be ignored, and from the study of his works some revival in interest in classification may be expected in the United States.

Eaton, Thelma / Kaula, P.N., ed., 1965, Sec. S88.

9.3.20

Ranghanathan's contraptions to classification make briefly the picture of the classification as it is today.

Davison, Keith, 1966, p.26.

9.3.21

The whole Prolegomena is a search for and statement of meaningful subject sequences, and their embodiment in the symbolism of notation

Vickery, B.C., 1969, p.170.

9.3.22

Ranganathan has pioneered faceted classification and faceted notation, conscious and consistent citation order, schedule of inversion, valuable postulates such as the 'five fundamental categories.'

Mills, J., 1970, P.144.

9.3.23

His explorations in the organisation of knowledge have led to the creation of a new approach to classification based on facet and phase analysis. Indeed, upon his creative enquiry into the nature of documentation, rests the structure of modern library classification.

Lancour, Harold, quoted by Parkhi, R.S., 1972, p.193.

9.3.24

At no time did Ranganathan ignore his predecessors. Always he sought to build on what his predecessors had done. I dare say that no body in the international library scene paid more homage to the work of Otlet and La Fontaine in creating the UDC.

Foskett, D.J. / Dudley, E., 1974, p.24.

9.3.25

Vickery commended Ranganathan's great contribution to the science of indexing for the introduction of new concepts like 'facet', 'isolate', 'focus', and many more. Such terms have their concrete meanings not only for Colon Classification but for the entire theory of library classification in the abstract.

Vickery, B.C. / Dudley, E., 1974, p.10.

9.3.26

Learning classification should begin with the presentation of an ideal, with a thorough grounding in principles and a demonstration of how they should be applied. To achieve such aims there is nothing more than Colon Classification and the body of theory on which it is based.

Langridge, D.W.,/ICRP, 1985, p.602.

9.3.27

Ranganathan was the first to make full use of clearly defined set of categories that were also the most generalized ever proposed for bibliographic purposes.

Langridge, D.W., 1989, p.39.

9.3.28

The beauty of Ranganathan's system is its economy. With the five categories plus rounds and levels we can perceive order among the millions of ideas which, as he so graphically puts it in his *Prolegomena*, 'confuse and taunt us at the phenomenal level.'

Langridge, D.W., 1989, p.42.

9.3.29

Ranganathan deduced... from first principles and built up a complete theory of classification that was adequate, testing it all the time by practical application in his Colon scheme.

Langridge, D.W., 1991,p.14.

9.3.30

What Ranganathan did provide for library classification was a rationale and a vocabulary for classification construction. Facet analysis, as a term and a working proposition in classification making, began with him.

Comaromi, John P. / Sharma, R.N., 1992, p.11.

9.3.31

The third basic principle introduced by Ranganathan, and it is perhaps the most important, is what he called symbiosis between classification and catalogue, or index.... This symbiosis pioneered by Ranganathan, resolves the long conflict between the alphabeticals and the classifiers... I stress this symbiosis as Ranganathan's most important contribution to indexing because it exemplifies a characteristic found in all his work—his ability to see the many-sided connection of each phenomenon in information transfer. In current jargon, we might call it the system approach. But Ranganathan expressed it more movingly, in lines from Francis Thompson that he quoted in many of his books:

"All things by immortal power,

Near or Far,

Hiddenly

To each other linked are,

That thou canst not stir a flower

Without troubling of a star."

Vickery, B.C. / Dudley, E., 1992, pp.9-10.

9.3.32

...an important element in the process of learning consists of combining analysis and synthesis; exactly, in fact, Ranganathan saw the process of making and using classification schemes. All my own experience confirms that the use of this method, which we know, of course, as "facet analysis", makes it a relatively straight-forward matter for librarian/information specialist to come to grips with the subject of a user's enquiry. This is of the greatest value precisely because it is user friendly: it inspires confidence in the user, that the librarian has the ability to understand the subject of the enquiry and user's information needs.

Foskett, D.J., 1992, p.230.

9.3.33

In his conceptualization of an analytico-synthetic approach to classification, Ranganathan was a paradigm pioneer of the first order. The success of his plan of action in solving the problem of an economical representation of knowledge is inestimable. The clearest evidence of this is that the most fundamental paradigm shift in classification in the twentieth century has been from largely enumerative to largely synthetic schemes. The gain in expressive power, coupled with saving in cost, made the shift compelling. The fact that the shift emanated from a plan of action, based on a firm philosophical foundation, made it attractive.

Svenonius, Elaine, 1992, p.180.

9.3.34

The search for unity among diversity characterized Ranganathan's approach to the universe of subjects; it also characterized his approach to classificatory language per se.

At the Elsinore Conference, Ranganathan called for an abstract study of classifications, the presumption being that there are general characteristics common to them. The search for an underlying sameness in different classifications continues to be an important focus of theoretical work in classification for its impact on standardization, evaluation and compatibility.

Svenonius, Elaine, 1992, p.182.

9.3.35

His arguments for the reexamination of traditional practice of library classification and for the introduction of a New Foundation are based on the recognition of the current knowledge as a dynamic continuum....He wanted to open up a new dimension in library classification so that it could stand a higher pressure from the field of knowledge than those classification systems virtually adopting enumerative schemes, having a rigid finality and still resting on arbitrary numbering at bottom.

Ingwersen, Peter and Irene Wormell, 1992, p.186.

9.3.36

The ignorance of Ranganathan's suggestions in the library world and the hammering critique against the "practicability" of his theories, are due to the fact that the majority of classifications do not feel the need for basing their work on a dynamic theory. Libraries confine their services to the feeding of readers only with the macro subjects embodied in books and have shown but scarce interest, also to reveal the micro-level of units of thoughts in their collections.

Ingwersen, Peter and Irene Wormell, 1992, p.186

9.3.37

It is certain that Ranganathan knew the limitation of

contribution to the future, both in classification in general and, in particular, in relation to the Colon Classification. Thus it should be noticed, that details in his classification system may meet obsolescence but not in underlying principles.

Ingwersen, Peter and Irene Wormell, 1992, p.187.

9.3.38

Although Ranganathan's name is primarily associated with theories of classification and with his own bibliographic classification scheme, the Colon Classification, he has also made significant contribution to modern practice in alphabetical subject indexing. His chain indexing is an attempt to arrive at a procedure for systematically developing an alphabetical subject index for a classified catalog (in card or book form).

Lancaster, F.W., 1998, p.54.

9.3.39

...Ranganathan's theories have had a profound effect on modern practice of subject indexing. One can see this clearly in the work of Coates (1960) who advocates a catalog or index free from the rigidity of pre-established subject headings. An index entry should be made fully co-extensive with the subject matter discussed...

Lancaster, F.W., 1998, p.55.

9.3.40

Ranganathan's theories can also be considered to have influenced PRECIS (Preserved Context Index System) developed by Austin.

Lancaster, F.W., 1998, p.56.

9.3.41

Ranganathan vigorously pursued the goal of finding

one best [emphasis his] subject classification system, the system which, once it was recognized for its excellence, would be adopted widely and used as a standard for all forms of subject retrieval of information.

Miksa, Francis L., 1998, p.73.

9.3.42

The CC has been influential for its theoretical contributions to classification, especially in its demonstration of the principles of facets. In this it has been pored over and its contents assimilated by the developers of other classification schemes.

Harvey, R., 1999, p.218.

9.3.43

Ranganathan was world's foremost classification theorists. He introduced a number of new ideas and terms, one of which was the term 'facet' and he can truthfully be described the 'inventor' of faceted classification

Hunter, Eric J., 2009.

SOURCES

Atherton, Pauline. (1965). "Ranganathan's classification ideas." *Library Resources & Technical Services* 9.

Batty, C. David. (1967). Introduction to Colon Classification. London: Clive bingley,

Davison, Keith. (1966). *Theory of classification.* London: C. Bingley.

Dudley, Edward, ed. (1992). *S.R. Ranganathan, 1892-1972*; introduction by M P Satija. New Delhi: Ess Ess Publications (first published by the Library Association, London, 1974).

Foskett, D.J. (1992). "Ranganathan and 'user-friendliness'." *Libri* 42(3): 227-234.

Gopinath, M.A. (1978). "Ranganathan, Shiyali Ramamrita". In Allen Kent, et al., eds., *Encyclopedia of Library and Information Science.* New York: Marcel Dekker, Vol.25, p.75.

Gorman, Michael. (1980). "Let us now praise: a reflective look at six persons who greatly influenced the art of cataloging." *American Libraries* 11 (April 1980): 203.

Gorman, Michael. (2000). *Our enduring values: librarianship in the 21st century*. Chicago, IL: American Library Association.

Harvey, Ross. (1999). *Organising knowledge in Australia: principles and practice in libraries and information centres*. Wagga Wagga, NSW: Charles Stuart University- Riverina.

Hunter, Eric J. (2009). *Classification made simple: an introduction to knowledge organization and information retrieval*, 3rd ed. Burlington, VT: Ashgate, p.36.

ICRP : Int. Conf. on Ranganathan's philosophy (1965 : Delhi) ed. by T.S. Rajagopalam. New Delhi : Vikas Delhi.

Ingwersen, Peter and Irene Wormell. (1992). "Ranganathan in the perspective of advanced information retrieval" *Libri* 42(3): 184-201.

Kaula, P.N., ed, (1965). *Library Science Today: Ranganathan Festschrift*. Bombay: Asia Publishing House.

Lancaster, F.W. (1998). *Indexing and abstracting in theory and practice*. 2nd ed. Champaign, Il: University of Illinois.

Lancaster, F.W., Mary Jo Zeter and Laura Metzler. (1992). "Ranganathan's influence examined bibliometrically" *Libri* 42(3): 268-281.

Langridge, D.W. (1989). *Subject analysis: principles and procedures*. London: Bowker-Saur.

Meadows, A.J., ed. (1991). *Knowledge and communication: essays on the information chain*. London: Library Association Publishing.

Maltby, Arthur. (1978). *Sayers' manual of classification for librarians*, 5th ed. London: Andre Deutsch.

Marcella, Rita and Arthur Maltby (ed.) (2000). *The future of classification*. Aldershot, U.K.: Gower.

Miksa, Francis L. (1998). *The DDC, the universe of knowledge, and the post-modern library*. Albany, N.Y.: Forest Press/ OCLC.

Mills, J. (1970). "Progress in documentation: library classification." *Journal of Documentation* 26: 144.

Palmer, Bernard. I. (1944). "New vistas in classification." *Library Association Record* 46: 182-183.

Palmer, Bernard. I. (1962). *Itself an education: six lectures on classification*. London: The Library Association.

Palmer, Bernard I. and A.J. Wells. (1951). *The fundamentals of library classification*. London: George Allen and Unwin.

Parkhi, R.S. (1972). *Library classification: evolution of a dynamic theory.* Delhi: Vikas,

Rajagopalan, T.S., ed. (1986). *Ranganathan's philosophy: assessment, impact and relevance.* New Delhi: Vikas Publishing House.

Rao, V.K.R.V. (1985). *"Foreword" to University library system in India / by K. S. Deshpande.* New Delhi: Sterling Publishers

Sayers, W.C.B. (1955). *Manual of classification for librarians and bibliographers,* 3rd ed. London: Grafton & Co. Sec 118.5.

Shamurin, E.I. (1959). *Essays on the history of library and bibliographic classification.* Moscow, Vol.2, p.326.

Sharma, R. N., ed. (1992). *Ranganathan and the West.* New Delhi: Sterling Publishers, xvii, 177p.

Shera, Jesse H. (1965). *Libraries & the organization of knowledge.* ed. by D. J. Foskett, London: C. Lockwood & Son.

Stecke, Mikee. (2002). *Ranganathan for Ias.* http://boxesandarrows.com/ranganathan-for-ias/

Svenonius, Elaine. (1992). "Ranganathan and classification science." *Libri* 42(3):176-183

Vickery, B.C. (1969). "[Review of Ranganthanan's Prolegomena to classification, 1967]." *Journal of Documentation* 25:170.

APPENDIX-I

AMERICAN LIBRARY ASSOCIATION
EXECUTIVE OFFICE
LINDA F. CRISMOND
EXECUTIVE DIRECTOR

50 EAST HURON STREET CHICAGO, ILLINOIS 60611 U.S.A.
EXECUTIVE DIRECTOR 312-280-1205 DEPUTY DIRECTOR 312-280-3208
COUNCIL/BOARD SECRETARIAT 312-280-3205 FAX 312-944-3897

AMERICAN · LIBRARY · ASSOCIATION · 1876 ·

EVERY BOOK, ITS READER

RESOLUTION IN HONOR OF S.R. RANGANATHAN ON HIS CENTENARY

WHEREAS, *Ranganathan in formulating the Five Laws of Library Science gave the profession for the first time a set of fundamental laws to which every information problem could be related;*

WHEREAS, *Ranganathan in developing the Colon Classification gave the profession for the first time an integrated set of canons for classification design according to principles;*

WHEREAS, *Ranganathan in articulating the Five Fundamental Categories (PMEST) gave the profession for the first time, in the concept of facet analysis, a universal foundation for all modern indexing and classification theory;*

WHEREAS, *Ranganathan in initiating the Chain Procedure (precursor to PRECIS) gave the profession for the first time a rational basis for the derivation of permuted term indexes;*

WHEREAS, *Ranganathan in his commitment to the promotion and protection of librarianship throughout the world gave the profession for the first time a worthy successor to the polymath library genius of our own Dewey;*

WHEREAS, *Ranganathan in achieving a degree of international recognition unparalleled in this century by any other librarian gave the profession for the first time a signal example of penetrating abstraction never divorced from profound spirituality;*

WHEREAS, *The ALA ALCTS CCS Subject Analysis Committee program of June 28, 1992, "Gearing Up for the Future" will commemorate the enduring contributions of Ranganathan in facet analysis as a father of the information professions;*

WHEREAS, *The international library community will honor his life and work at the ISKO 1992 Ranganathan Centenary Conference in the city of Madras; now, therefore, be it*

RESOLVED, *That the American Library Association send its greetings to the international conference in Madras and on behalf of the entire American library community, join in affirming his enduring contribution; and be it further*

RESOLVED, *That this greeting be conveyed by the ALA to the IFLA Section on Classification and Indexing.*

ADOPTED BY THE
COUNCIL OF THE AMERICAN LIBRARY ASSOCIATION (ALA)
January 29, 1992, San Antonio, Texas

Linda F. Crismond

Linda F. Crismond
Secretary to ALA Council

AMERICAN LIBRARY ASSOCIATION
EXECUTIVE OFFICE
LINDA F. CRISMOND
EXECUTIVE DIRECTOR

AMERICAN · LIBRARY · ASSOCIATION · 1876

50 EAST HURON STREET CHICAGO, ILLINOIS 60611 U.S.A.
EXECUTIVE DIRECTOR 312-280-3215 DEPUTY DIRECTOR 312-280-3208
COUNCIL/BOARD SECRETARIAT 312-280-3203 FAX 312-944-3897

MEMORIAL RESOLUTION EXPRESSING APPRECIATION FOR THE CONTRIBUTIONS OF DR. S.R. RANGANATHAN (1892-1972) ON THE 100TH ANNIVERSARY OF HIS BIRTH

WHEREAS, *S.R. Ranganathan devoted 48 years of his life working with the Indian Libraries; and*

WHEREAS, *He was instrumental in supporting many international programs including IFLA, FID and UNESCO projects which have helped libraries and information science to advance and improve; and*

WHEREAS, *S.R. Ranganathan was successful in introducing **Colon Classification, Five Laws of Library Science, Classified Catalogue Code**, library terminology, among many other contributions; and*

WHEREAS, *He was instrumental in establishing closer relations between the East and West, and encouraging cooperation at all levels of librarianship and library education; and*

WHEREAS, *S.R. Ranganathan succeeded in making library science an important subject for study and research; now, therefore, be it*

RESOLVED, *That the American Library Association on the birth centennial of an international giant, S.R. Ranganathan expresses the gratitude of its members to him for his contribution, many years of dedication and outstanding service to the promotion of international librarianship; and be it further*

RESOLVED, *That the American Library Association extends its best wishes to the Indian Library Association and Indian Librarians on the occasion of Dr. S.R. Ranganathan's birth centennial celebrations; and be it further*

RESOLVED, *That copies of this resolution be forwarded to the President of the Indian Library Association, Documentation Research and Training Center, University of Madras Library, and School of Library and Information Science University of Delhi, India.*

ADOPTED BY THE COUNCIL OF THE AMERICAN LIBRARY ASSOCIATION (ALA)
January 29, 1992, San Antonio, Texas

Linda F. Crismond

Linda F. Crismond
Secretary to ALA Council

APPENDIX-II

Remembering Ranganathan: A Sentimental Reflection

Nasser Sharify (1925-2013)
Dean Emeritus & Distinguished Professor
Pratt Institute, New York, New York

It was an afternoon in September of 1964 that I found myself in the presence of an intellectual giant. His small, fragile body wrapped in a delicate, light brown skin, mystic, like the clouds of the twilight. His angelic white robe protecting him, yet providing him the freedom of movement, like the white wind that goes where it goes. His mind, fresh and fluid, vast like the ocean, deep like the dawn. He lived with me for twenty-one days.

The University of Pittsburgh honored him with an honorary doctorate. He honored my home, and my family with his presence. Everyday I took him to the School of Library and Information Science, where as a junior member of the faculty, I taught cataloging and classification, and described Dr Ranganathan's colon classification every semester to my students. And he, as a distinguished visiting lecturer enriched the mind of the student and the faculty.

Every evening I cooked for him, a combination of vegetables, the imitation of what I was eating in 1947 and 1948 in New Delhi, while as a poet in residence and reporter of All India Radio.

I was lost in the complexity of hundreds of life's questions, and he was the answer, clear, thoughtful, and precise. We talked and talked every night on the terrace of my home about language, religion, and theory of classification. He told the tales of life, and played with my children, affectionately, warmly, childishly.

Forty-two years have passed. I still remember every day of those twenty-one unforgettable days that an Indian intellectual giant lived in my home in 995 Summer Place, Mount Lebanon, Pittsburgh.

Author Index

Glossary

Abstract entity : In contrast to a concrete entity an abstract entity is an intangible conceptual object which cannot be perceived by any of the sense organs. An abstract entity is a construct of the mind, and outside the mind it has only manifestations. Examples are goodness, love, bravery, honesty. In J. Kaiser's terms it is a process or action.

Adapting a KO system : Making changes in a standard classification system here and there to suit local conditions. It may also involve extension of some classes to classify local subjects for which there is no satisfactory provision in the system used by the library.

Agglomeration : A mode of formation of federated multidisciplinary subjects. Subjects by this mode are a group of main classes which are near neighbors and are bound either by related subject matter, or employ similar research methodology. Examples of Agglomerates are, Social sciences, Bio sciences, Behavioral sciences, etc. In his CC Ranganathan also calls them partially comprehensive main classes.

Anteriorising common isolates : In the CC some forms of approach documents are designated by what are called anteriorising common isolates. These ACIs when applied to a class number decrease its ordinal value and bring it to the fore position. Such documents such as bibliographies, dictionaries, periodicals, glossaries, syllabi, biographies etc. are considered as approach documents to study the subject proper. The anteriorising position is obtained by fixing the ordinal value of ACI digits. For example, Ba, Bibliography of Mathematics files before B Mathematics on the shelves, so will do Bk Encyclopedia of mathematics.

APUPA pattern : A pedagogical order of documents on the shelves or entries in a classified catalog which is logical and its order is in the way a learner goes about the subject. This pattern arranges the documents from general to specific and to advanced subjects. It is ingeniously obtained by fixing the ordinal value of common isolates and the indicator digits.

A = Alien, P = Penumbral, U = Umbral. Arrangement of documents on the shelves is in the order in which core documents represented by umbral region, having 100% subject matter density, are preceded by alien and penumbral regions and followed by penumbral and alien regions. P on the left of U refers to the approach subjects to the core documents such as bibliographies or glossaries of the subjects, while penumbral on the right of umbral region represents advanced subjects such as criticism, research, research centers or professional associations. A represents the related subjects in the discipline. For example, if physics is an umbral region, then A on the left is mathematics and on the right is astronomy. Ranganathan has been able to achieve this self learning pattern by assigning different ordinal values to the common isolates (CIs) divided into two groups of ACIs and PCIs.

By using two types of common isolates in the CC Ranganathan is able to achieve somewhat pedagogical sequence of documents on the library shelves. Here U stands for core documents for the study of the subject, while Ps on both the sides denote documents of lesser subject density. P on the left of U is zone of approach documents to reach the core U, while P on its right is for advanced studies say, research, critical studies or advanced centers for study of the subject. A on both the sides represents closest neighbouring subjects. Thus a learner makes his/her way from preliminary documents to core documents and finally to advanced documents. APUPA pattern is considered as an aid to self learning. This could only be achieved by dividing common isolates of two categories of anteriorising and posteriorising common isolates.

A P U P A P U P A P U P A P U P A P U P A P U P A

Array : A group of cognate entities/classes of equal rank, having the same genus, and arranged in some predictable/systematic and helpful order.

Ascertainable : Something that can be known or described objectively, or can be demonstrated concretely.

Ascertain-ability Canon : A canon in the Idea Plane for the choice of characteristics which mandates that the characteristics we choose to divide the universe /group of entities should itself be ascertainable and concrete, that is knowable. It should be objective and demonstrable. Human beings cannot be divided on the basis of their previous birth as it is not knowable. Date of death for living persons is not knowable. Hence these should not be used as characteristics. But date of birth is knowable. It can be used as a characteristics to divide a universe of human beings.

Asymmetrical relations : A phase relation in which one phase (secondary) is used to study the exposition of the other (primary) subject. Bias, Influencing and Tool relations are asymmetrical.

Attribute : Any quality or aspect of an entity. An entity has numerous attributes which go on increasing when we move from general to specific. An attribute becomes a characteristic when used as the basis of division in classification.

Author number : An alphanumeric number denoting the name of the author/editor/any heading for alphabetical sub-arrangements of the books having the same class numbers. Strictly speaking, it is a part of the book number.

Author number vs Book number : Quite often the author number alone is able to individualize a book within the same specific class. In that case, it is a book number. But more often than not, it fails to do so. It may further require specification by addition of work number (title) or author's initial in case of biographies. So in such cases, the author number is a part of the book number. Also it may be borne in mind that author number is not always derived from author's name. In case of biographies, it is derived from the subject i.e. name of the biographee, or it may be derived from the title of the book in case cataloguing entry is made under the title. Similar is the case with critical works of literature. Book number = Author number + Work number

Automated classification system : As contrasted from usual print systems, automated library classification systems are in a machine readable data format. Their standard for formatting is *MARC21 Concise Format for Classification Data* (2003).

Autonomy to classifiers : Inbuilt provisions in a classification system to carry on the work of classification by a classifier in face of non-availability of class numbers/ isolates for new subjects. It is mostly provided by hospitality and synthetic devices. It also means freedom to classifiers to make choices where needed.

Base of notation : Total number of digits in a notational system. Base of notation in DDC is only 10, while in CC it is 74. In the Library of Congress Classification it is 26+10. Longer the base, larger the capacity of notation to provide unique class numbers.

Basic subject : A subject which is usually a main class or the first facet in the facet formula. It is a subject without an isolate idea. Main classes taken together form the first array of the division of the universe of knowledge. Basic subjects are postulated by the classification system. Their number and boundaries vary with time.

It is a subject without any isolate idea e.g., Physics, Marxian economics, or Algebra. These are limited in numbers and vary in each classification system. Within each system these may vary from edition to edition.

Book number : A device to sub-arrange documents in a library having the same ultimate class number. Mostly two alternate systems are popular for book numbering, namely alphabetical by author, and chronological by the year of publication. Alphabetical systems alphanumerically encode the heading under which the documents have been cataloged by AACR. Chronological systems sub arrange documents by the year of publication.

For alphabetical systems mostly Cutter tables are used, whereas chronological method was invented by W.S. Biscoe for the DDC, but perfected by S.R. Ranganathan for his CC. Apart from these two there are other numerous well known but less used system designed for special materials such as literary works, periodicals, biographies, fiction etc. In the Library of Congress Classification book number is an integral part of the Call number. These are also known as author or cutter numbers. Book numbers may also be designed locally.

Boolean operations : Logical or algebraic operations in online post-coordinate searching and retrieval involving variables with two values A and B to perform a search using operators AND, OR, NOT to retrieve a desired grouping.

Broad classification : A classification whose subdivisions are not detailed and therefore only make broader groups of documents on the shelves. It also means classifying books broadly without making use of detailed subdivisions of the system employed. For example, using abridged DDC instead of the frill edition.

Broken order : Localized arrangement of documents on the shelves in which related subjects are brought together irrespective of their place in a standard classification scheme. For example, most of the DDC classified libraries place 400 languages alongside 800 literature thus breaking the sequence. (See also Shattered order)

Browsing : Browsing is to look at library collections without any specific purpose – a sort of window shopping. Browsing results in incidental discoveries of valuable books in the library stacks. Browsing is a pastime of scholars who visit a library. Open access to shelves and a systematic classification are essential for browsing.

Call number : A composite number comprising of class number, book number and collection number which provides a unique and complete shelf address of the document in a library. It consists of section/collection number, class number and the book number taken in this order. Every document has its individual call number as is your telephone number or motor vehicle registration number.

Call number= Collection number + Class number + Book number.

Canonical Class : Some main classes are first divided into traditional classes instead of directly dividing them into categories. Thus a canonical class is a sort of basic class which has its roots in tradition. For example, mathematics is divided into its canonical classes of Arithmetic, Algebra, Geometry, Analysis etc, and Physics is divided into canonical classes such as Mechanics, Heat, Light, Electricity.

Canons : Normative principles applicable to a sub-discipline, e.g. canons of cataloguing; canons of books selection. Ranganathan has formulated canons for work in all the three planes of classification work. (See Appendix-I to Chapter 2, pp. 59-63). Also there are canons of book selection, and canons of cataloguing formulated by Ranganathan.

Capacity of notation : A quantitative measure of the total class numbers a notational system can provide. For example, quantity of three digit class number the DDC can provide is (10^3) 1000, while in RIC it is (26X3) 17576. Larger the base of the notation higher its capacity.

Cardinal digits : Numbers or symbols which depict measure of quantity or status of some entity. Cardinal numbers impliedly are also ordinal in nature, e.g., 1, 2, 3 ... are both cardinal and ordinal numbers.

Category : An umbrella term for very broad division of knowledge. A category is very broad and general division of the universe into homogeneous groups at the seminal level. It is a concept of high generality and wide applications which can be used to group other entities or concepts. Categories are ultimate generic or seminal ideas at the bottom of all the patterns.

Ranganathan's postulates that all the concepts in the universe of knowledge essentially fall in any of the five fundamental categories. He further believed there are five and only five fundamental categories in the universe of knowledge denoted by PMEST. Many modern library scientists do not believe in this postulate of Five Fundamental Categories. They equate categories with facets, and number of facets is much more in the universe.

A category is mostly taken synonymous with facets in the modern classification theory. But in Ranganathan's CC the facets occur within a category.

Chain : A sequence of classes in successive

subordination or in genus-species, or hierarchical order. In a chain entities get arranged automatically in their decreasing extension. Chain moves vertically downwards arranging entities in successive decreasing extension or increasing specificity. A family lineage forms a chain.

Characteristic : It is an attribute, basis or criterion of division or grouping in classification. If a group is divided into Hindus, Muslims, Christians, Sikhs, etc. then religion is the characteristic. It is a sort of a hammer to break the mass of knowledge into constituents. Quality of the characteristics and the order in which these are applied determine the utility value and aptness of the classification thus produced.

Chronological book number : Book numbers which sub arrange books in order of the year of their publication. Chronological book numbers, which originated from the accession order, have been elaborated by W.S. Biscoe, J.D. Brown. S.R. Ranganathan took it to almost perfection.

Chronological device (CD) : A device to (Time) from new isolates by converting a chronological facet into personality facet.

Chronological order : It is the arrangement of entities in an array in historical order, or as they occur in time. For example, Indian prime ministers, Nehru, Shastri, Indira Gandhi... Manmohan Singh, and Modi are arranged in chronological order. People standing in a queue are also in this order, so is the principle of "first come first served". It is also called historical order or time sequence.

Citation order : Order of the facets in a compound subject or subject heading showing their syntactical relations. PMEST is one order; concrete/abstract order given by J. Kaiser (1911) is another. All the principles for the facet sequence proposed by Ranganathan such as the Wall-Picture principle, or the cow-calf principle are also for citation order. Comprehensive citation order formulated by the CRG, London is: Thing-Kind-Part-Property-Material-Process-Operation-Patient-Product-Byproduct-Agent-Place-Time. It depicts syntactical relations among facets.

Class : A set of entities having at least one characteristic in common. A class can be small or big, even universally big, e.g., all the Indians make one class, and all Christians make another class. A class may even consist of one member only.

Classification : It is a process of dividing or grouping entities on the basis of likeness or some underlying relation. Ultimately, classification is organization and co-relation. It is grouping, selecting, sorting, ordering, tabulating, ranking, mapping, structuring. In context of library science it is also making classification schedules and operating classification systems.

Classificationist : A person who designs a classification system, an engineer or architect of a knowledge organization system

Classifier : Any person who classifies. An individual who applies a classification system to the library documents in accordance with the policy of the library. A classifier is an operator of the system as distinguished from the classificationist who is a designer of the system.

Collateral arrays : Two or more arrays are said to be collateral to one another if all the members in all these arrays are of equal rank and their immediate parental classes emanate from the same source. For example array that you and your siblings form is collateral to the one formed by your first cousins. In the DDC the array formed by 310/390 is collateral to the array 510/590.

Collection number : A symbol and part of the call number which denotes and refers to the section of the library holding a certain type of documents, such as

Manuscripts section, Textbooks section or Periodical publications section. The library's holdings are divided into section for convenience of management and safety of documents. This division makes a library a cluster of libraries within : libraries within a library. Ranganathan recommends the following symbols /notation for the section/collection number :

R Reference

RR Rare book

T Thesis

Tx Text

G Government publication

RP Reports

For departmental libraries Ranganathan suggests the following convention:

BD Mathematics Department

DD Engineering Department

LD Medical College

RD Philosophy Department

YD Sociology Department

ZD Law Department

But for the abnormal books Ranganathan gives the following rules:

Underline the book number for small sized books

Over line the book number for large sized books

Both underline and over line the book number for abnormal books

Encircle the book number for worn out and fragile books.

Common auxiliaries : Known by various names in different classification systems these are non-subject recurring features of documents. These are subdivisions commonly applicable to the class numbers in the main schedules. Their name and notation remains the same wherever applied. In the CC these are known as common isolates, and in the DDC, standard subdivisions. These make the system synthetic and notation mnemonic. Over the years their number and variety have increased. In the DDC there are now six such tables. Ranganathan once envisaged to convert all the special isolates (subject divisions) into a few common isolates. Indeed in the CC-7 the tables and number of various common isolates is amazing.

Common isolates : Some recurring non subjects divisions for the forms of documents are applicable across the schedule. Examples are: bibliographies, dictionaries, glossaries, journals, research, professional associations, critical studies etc. They get meaning only when get attached to a class numbers. By themselves they do not make any class numbers. In the CC these all of two types : ACIs and PCIs.

Complex subjects : Two phased subjects such as "psychology for nurses". These are formed by loose-assemblage mode of formation. An interdisciplinary subject comprising of two phases, e.g., Relation between history and geography; Comparative study of Indian and British Constitutions. Earlier fused subjects were also seen as complex subjects. Now, fused subjects are mostly basic subjects.

Compound subject : A subject comprising of a basic subject and one or more isolate ideas, e.g. Agriculture of wheat, Library science in India in the 21st century. Number of isolates attached to a basic class determine the depth/ intension of the subject. Their number in the universe of knowledge is almost infinite.

Concomitance canon : A canon in the Idea Plane for the succession of characteristics mandates that the characteristics to be applied one after the other to the same group of entities should not produce the same grouping. It means the two characteristics that we apply should not be the two sides of the same coin. Crows cannot be divided on the basis of their colour. As crows and their colour are concomitant.

Concomitant : Happening at the same time; providing the same result; something synonymous in action.

Concrete : As contrasted from abstract, concrete is an object or phenomena which can be perceived by any of the sense organs, e.g. Table, music, pungent odour, sour, soft. It corresponds to thing or entity in Kaiser's terms.

Concreteness : Quality of an entity of being perceived by any of the five senses; something objective, not subjective.

Context Canon : A canon in the Verbal Plane which recommends that classes should be listed and read in the context of upper class. For example,

Salts

Single,

Double,

Complex

means single salt, double salt and complex salt respectively. It is for elegance and brevity of library classification schedules.

Consistent sequence : A canon in the Idea Plane for formation of arrays of classes. It mandates that the order of classes once chosen should be maintained consistently whenever the same set of classes occurs elsewhere. The entities child, adult, old people occur in many classes such as medicine, psychology, Education, sociology, so their sequence should be the same in every class.

Consistent succession of characteristics : A canon in

the Idea Plane for the succession of characteristics mandates that the sequence of characteristics once determined should be applied consistently in other similar situations. That is the order of characteristics should not vary from time to time or from group to group. It means if Language-Form-period-Work is the sequence of characteristics for English literature then it should be the same for classifying literature in all the languages of the world.

Controlled vocabulary : A set of select terms, free of homonyms and synonyms, having their own syntax rules. It is also known as Indexing Language. Classification, thesauri, thesaurofacets, subject heading lists, taxonomies, ontologies, folksonomies, FAST are all examples of CVs.

Copy cataloguing : The act of using or adapting the cataloguing record(including class number) prepared by some outside centralized or commercial agency. Examples are downloading data from MARC records on the web or using CIP record given in the document. National bibliographies, or the bibliographic utilities like the OCLC can be used for this purpose

Cross reference : A direction or reference from one term to another in a controlled vocabulary. These references are either to direct the users to the equivalent but preferred terms (see), or to advise them to search under related terms (see also) to widen the search. Cross references can be both individual and general.

Currency Canon : A canon in the Verbal Plane recommends that the terms used in the KO system should be current ones and should be revised from time to time to reflect the current usage. This is necessary for efficient retrival, and also for chain indexing.

Cutter mark : An alphanumeric number taken from any of C.A. Cutter's Author table to convert the Author's name or for that reason any heading, into alpha-numeric symbols for brevity and convenience of shelving and location of the documents.

Cutter author numbers : Alpha-numeric table of authors and their notations designed by C.A. Cutter (1837-1903) to alphabetically sub-arrange books within the same class. Many varying tables of Cutter Author numbers are available. The Library of Congress Classification (LCC) uses these numbers in a very simplified way — usually an alphabet followed by a single decimal numeral. The Cutter numbers in the LCC numbers are used both for alphabetical subject divisions in the ******* as well as book numbers on the shelves.

Cuttering : An eponymous (named after Charles A. Cutter) process of assigning the author number for alphabetical sub-arrangement of books having the same class number. Sub-arrangement code may or may not be taken from Cutter's table. For example, many libraries only use first three initial letters of author's name/heading for sub-arrangement. A book by B.K. Sharma gets the Cutter code SHA. Cuttering has become an eponym in LIS terminology.

Decreasing Extension Canon : A canon in the Idea Plane for formation of chain of classes which mandates that entities in a chain should be kept in order of their increasing specificity, or decreasing generality. For example, World-Asia-South Asia-India are arranged in order of decreasing extension. Adherence to this canon is rather automatic as by definition chain is a sequence of entities in successively decreasing extension or increasing subordination or specificity.

Delivery of Books Act : The Delivery of Books and Newspapers (Public Libraries) Act, 1954 (Amended 1956) mandates every publisher in India to deliver free of charge a copy of publication within 30 days of the release to some designated libraries in India. The National Library at Kolkata and three public libraries in Mumbai, Chennai and Delhi are the legal depositaries of books under the Act.

Dependency order : A citation order of arranging facets/entities in an order in which an entity depends for its existence on its immediately previous entity. Wall-Picture principle as exemplified by Production—Distribution—Consumption order in economics is a dependency order. French philosopher Auguste Comte (1798-1857) suggested dependency order in the arrangement of main classes. Ranganathan order of main classes in science (A/M), in the order of theory-practice, is also a dependency order.

Depth classification : A fully detailed or minute classification which aspires to faithfully translate the specific subject of the document into artificial notation of the system. Its objective, as contrasted from a broader classification, is to individualize each and every document on the shelves. In other words, it is a classification which is capable of providing class numbers co-extensive with the subject of the document. Special subject classifications are usually depth classification.

Devices for sharpening or creating isolates : To make some vague or broad isolates more specific, or to altogether create new isolates, if required Ranganathan formulated some conceptual devices. These are Subject device (SD), Chronological device (CD), Geographical device (GD), Superimposition device (SID), Alphabetical device (AD) and Classic device (ClD). These devices provide autonomy to classifiers and help to continue the work of classification even if some isolates are not found enumerated for the new concepts. On the dint of such devices Ranganathan called his classification as a self-perpetuating one. These devices empower the classifier with autonomy.

Dichotomy : Simplistically dividing entities into two groups at every step, e.g. all the entities in the world are divided into two groups of living and non-living, or into males and females.

It is also known as tree of Porphyry after the Neo-platonic philosopher (c. 234–c. 305 AD)

Division by dichotomy

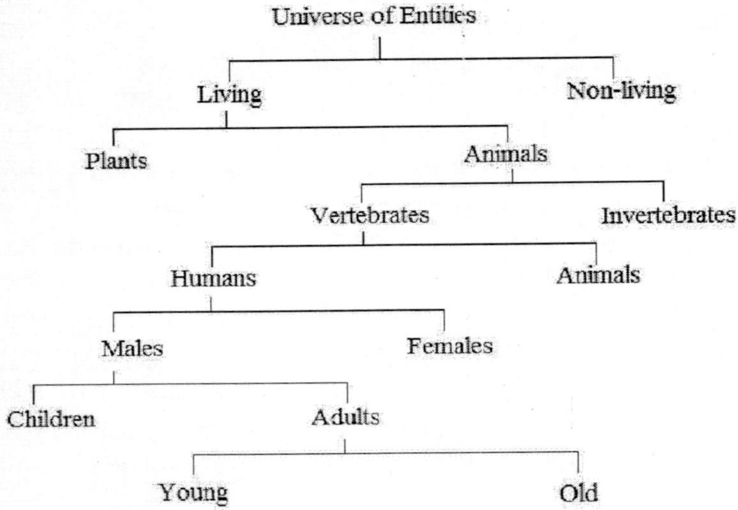

Dictionary catalogue : Catalogue in which all sorts of entries are filed in a single A/Z dictionary order.

Differentiation Canon : A canon in the Idea Plane for the choice of a characteristics mandates that the characteristics we choose to divide the universe /group of entities should be able to divide the universe at least into two groups. It also means that the characteristics of division should not be common to all the entities. Human beings cannot be divided on the basis of having two legs, but they can be divided by their skin color. Color differentiates human beings.

Digit : A single character in a notation(whether semantic or indicator) say 9, A, or + : , etc.

Discipline : A broader area or compartment of the

universe of knowledge forming a major cohesive area of knowledge based upon a particular research methodology or having similar objects of studies.

It is the first order division of the knowledge into organized and coherent chunks of knowledge for convenience of study and organizing knowledge. The three primitive disciplines are natural sciences, social sciences, and humanities. Now all our classification systems are discipline based.

Dissection : A process of formation of specialized subjects by breaking a larger subject into smaller area once at a time. Example are say dividing literature into poetry, Plays, fiction, prose, satire, or say dividing the earth into its seven continents, namely Asia, Africa, Europe, Antarctica, Americas, Australia, etc. Resulting subjects form an array of classes of equal rank.

Distillation : A mode of formation of unitary type interdisciplinary subjects. Such subjects are formed when the similar process or methods used in different disciplines are gathered into a coherent theory as in the distillation of a new liquid from various compounds. Examples are Research methodology, Management science, Career-ology which are newly postulated main classes in the CC.

Documentation Research and Training Centre (DRTC, Bengaluru) : DRTC (http://drtc.isibang.ac.in/DRTC/) was established in January 1962 as a division of the Indian Statistical Institute. P.C. Mahalanobis, in full Prasanta Chandra Mahalanobis (1893-1972), Indian statistician who was instrumental in formulating India's strategy for industrialization in the Second Five-Year Plan (1956–61) was an influential member of the Planning Commission and was then Director of Indian Statistical Institute. He, who had all along been engaged in perspective planning, sensed a strong correlation between industrial productivity and research in the country. He was convinced that quality research (both basic and applied) in turn depends on prompt and pinpointed documentation services to researchers. Therefore as early as 1956, he had requested Ranganathan, who was then in Zurich, to come back to India and establish a school for training manpower to provide information services to industry. S.R. Ranganathan in early 1960s was already imparting training in librarianship at Malleshwaram, a suburb of Bangalore. Later with the goodwill and support of Prof P C Mahalanobis his library school was merged with Indian Statistical Institute and named the DRTC. Thus was born the DRTC at the Bangalore centre of Indian Statistical Institute. The DRTC has grown into a world class institute of higher learning, training and research in all aspects of information management. In its early days it did lot of research on classification theory, though at present it focus has widened on rather comprehensively to include both the traditional and modern aspects of library and information science, and big data (http://drtc.isibang.ac.in/DRTC/)

e-documents : It is an abbreviated term for electronic documents, that is documents that exist only in electronic or digital form such as data stored on a computer, network, backup, archive or other such computer readable storage media. Examples of documents subject to e-discovery are emails, voicemails, instant messages, audio files, data on handheld devices, animation, multimedia, metadata, graphics, photographs, spreadsheets, websites, drawings and other types of digital data. An electronic document is any electronic media content (other than computer programs or system files) are intended to be used in either an electronic form or as printed output.

Educational and scientific consensus : A great US librarian and classificationist H.E. Bliss (1870-1955) tried to discover an order of main classes based upon the consensus of educationists and scientists. He used such an order in his system of Bibliographic Classification (BC,1940-1953).

Empty – Emptying Digit : A digit which is both empty and emptying U, W and Y are Empty-Emptying digits in the CC. These are used for interpolation in an array.

Empty digit : A digit having only ordinal value and without any semantic value. In the CC 0,9,z and Z are empty digits in lower order arrays. It means these are not used to denote any isolate number.

Emptying digit : A digit which takes away the semantic power of the preceding digit but allows it to retain its ordinal value. T,V and X are Emptying Digits in the CC. For example K in the digit pair KX has nothing to do with Zoology, but KX will file between K and L. In fact KX becomes a fused pair treated *de jure* as a single digit.

Energy : A Fundamental Category of CC which menifests action or problems, e.g., designing, repairing, surgery, solving, welfare actions, etc.

Entity : Any abstract or concrete object or phenomenon that exists. In this universe anything we experience or perceive is an entity.

Enumeration Canon : A canon in the Verbal Plane recommends that scope of classes in a schedule of classification should be indicated by listing all the subclasses, not by any definition. This is to avoid controversies or any ambiguity on boundaries of classes in a classification system.

Enumerative classification : A classification systems which lists in a systematic way all the basic, compound and the complex subjects of the past, present and likely future: a kind of classification which is a systematic list along with their ready-made class numbers of all the subjects of the past, present and the foreseeable future. The Library of Congress Classification (LCC) is considered as the most outstanding example of this species of classification. However, the age of such systems has come to a close giving way to faceted system. The LCC thrives on its institutional strength.

Environmental basic subject : In the CC a main class studied from the view point of a unique environment. For example, Desert biology, or High altitude engineering, or Deep space physiology.

Evolutionary order : Order of classes in the natural, chronological sequence of their origin and development in time. This order is taxonomic and cosmic, for example systems of governments such as Anarchy, Feudal, Theocratic, Monarchy, Oligarchy Democracy, and Welfare state are listed here in an evolutionary order.

Exhaustiveness Canon : A canon in the Idea Plane for formation of arrays of classes mandates that the array of classes should be exhaustive of its immediate universe. It means no entity should be left out in listing of eligible and relevant entities in the array. If we divide the universe of human beings into males and females then it is not exhaustive as it leaves out the third gender. In practical classification adherence to this canon is secured by listing 'others' at the end of the array.

Exclusiveness Canon : A canon in the Idea Plane for formation of arrays of classes. It mandates that an entity should belong to one and only one array. It means that dogs should either be kept under Canidae or domestic animals, not under both. Its violation results in what is called cross classification. But in electronic databases/OPACs exclusiveness is no more necessary. Its violation is a boon which may provide an extra access point.

External notation : Another name for book/author numbers. A notation other than for the class number. It is termed so as it denotes some external characteristics of the document whereas the internal characteristics of the document are denoted by the class number.

Facet : A subgroup of equally ranked entities obtained by the applications of single characteristics to a group. A facet is mostly taken synonyms with category in the Western literature. However, on the Ranganathan's CC the facets occur within a category. In Literature there are four facets, namely, Language, Form Author and Work of the Personality Category.

Facet analysis : The process of breaking a subject into its constituent topics and assigning each concept to any of the pre-determined category. Another name for subject analysis.

Facet formula : A generalized citation order of categories and facets which holds true across the main classes. It shows syntactic relations. In the CC, it is famous as PMEST order. Kaiser's order of Things-process is the skimpiest facet formula

Faceted classification : Opposed to an enumerative classification, a faceted classification system is that which only enumerates basic subjects and their constituents divided into facets in addition to some common sub-divisions separately. It provides syntactical rules for their combination to synthesize (construct) compound and complex subjects. Current trend in classification is towards finely faceted systems.

FID : FID was established on 12 September, 1895, in Brussels, as the International Institute of Bibliography (originally Institut International de Bibliographie, IIB) by two Belgian lawyers, Paul Otlet (1868-1944) and Henri La Fontaine (1854-1943). Its headquarters shifted to The Hague after 1934. It has gone through a number of changes in name as under to reflect change of scope of the field in which it operates:

1931 : The International Institute for Documentation (Institut International de Documentation, IID).

1937 : The International Federation for Documentation (Fédération Internationale de Documentation, FID).

1988 : The International Federation for Information and Documentation (Fédération Internationaled' Information et de Documentation, FID)

FID was dissolved in 2001 due to financial constraints.

Its Committee on Classification FID/CR did lot of research work in classification and instituted a Ranganthan Award for Classification Research in 1976 for an outstanding worker in classification and Indexing. Ranganathan was its honorary Vice-president.

Filiatory sequence canon : A canon in the idea plane for arrangement of entities in the schedule of classes according to their filial affinity. It means all the members of a family should be kept together before forming any collateral family. This applies only to the making of schedules, not in any abstract classes.

Filiatory sequence is a linear arrangement of entities in multiple hierarchies according to their filial affinity. In schedules comprising of many merged/coalesced arrays and chains, a chain should be completed before a new array starts. Simply speaking, in listing members of a large family, children should be placed close to their parents. The term filiatory (derived from filial) does not exist in English dictionary—it is self coined by Ranganathan

Fission : A process of formation of specialized subjects by breaking successively a larger subject into smaller and smaller areas as in a nuclear fission. This denuding process is vertical. Examples are breaking of disciplines into main classes, and dividing and subdividing a main class further into its organized and coherent classes. For example : Social science — Economics — Financial economice — Money and Banking — Money — Coins — Gold coins.

Fixed location systems : A pre-dewey method of arranging books on the shelves which assigned a fixed/ permanent place to a book in the library. For example, call number 4.3.22 meant that it is the 22nd book on the third shelf of 4th Almirah in the library. Though broadly divided by subject it was difficult to maintain subject collocation when an allotted shelf/almirah to a subject was filled. Libraries had to be "reclassified" to maintain subject grouping that involved lot of wastage of time and labor. Melvil Dewey invented relative location method to completely solve these problems. Now all classification systems follow this relative location system

Focus : An individual entity/isolate in a facet. For example, in the Language facet in the Main Class O Literature English language is the focus, so is, say, German or Sanskrit language

Form classes : A non-fiction publication always has a subject and form (of its presentation). In "Journal of Commerce" journal is the form, and commerce is the subject. But sometimes the form itself becomes the subject, then it is a form class. In *History of Journals,* journals is the subject, whereas history is its form. "Cyclopediology" is the subject on the form cyclopedias. All the library classification systems reserve a place, usually among the generalia class, for such subjects. In the DDC 030, 050, 060 and 090 are form classes. In the CC form main classes are denoted by a/y.

Form of the document : In the CC it refers mostly to the internal format or the mode of presentation of the subject, e.g., a book in pictures, or in data tables, or the subject presented in a dictionary or chronological order. It also refers to the external formats such as microfilm, or CD-ROM.

Fusion : A mode of formation of unitary multi-disciplinary subjects by permanently fusing two subjects to form a new subject with new characters. The process may be like cross breeding of subjects to form a subject with new genes. Of the numerous examples some are, Geophysics, Biochemistry, Medical jurisprudence, Social darwinism. This seems the most trendy mode of formation of new subjects due to team and collaborative research. This multidisciplinary mode is antidote to too much specialization which has acquired morbid depths and isolates professionals working in the same field.

General classification : Library classification for all subjects and all forms of documents such as the CC or DDC.

Generalia class : In the universe of knowledge, there are no generalia subjects, each subjects has its unique place there. But there are generalia documents which cover topics across many subjects. A newspaper covers everything under the sun. Limca book of facts is not confined to one subject. A library classification has to provide a place to such subjects which usually precede the disciplinary classes. It is termed as Generalia class. In the DDC, the Division 010-090 is reserved for such documents. Generalia classes also include form classes. In the CC these classes are denoted by a/y.

Genus and species : Genus is any original universe to be divided into species by adding some characteristic to the genus. These are relative terms. A father is a genus for the children; when children become father/mother they will be genus for their own children. Table is Genus, and dining or study tables are its species.

Helpful sequence : Order of entities in an array which is helpful or of some aid to majority of the library users. However, no one order can be helpful to all the users. Ranganathan has given eight systematic orders in which entities in an array can be helpfully arranged. This order prevails mostly in the main classes, their branches and further subdivisions of equal rank in an array.

It is a systematic arrangement of entities of an array in a way which is helpful to majority of users. There is no one order which is helpful to all users. Ranganathan has formulated eight principles for helpful order to be applied suitably depending upon the nature of entities. At the same time, Ranganathan has stipulated that exception for helpful order may be made "When any other overwhelming consideration rules it out".

Hierarchy : A system or arrangement of classes according to their successive rank or status. A chain depicts a hierarchy of classes. The World, Asia, South Asia, India, North India, Delhi are in hierarchic order. Genus-species, or whole-part relations are also hierarchic. A family lineage is also hierarchic.

Homonym : A word having the same form, spelling but many different meanings. For example, cricket is a game as well as an insect. Bridge is a game as well as a pathway connecting two sides of a water body, or another path. It is a case of many (things) – one (word) mapping between things and words. A terminology should be free from homonyms.

Hospitality of notation : An essential quality of every notation to accommodate new subjects at their proper places without disturbing the existing ones. Ranganathan tackled the problem of hospitality in two dimensions of arrays and chains separately. In the array he used the traditional Gap device, but for extrapolation he invented what was called octave device later raised to sector device by earmarking 9,z Z as the sectorising digit. Later he also invented the empty and emptying digits devices for interpolation of new subjects. In the chain the fraction device used by the DDC is applicable to all the hierarchical notations. By using so many devices for hospitality Ranganathan made the CC notation most hospitable of all notational systems

Hybrid systems : A new breed of classification systems with enumerative antecedents with grafting of features and facilities of a faceted system. The current edition of the DDC falls in this category.

Idea plane : The first and the most important phase of classification designing work which settles the theory, prepares plans and blueprint of the entire work. The work in the Idea plane ends with a systematic network of classes in arrays and chains.

IFLA : Founded in Edinburgh, Scotland, in 1927 The International Federation of Library Associations and Institutions (IFLA) is the leading international body representing the interests of library and information services providers and their patrons. As the global voice of the library and information profession, it has now over 1500 members in approximately 150 countries around the world. IFLA was registered in the Netherlands in 1971. The Royal Library, the national library of the Netherlands, in The Hague, is its headquarters. In 1992 IFLA held its annual conference in New Delhi, India to commemorate the birth centenary of Dr. S R Ranganathan. Its section on Classification and Indexing promotes research and studies in this area.

Index : A list of concepts and names in a predictable order for retrieval of information; a tool to navigate the body of its information to locate terms and concepts. Majority of indexes are in alphabetical order.

In context of a classification system, it is the alphabetical key to all the terms and concepts in the schedules and auxiliary tables along with their class numbers. A good index, as of the DDC, is not only an alphabetical approach but also presents a supplementary or alternative structure of knowledge. The CC 6th edition has many indexes

Indexing : The process of applying an index, or tagging description, to items in the information store with pointed references for full retrieval and recall.

Indexing language : A set of select vocabulary showing semantic and syntactical relations used for knowledge organization and information retrieval. Also known as controlled vocabulary. The CC, DDC, LCSH and Art and Architecture Thesaurus (AA&T) are outstanding examples of controlled vocabulary. (See also Controlled vocabulary).

Information : Data or signals intercepted by the sense organs from the environment and processed by the brain into meaning: something communicated or obtained through reading and observation. It is structured and inferred data.

Internet : Internet is a global system of interconnected computer networks that use the standard Internet protocol suite (TCP/IP) to link several billion devices worldwide. It is an international network of networks that consists of millions of private, public, academic, business, and government packet switched networks, linked by a broad array of electronic, wireless, and optical networking technologies. The Internet carries an extensive range of information resources and services, such as the inter-linked hypertext documents and applications of the World Wide Web (WWW), the infrastructure to support email, and peer-to-peer networks for file sharing and telephony.

Intra-array relations : A relation more specialized than intra-facet relation occurring between two isolates of the same array of the same facet and within the same category. E.g.: Relation between college and university libraries, or difference between Protestant and Roman Catholic sects.

Intra-facet relations : Interactive relation between two facets of the same category in the same main class, e.g.: Relation between anatomy and physiology, or comparison between Academic and Public libraries, or relation between Christianity and Islam.

Inversion principle : The order of facets in the facet formula is reverse of their shelving order to achieve general to specific order in filing documents.

It is arrangement of the books on the shelves in reverse order of the citation of facets in the facet formula. The CC and UDC follow this principle. In CC the books on the shelves are arranged in the order of TSEMP. In other words, the facets in the PMEST move from concrete to abstract, or specific to general whereas the books on the shelves are arranged in general to specific, or abstract-concrete order.

Isolate : In the CC, it is the smallest unit of knowledge which cannot be further subdivided and cannot stand of its own, for example, child, wheat, oxygen, research are a few examples of isolates. An isolate has to be combined with a basic facet to make any meaning. All the isolates have been divided into two kinds: special and common. Special isolates are exclusive or unique to a given main class.

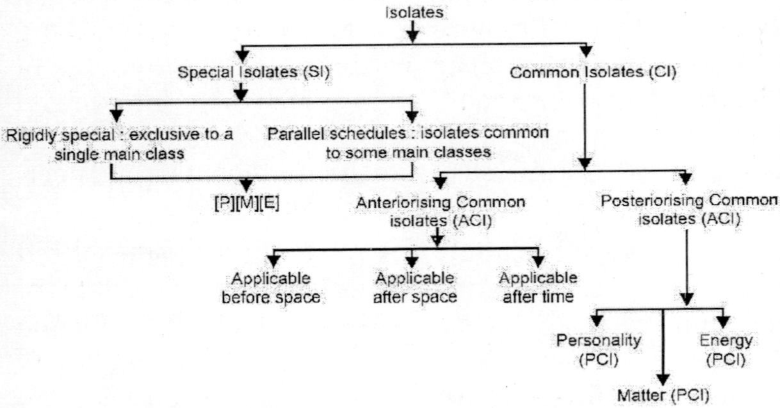

Jevons, W.S. : W.S. Jevons (1835-1882) was a British

economic thinker, philosopher and logician. In economics, he is known for his Law of Marginal Utility. He did much investigations on the "Laws of Thought". His textbooks on logic were widely used. Of his works on logic and scientific methods, the most important is his *Principles of Science* (1874). In library classification he is known for his declaring 'classification as an absurdity'.

Keyword : A word or phrase, usually for free text searching, which is deemed significant to describe, tag and spot the concepts in the body of the text. Keywords are predecessors of subject headings. These are still used for indexing and retrieval.

Knowledge : Sum total of ideas, facts, fiction, expressed feelings, myths, experiences conserved by the human societies. It is generated through discoveries, inventions, experimentation, observation, imagination and speculations. What is known to the society and is held in its collective memory may be called knowledge. It is mostly recorded in print and electronic media and is manifested in all cultural concepts and information bearing objects. Knowledge is what I know, whereas information as what we known. Knowledge is cultural.

Knowledge classification : The process of outlining, structuring and mapping the entire knowledge in abstract or some part of it. It helps to study its evolution and cognitive structure, nature and growth. It is a province of philosophers and scientists. Modern library classifications are based on knowledge classifications. Knowledge classifications are mostly enumerative in nature.

Lamination : A process of formation of specialized subjects by specifying a main class by a topic or restricting its area, e.g., Cultivation of wheat (Agriculture), Human diseases (Medicine). It is done by superimposing one or more laminas of a isolate on a main class. Such subjects are termed as compound subjects in the CC. Thus lamination is the process of turning a basic subject into a compound subject. Theoretically there is no limit on the number of laminae a basic subject can have. Number of laminated subjects is almost infinite in the universe of knowledge.

Language inequality : Refers to the situation when a commentary on a book of literature/languages is written in a language other than of the host book. For example, a book of Hindi literature written in English or Gitanjali by Tagore translated into French, and for that reason, in any language, other than Bengali; Shakespeare's Hamlet in Hindi or in Spanish are instances of language inequality. Similarly, a book on Hindi grammar written in English is also a case of language inequality.

Length of notational base : It is the number of distinct digits a notational system has. The length of base of the DDC notation is 10, while of RIC it is 26. The CC using so many digits has the lengthiest base of notation among all library classifications. Larger the base shorter the class numbers. That is length of base leads to provide shorter class numbers — latter is always welcome by librarians and library users. Larger the length of base of a notational system more its capacity to generate unique class numbers.

Levels (of Facets) : See Rounds and Levels

Library classification : Systematic arrangement of books and other reading material in a library or entries in a catalog in a way useful to the users. Modern library classification is knowledge classification as applied to books and other packages of information for storage and retrival.

Literary forms : A book of creative literature is read for its form and aesthetic pleasure, rather than for its subject, whatever it could be. Literary forms such as Poetry, Fiction, Essays, Satire, are the primary forms, whereas documentary forms such as dictionary, encyclopedia are secondary or auxiliary forms of the documents.

Literary warrant : In library classification, a term and principle given in 1910 by a British librarian Sir Wyndham E. Hulme (1859-1954) which means that a scheme of library classification should be based on and guided by the published literature, i.e., should be only empirical in listing classes and their sub-divisions instead of theoretically dividing the universe of knowledge. It also means that a knowledge Organization System (KOS) should not include those classes on which there is no published literature. The Library of Congress Classification is the best example of a system based on literary warrant.

It also means that classification making should be an inductive, not deductive process. The LC is the best example and method of application of this principle: the scheme was designed by actually classifying books available there, and now it is revised and updated by classifying new books acquired in the library. It means what is not in the LC is not listed in the LCC.

Loose assemblage : A mode of formation of loosely gathered *ad hoc* multidisciplinary subjects. In such mode of formation a subject is studied in relation to others, or is exposed in view of the specific needs of others, such as geometry for painters, Psychology for nurses, Law for doctors. Such subjects are called conflex subjects.

Main class : It is a conventional area of knowledge carved into an accepted, coherent broad field of specialization which gives context to a topic from a specialization aspect of the field. Forming the first array of the division of knowledge in any library classification, the main classes are postulated conveniences to control the universe of knowledge and study it in parts.

Main classes like a classification system are social. Therefore, number of main classes and their order varies from classification to classification. Main classes make a broader map of knowledge. Ranganathan prefers the term basic subject. The CC is based on the following types of main classes:

Main basic subjects

Non-main basic subjects

These are further divided into 10 species. On the basis of their modes of formation the following 10 types of basic subjects have been identified

1.	Main basic subjects	2.	Non-main basic subjects
1.1	Traditional (Law, Physics)	2.1	Canonical classes (Algebra, Geometry)
1.2	Newly emerging (Library & Information Science)	2.2	System constituents (Marxian economy)
1.3	Fused (Biotechnology)	2.3	Environment constituents (Desert farming)
1.4	Distilled (Research methodology)	2.4	Special constituents (Gerontology medicine)
1.5	Subject bundles (Ocean sciences)		
1.6	Agglomerates (Social sciences)		

Matter : A category in the CC comprehending material or a thing acting as medium on which action takes place. In Gold coin, wooden table, marble house or cataloguing microfilms, gold, wood, marble and microfilms represent the matter category respectively.

Micro documents : Compared to macro documents such as books, monographs, micro documents are small packages of information and knowledge such as journal articles, conference papers, or brief research reports, standards and patents, etc. Micro subjects have more intension and less extension. They require depth classification for their organization and retrieval.

Mixed notation : A kind of notation which uses more than one kind of symbols to denote classes. CC, UDC, Library of Congress employ mixed notation of Alphabets, numerals and even punctuation marks. Of all the notational systems that of the CC is the most mixed one.

Mnemonic notation : A notational system having some in built aids to memory, or which is symmetrical. In LCC we have G for Geography, M for Music, T for Technology. CC & DDC try to denote the same concept by the same digits where has it occurs in the schedule. For example in the CC Physiology is always denoted by ': 3' in Medicine, Biology, Animal husbandry, etc. A faceted classification is mnemonics by default. There are three types of mnemonics: alphabetical, scheduled and seminal.

Modulation canon : A canon in the Idea Plane for formation of chain of classes mandates that a chain of classes should be formed in proximate steps; no link should be missing, or there should be no jump but only proximate steps. In other words, there should be no interruption or gap in the chain. For example, the chain, World-Asia-South Asia-New Delhi is not modulated as the link India is missing between South Asia and New Delhi.

Natural language : Everyday language as distinguished from controlled vocabulary, or even notational language - later is termed as an artificial language of ordinal numbers. Ranganathan called it a metalanguage as all indexing languages are derived from it.

Notation : An adjunct of library classification to denote classes and their subdivisions and their auxiliary aspects by a series of short symbols: a system of brief symbols to translate subjects and their subdivisions into ordinal numbers for mechanization of the classified arrangement of subjects on the shelves, or in a classified catalogue. Knowledge classification doesn't need notation.

Notational Plane : The third and the last phase of designing a classification system. Here notation, in the form of short hand symbols, is assigned to the concepts given names and terms in the verbal plane. Ranganathan calls it the servant of the idea plane, but it is the most visible plane of work which faithfully executes the policies and decisions of the Idea plane. A good classification needs an equally good notation. But a bad notation may mar a good classification.

Notes : A variety of explanations, suggestions or instructions appended to an entry in the classification schedules or auxiliary tables. Notes guide and aid the classifier in clear interpretation of the entry for uniformity and consistency in application of the system. Notes enhance inter-indexer consistency in using the system. The CC lacks in such notes in the schedules which however are given in the rules part for inter-indexer consistency in application of the system.

One Place Theory: To collocate all the abstract aspect of a concrete subject around it. Given by the English librarian James Duff Brown for his Subject Classification it is an alternative approach to division by discipline. But it did not work well in mapping knowledge and shelf arrangement of books.

Online Classification : Library classification system prepared as an electronic database and available on the web. Usually electronic systems such as WebDewey have many additional features over and above their print versions. Many products and services can be based on an online classification system. The CC so far is not available online

Ontology : A complex, deep and multi-hierarchical knowledge organization system to describe a knowledge domain depicting seminally deep and wide inter-relations between concepts and terms.

Ordinal value : A system or series of symbols which have no quantitative(cardinal) value but show only the order. Digits of notation of a library classification always have only sequential value, not any substantive or cardinal value. Digits determine the place of the subject, not any measure of its cardinal status or quality. For, example in the DDC 200 means it will file after 100, but in no way is better or weighty than 100. So is the case with the CC which uses the symbols A/Z. Ordinal notation is again of two types: semantic digits which denote subjects, while Indicator digits are signposts to indicate the type of facets in a faceted class number.

Osmosis Method : An administrative or procedural method, suggested by Ranganathan, for reclassifying or re-cataloguing a library without disrupting its services. By this method, only those documents which are in circulation are given new classification numbers. Documents which are no more in current use never get reclassified and may be sent to a depository. Thus this method reduces cost of reclassification and identifies documents which are obsolete or no more in active use. Its disadvantages is that this method is slow and burdens the library in managing two parallel collections having new and old class numbers for some time.

Outsourcing Technical Services : Getting the technical work of processing of documents done by an outside agency on contract basis.

Parallel Sequence : There are libraries within a library each classified by the same system which results in parallel sequence of documents brought together in separate sections by some similarity of format or purpose of service.

Permanence Canon : A canon in the Idea Plane for the choice of characteristics mandates that the characteristics we choose to divide the universe/group of entities should itself be permanent. It should not be fluctuating or keep varying, as the color in chameleons. Color of clothes we wear may not be constant, but our skin color is. Hence latter, not former can be used as a characteristic to divide human beings.

Personality : The first category in the CC facet analysis and synthesis which stands for thing, entity in wholeness of the subject. A sort of fulcrum of the subject on which the subject is built. For example, in Library science, kind of the library is the personality, in agriculture, crop is the personality. In Sociology the Social group is the personality, and in psychology an individual is the personality. In a subject the personality may be latent, or diffused but in fact it is not absent. For example, in Social welfare category personality is diffused, so is in human diseases.

Phase : Dictionary meaning of Phase is a visible stage or process of development. A phase is that portion of the complex class which has been derived from any single basic class. The portion could either be a compound subject or even only a basic subject.

Phase analysis : Analysis of a complex class into its constituent phases and to determine the precedence of one phase over the other.

Phase relation : Any incidental or *ad hoc* relation between two components of a complex class. The CC recognizes six types of relations between two phases of a complex class, namely General, Bias, Comparison, Difference, Tool and Influencing. *See also* Asmmetrical relations.

Phenomena : Any existence, abstract or concrete, in the universe; a fact or event in nature or society. It is any observable occurrence. In scientific usage, a phenomenon is any event that is observable, however common it might be, even if it requires the use of instrumentation to observe, record, or compile data concerning it.

Planes of work (Three) : Division of the work in designing classification systems into three distinct but consecutive and accumulative phases, namely Idea plane, Verbal plane and Notational plane.

PMEST : A famous acronym for Ranganathan five fundamental categories showing their order and intra relations in the specific to general order.

Porphyry Tree : Dichotomous method of classification invented by the Greek philosopher Porphyry (232-304 CE). It divides the universe into two antithetical groups at every step of division, e.g., Living, non-living; Male, Female; Metals, Non-metals; Organic, Inorganic. *See also* Dichotomy.

Post-coordinate indexing : In a search strategy relating two or more terms together at the time of search, now usually using Boolean operators. Uniterms or thesaurui are used for Post-coordinate indexing.

Posteriorising Common Isolates (PCIs) : Some documents such as research in or critical studies of the subject, its research centers or professional associations are better read after the full study of the core subject. Such aspects are denoted by posteriorising common isolates and get placed after the core subjects. In the CC, these are again of three kinds: personality, matter and energy indicated by their respective indicator digits.

Postulate : An assumed or self evident law or regularity at the lowest level of normative principles. It is a working assumption to start with. It can neither be proved, or disproved. It is either helpful or unhelpful. Its foremost example is the postulate of 'Five and only five fundamental categories'. Sometime it is too obvious to be proved, e.g., the assumption in the CC that every compound and complex subject has a basic subject. It is just like saying every child has a parent. With experience or discovery of new facts a postulate may be replaced by a better one.

Postulational approach : Work of classifying or

designing classification systems based on a pre-mediated theory in the form of Normative Laws, Canons, Principles, and Postulates.

Pre-coordinate indexing : Use of two or more terms in a pre-determined sequence before search to be used as a single whole. A classification number say of DDC, or terms from the LCSH or headings derived by chain indexing are used for pre-coordinate indexing. It is used both in online and manual environments.

Primary phase : The first phase of a complex subject which enshrines the subject *per se* of the document.

Principles : Rules for regulating the work of some normative laws. For example, Principles for helpful sequence, or Cow-Calf Principle for facet sequence, or Principles of alphabetization of entries in a dictionary catalog.

Pure notation : A notational system which uses only one kind of symbols. The DDC using Indo-Arabic numerals and the RIC using Roman alphabets are examples of pure notation. These days a pure notation finds it extremely difficult to cope with the growing knowledge and subsequently very complex classification systems. Pure notation is on its way out in practice.

Reclassification : It is the process of replacing class numbers of the whole collection by a newly selected classification system, or modifying class number of a few books according to a new edition of the system already in vogue in the library. Reclassification is a costly, time taking process, so mostly dreaded and avoided by librarians. *See also* Osmosis method.

Relevance canon : A canon in the Idea Plane for the choice of characteristics mandates that the characteristics we choose to divide the universe /group of entities should be relevant to the ultimate purpose of classification. A group of athletes can be selected on the basis of their height or weight, but not on the basis of their color, religion or educational attainments. Latter three characteristics are not relevant for athletics.

No classification is universal. A classification relevant for one group of users may be less relevant, or not useful, to another group. Therefore the characteristics selected to divide a group should be relevant to the purpose of classification. Relating choice of characteristic with the end purpose of classification is a subtle task.

Relevant succession canon : A canon in the Idea Plane for the succession of characteristics mandates that the sequence of characteristics to be applied one after the other to the same group of entities should be relevant to the purpose of classification. If the purpose of classification is to serve world literature historians then 'period' should be the first characteristic applied to the publications on literature. In an Indology library Indian-ness should be the first characteristic and subject should be the secondary characteristic

Reticence Canon : A canon in the Verbal Plane recommends that the terms used by the classificationist should be reticent, not judgmental. The terms used in a schedule should be neutral and need not reflect the personal opinion of the classification designer. Terms major, or minor authors should be avoided to classify literary authors.

Reticence means non-critical; non-judgmental. Terminology of a controlled vocabulary/indexing language should be reticent, that is it should not be critical or judgmental. It should not reflect the personal opinion or inclination of the classifier/indexer.

Rigidly faceted classification : A faceted classification in which every facet has to be there, or is indicated by dummy digits to avoid cluttering of facets. The first three editions of the CC were rigidly faceted.

Rounds and Levels : It is not necessary for the subject of a document to be composed of all the five categories. It may comprise of any number of categories from one to five depending upon how far it is compounded or micro. On the other hand, a category may also occur more than once in the same subject. A category usually manifests itself more than once in micro subjects. Therefore number of facets in a subject may be more than the number of categories. Recurrence of a category is accounted for and accommodated by the ingenious postulate of Rounds and Levels. The PMEST formula is, in fact, comprised of many so called rounds and levels of facets. For example, in class O, Literature, the category [P] personality occurs four times (Language, Form, Author, and Work), each at the same hierarchic level. In the subject, 'Treatment of human diseases', both diseases and treatment are manifestations of the first and second rounds of energy, respectively, in the sixth edition. A subject aspect 'Summer of 2016' manifests two levels of Time facet. Thus, in a facet formula, facets of the same category may occur more than once to be accommodated in a logical citation order of rounds and levels. Ranganathan postulated that:

- Space and time occur only in the last round of the facet formula;
- Categories [P], [M], and [E] can occur in various rounds;
- Levels occur only within a round;
- Within a round [P] and [M] can also occur at many levels;
- Energy always completes a round. It has no level, but only rounds.

To mechanize the arrangement of categories and their recurring but scattered facets, Ranganathan after a long trial, finally settled on the general, all encompassing, and very handy facet formula famous as PMEST. Rounds of categories and, within a round, levels, are arranged by the Principle of Dependency, which Ranganathan formulated as the Wall-Picture principle: since there cannot be any mural without a wall, so the wall is made the first facet. The master Wall–Picture principle has various corollaries formulated in such axiomatically worded principles as the Whole–Organ principle (whole–part relationship) and the Cow–Calf principle (principle of appurtenance) to arrange rounds and levels of facets; the more complex Actand-Action-Actor-Tool principle is obtained by a mix of the above principles. Actand or Actee is someone on which action is performed. For example, Actand is a patient on which Action (surgery) is performed by the Actor (doctor) with laser (Tool).

In the sequence, the basic facet, invariably represented by the main class or its amplification by system (Sm), environment (Env), or specialization (Sp), precedes other facets. The grand general facet formula may be represented as follows:

(BF), [1P1], [1P2], [1P3], [1P4]; [1M1]; [1M2]; [1M3]: [E], [2P1], [2P2]; [2M1]: [2E], [3P1]....:[3E]. [S1].[S2]'[T1]'[T2]

Numbers prefixed to a category indicate its round, while numbers suffixed to a category indicate its level, e.g., [2M1] is 2nd round 1st level Matter:

In the current edition of CC, the total number of facets and their general sequence is as follows:

> Field of study → System → Environment → Specials → Object of study → Kinds/Parts of object → Properties of object → Action on the object → Kind of action → Method of action → Agent of action → Instrument of action → Space → Space qualifier → Time → Time qualifier.

This compares well with thee CRG/BC-2 facet

sequence formula: Thing-Kind-Part-Property-Material-Process-Operation-Patient-Product-Byproduct-Agent-Space-Time.

Sarada Ranganathan Endowment for Library Science (SRELS) : Founded by Ranganathan in 1961 in memory of his wife Vangal Lakshmana Sarada Ranganathan (1908-1985) is a registered Charitable Endowment at Bangalore with the following aims and objectives:

- To improve the library and information services in India.
- To train library and information service personnel.
- To promote the provision of efficient library and information service.
- To apply research results of library and information studies.

The Endowment is implementing these objectives by publishing books, reports and the periodical *SRELS Journal of Information Management* and by organizing Workshops, Lectures and Seminars. The Endowment organises three series of lectures:

Sarada Ranganathan Endowment Lectures (1965)

Dr.S.R.Ranganathan Memorial Lectures (1973)

Curzonco-Seshachalam Endowment Lectures (2001).

As a publisher it has *inter alia* published the 7th edition of the CC7 (1987), and has republished most of the Ranganthan's earlier books to make these available to the students and scholars

Schedules : The *terra firma* of library classification system which systematically lists classes and their subdivisions along with their notation and notes.

A printed or otherwise recorded (as an electronic databases) it is a series of lists of subjects and their subdivisions arranged in a systematic, usually general to specific order with unique notation for each entry. Considered as core of a classification system, the other parts such as index are considered adjunct to classification. In the UDC, it is called main tables.

Secondary phase : The second phase of a complex subject which usually affects the exposition of the primary phase. It gives the phase relation its name – i.e. determines the kind of phase relation. *See also* Asymmetrical relations.

Semantic relations : Subject, substantive and *a priori* relations in library classifications and other controlled vocabularies which are mostly controlled by hierarchical or collocation relations. These are relations among classes in arrays or in chains

Shattered Order : For too many breakages in the standard order to bring together related subjects the term coined by Arthur Maltby is shattered order. It is going beyond broken order. Such a broken order is sometimes necessary to produce Reader's Interest Classifications

Shelf arrangement : Arrangement or display of books/documents on the shelves by some predetermined systematic order. Since ancient times, the librarians have tried many shelf arrangement systems ranging from size of the book, language or author and subject. These days though shelf arrangement is mostly in classified order supplemented by alphabetical or chronological suborders within a class, yet for so called non-book material many other arrangement systems are prevalent in libraries. Ranganathan arranges his documents in what he calls APUPA pattern.

Social epistemology : A term said to be coined by the famous US Professor, and a great admirer of Ranganathan Jesse H. Shera (1903-1982), it is study of the nature of knowledge and its impact on society and vice-versa.

Space : The fourth fundamental category of the CC

which manifests surface of earth in its various divisions such as political boundaries, or physio-geographic features such as deserts, mountains, woods, water bodies, etc.

Special classification : A depth classification for a narrow specialized area of knowledge say, medicine, law, social sciences, etc. It also refers to a classification for specific form of documents such as braille books government publications, fictions or maps, standards or patents.

Special isolates : In the CC subject subdivisions of a main class under various facets are called special isolates. Each main class has its own unique isolates under P, M and E categories. These have no meaning in other main classes. For example, rice, wheat, maze etc. are special isolates in the personality of J Agriculture in the CC.

Specialization : Intensive knowledge and skills about a narrow area of knowledge.

Specials basic subject : To classify all the aspects of a subject from the view point of a specialization, for example, in Medicine we have Child medicine, or Old age Medicine, or we could have Sports medicine. Similarly in economics we have small scale economy ,or large scale economy, or Tropical farming in Agriculture.

Species (plural unchanged) : A group of bio entities with a same genus and who can interbreed among themselves. The term has been used by Ranganathan to designate various stages of development of library classification in its march from enumerative systems towards refinement and sophistication of a freely faceted classification.

Subject : An organized and systematized coherent body of ideas. It is a general context or field of focus of study. It is a topic or theme of any depth or breadth for study or research. Subjects have similar objects to study or are amenable to a common research method. According to Ranganathan, subjects are of three kinds: Basic, Compound and Complex.

Subject analysis : See Facet Analysis.

Subject bundles : A mode of formation of loosely and temporarily gathered multidisciplinary mission oriented subjects. Subject bundle usually come in the arena of big science. Examples are Tenesse Valley project, Mars missions, Antarctica expeditions. Such subjects are disbanded after completion of the project.

Subject catalogue : Part of the catalogue providing subject access to unknown items.

Succession : Order; sequence; coming one after the other.

Symmetrical relation : A phase relation where phases are reversible in position and their relation is mutual. General, Comparison and Difference relations are symmetrical. *See also* Asymmetrical relations.

Synonyms : Different words having the same or almost the same meanings. For example, Shut, Close. It is a case of many (words) for a single concept mapping between words and meaning or things. Every language of the world abounds in synonyms which have to be removed in vocabulary control for indexing and classification.

Syntactical relations : A sort of grammatical, *a posteriori* relations in a compound subject. These are achieved by an imposed citation order on the facets of a compound subject. Citation order of components in a compound subject which are mostly determined by the logical principle of dependency of facets. PMEST is the grand model for such relations, and for facets within the PMEST. Ranganthan gave many principles for facet sequence, such as wall-picture principle.

Systems basic subjects : A system in Colon

Classification represents a view point or unique way of doing something. In medicine Homeopathy, Allopathy and Ayurveda are different systems. In Economics, Marxism, Capitalism are two different systems. Only the CC has the provision to classify all the aspects of a subject from the viewpoint of a particular system

Taxonomic relationship : A genus-species relationship or relationship between an entity and its kinds.

Taxonomy : Any sort of classification structure. Generally speaking, it is a, science of classifying and naming living organisms of plants and animals. Scientific classifications are taxonomic.

Telescoped array : A chain of classes in the Idea and verbal planes represented as an array in the notational plane is a telescoped array. It brings brevity in notation. For example, Word, Asia are linked in a chain, but by denoting these by equal number of digits 1 and 4, respectively, Ranganathan makes the array 1/9 in space isolates as a telescoped one. In many classes such as I Botany, K Zoology Ranganathan frequently makes use of telescoping for brevity of notation

Term : A technical and standardized name given to a concept.

Terminology : A system of standardized names given to concepts and entities for unambiguous communication.

Thesaurus (IR) : A highly structured and controlled subject vocabulary which shows equivalence, hierarchical and other associative relations with other terms in the thesaurus. It is also used to index and retrieve documents where physical arrangement is not necessary. A literary or desk thesaurus is used by writers to make a better choice of words.

Time : The fifth fundamental category of Ranganathan which manifests time in various aspects. Time could be chronological, calendar, seasonal, diurnal, or even social such as war time, future time or geological such as the ice age, or Jurassic age.

Topic map : A kind of ontology in a standard format for representing complex knowledge organization systems comprising of topics (concepts), associations (relationships) and occurrences (attributes).

Universal Bibliography : An ideal bibliography of all subjects in all languages published anywhere at any point of time. Such a bibliography is a utopian dream. Many have dreamt of such a project but could never execute it due to too obvious reasons. Founders of IIB (1895) gave up this project even after collecting 12 million references. *Bibliotheca universalis* (4 vol., 1545–49), an index in Greek, Latin, and Hebrew of writings in all languages compiled by Swiss naturalist Konard von Gesner (1516-1565) is considered to be a universal bibliography of its time.

Universe of Knowledge : Refers to the entire corpus of knowledge known to mankind. An assumed term referring collectively to everything.

Verbal Plane : The second phase of designing KOS systems which involve assigning standardized terms to all the concepts arrived at and arranged in arrays and chains in the Idea Plane. Terms given to each terms are unique ,that is, free from homonyms and synonyms. Canons of verbal plane prescribe that the terms should be current, familiar, reticent and should be written and read in the context of the above link.

Vocabulary control : The process of formulating controlled vocabulary, authority list, thesaurus, etc. for terminology management.

WASPish bias : Western, Anglo-Saxon Protestant bias in the DDC and other western library classifications. In fact every KO system is value loaded and cannot escape any social or ideological bias that naturally creeps in. Every KOS holds mirror to its time and place.

Web directory : Web directory, also called link directory, is a directory on the World Wide Web. It specializes in linking to other web sites and in categorizing those links. A web directory is not a search engine and does not display lists of web pages based on keywords; instead, it lists web sites by category and subcategory. Most web directory entries are also not found by web crawlers but by humans. The categorization is usually based on the whole web site rather than one page or a set of keywords, and sites are often limited to inclusion in only a few categories. Web directories often allow site owners to submit their site for inclusion, and have editors who review submissions for fitness.

Web search engine : It is a software system that is designed to search for information on the World Wide Web. The search results are generally presented in a ranked list of results often referred to as search engine results pages (SERPs). The information may be a mix of web pages, images, and other types of files.

Work facet : In the facet formula for O Literature the work facet denotes the title of the work. As in Shakespear's Hamlet O111,2J64,H, the digit H which stands for Hamlet is the work facet.

Work number : The end part of the cutter number which usually denotes the title of the document. For example, in the Booknumber H986C of "Crome Yellow" by A. Huxley the C denotes "Crome", and H986 Huxtley.

World Wide Web : Abbreviated as WWW or W3 commonly known as the Web, is a system of interlinked hypertext documents that are accessed via the Internet. With a web browser, one can view web pages that may contain text, images, videos, and other multimedia and navigate between them via hyperlinks. Sir Tim Berners-Lee, a British computer scientist and former CERN employee, is considered the inventor of the Web whose1989 proposal was meant for a more effective CERN communication system. Later Berners-Lee eventually realised the concept could be implemented throughout the world.

Index

All entries are in context of Ranganathan or the Colon Classification. g means defined in Glossary

S

T